Liberalism without Illusions

Liberalism without Illusions
Renewing an American Christian Tradition

Christopher H. Evans

BAYLOR UNIVERSITY PRESS

Cover Design by Nita Ybarra
Cover Image: Small boy at mealtime in the camp for white flood refugees, courtesy of the Library of Congress.

Library of Congress Cataloging-in-Publication Data

Evans, Christopher Hodge, 1959-
   Liberalism without illusions : renewing an American Christian tradition / Christopher H. Evans.
      p. cm.
   Includes bibliographical references and index.
   ISBN 978-1-60258-208-8 (pbk. : alk. paper)
   1. Liberalism (Religion)--United States. 2. United States--Church history. I. Title.

   BR517.E82 2009
   277.3'08--dc22

                                        2009029957

To the members and friends of

Christ Episcopal Church, Pittsford, New York

Contents

Acknowledgments   ix

Introduction   1

1   Why Do Americans Distrust Liberals?   19

2   Evangelical and Modern: Christian Liberalism
in the Nineteenth Century   33

3   Christian Liberalism and the Social Gospel Heritage   55

4   The Diffusion of Liberal Theology   79

5   Did Liberalism Win?   99

6   Does Liberal Theology Still Matter?   117

7   Liberalism without Illusions   141

Epilogue: Past Imperfect   161

Notes   165

Selected Bibliography   193

Index   203

Acknowledgments

This book would not have been possible without the support of the people of Baylor University Press, in particular, Carey Newman, Jenny Hunt, Diane Smith, and Myles Werntz. As an editor, Myles was a wonderful conversation partner in the process of writing, and I am grateful for his critical read of the manuscript at various stages of its evolution. Many of the book's arguments emerged through years of teaching on the faculty of Colgate Rochester Crozer Divinity School. Not only am I grateful for the opportunity to teach at a theological seminary identified with the tradition of theological liberalism, but for the privilege to work with many wonderful colleagues who have supported me and fueled my spirit in numerous ways. In particular, I give thanks for all the ways that my students, past and present, have engaged me in conversation and challenged my own theological assumptions.

Additionally, many persons helped give shape to this project through conversation, friendship, and, in some cases, the reading of the manuscript. Among them, I give thanks to G. P. Dickerson-Hanks (who read and commented on an earlier draft of the manuscript), Dianne Reistroffer, Ellie Stebner, Bill Herzog, Bob Hill, Winifred Collin, the anonymous reviewers at Baylor, and my good friend and partner in coffee consumption, Dale Davis. I count my blessings every day for the support of my wife, Robin Olson, and for our children, Peter and Andrew.

Finally, I am very fortunate to work part-time as a parish associate at Christ Episcopal Church in Pittsford, New York. This wonderful faith community welcomed me to its staff a few years ago, and I cherish the creative outlet that this church provides to my ministry. It is with deep gratitude that I dedicate this book to that congregation.

Introduction

In 1907 Walter Rauschenbusch concluded his book *Christianity and the Social Crisis* by asserting that the goal of a just society was within humanity's grasp. "If at this junction we can rally sufficient religious faith and moral strength to snap the bonds of evil and turn the present unparalleled economic and intellectual resources of humanity to the harmonious development of a true social life, the generations yet unborn will mark this as that great day of the Lord for which the ages waited, and count us blessed for sharing in the apostolate that proclaimed it."[1] Writing at the height of the American Progressive Era, Rauschenbusch reflected a pervasive spirit of optimism that characterized many religious leaders of the day who were part of what scholars label the social gospel. Yet for all of Rauschenbusch's idealism, his Christian faith gave him a somber view toward the ultimate perfectibility of humanity in the realm of history.

> In personal religion we look with seasoned suspicion at anyone who claims to be holy and perfect, yet we always tell men to become holy and seek perfection. We make it a duty to seek what is unattainable. We have the same paradox in the perfectibility of society. We shall never have a perfect social life, yet we must seek it with faith. . . . At best there is always but an approximation to a perfect social order. The kingdom of God is always but coming.[2]

Twenty-five years after Rauschenbusch wrote these words, Reinhold Niebuhr, in his book *Moral Man and Immoral Society*, stated arguments that many saw as a direct challenge to the optimism of the social gospel. For all of Niebuhr's emphasis on classical Protestant notions of sin and his critique of the social gospel's emphasis on human progress, his conclusion to *Moral*

Man echoed aspects of Rauschenbusch's *Christianity and the Social Crisis*: "We cannot build our individual ladders to heaven and leave the total human enterprise unredeemed of its excesses and corruptions." While he believed that the pursuit of a just society was an unobtainable illusion, "it is a very valuable illusion for the moment; for justice cannot be approximated if the hope of its perfect realization does not generate a sublime madness in the soul."[3]

Moving ahead in the twentieth century to 1968, Martin Luther King Jr., in his final Sunday sermon at the National Cathedral in Washington, D.C., reflected upon a similar paradox. In a subdued tone, King affirmed the hope that America stood at the crossroads of a great moral opportunity "to help bridge the gulf between the haves and the have-nots." The question for King was *not* whether America had the means to solve the problems of racism, militarism, and economic injustice that plagued the nation; "the question is whether America will do it. . . . The real question is whether we have the will."[4]

For all the different historical contexts behind their careers and writings, Rauschenbusch, Niebuhr, and King articulated remarkably similar theological premises. Each person committed himself to engage the social, political, and religious forces that shaped his particular historical era. Each had a passion for justice that rooted him in a belief that it was possible to change the course of human history. And each one approached his social engagement out of a deeply rooted Christian faith. Amidst their differing public careers they mused over theological questions that have plagued Christians for thousands of years—the nature of sin, the role of the church, the nature and purpose of God, and the responsibility of Christians to the larger society. At the same time that Rauschenbusch, Niebuhr, and King sought ways to apply their understanding of Christianity to the problems of the contemporary world, they also reflected an openness to the world, critiquing and embracing a wide range of intellectual sources and influences. They were paradigmatic of one of the most prominent, and most underappreciated, movements in American Christianity: theological liberalism.[5]

In the early twenty-first century, discussions about the nature of theological liberalism surround the same theme of paradox that permeated the lives of Rauschenbusch, Niebuhr, and King. On one hand, liberalism is acknowledged as an indisputable part of the Western Christian tradition. In his introduction to his definitive three-volume history of American theological liberalism, Gary Dorrien asserts that "liberal theology has been and remains the most creative and influential tradition of theological reflection since the Reformation."[6] To interpret Christianity over the past two centuries without a discussion of liberal theology is tantamount to discussing the Reformation without Martin Luther.

On the other hand, many religious leaders within a variety of churches question the relevance of Christian liberalism, seeing it as an aberrant movement that has sucked the life and vitality out of Christianity. In his 1937 book *The Kingdom of God in America*, H. Richard Niebuhr provided what many see as the classic critique of the liberal Christian heritage. Frequently identified with the tradition of Christian realism (or neo-orthodoxy) that arose in the aftermath of World War I, Niebuhr castigated liberalism for what he saw as the movement's superficial beliefs in human progress and the way it drained the vitality out of classical Christian doctrine, particularly surrounding God's sovereignty and the redemptive power of Jesus Christ. Many commentators overlooked the nuances within Niebuhr's critique and seized upon one sentence that became a classic condemnation of liberal theology: "A God without wrath brought men without sin into a kingdom without judgment through the ministrations of a Christ without a cross."[7]

The consequences of Niebuhr's epitaph to liberal theology have been reflected in subsequent developments in American religion. Since the 1970s, no theme dominates studies of American religion more than the question of the declining religious and cultural impact of mainline Protestantism.[8] These denominations are associated with churches that emerged out of the sixteenth-century European reformations and whose roots, in most cases, extend back to the colonial era. By the 1930s most of these traditions became centers for propagating many of the key tenets of liberalism, especially an embrace of modern intellectual theory, theological and religious pluralism, and an openness to the wider intellectual and popular currents within the culture. The past generation has witnessed a time in which the voices of liberal mainline Christianity have eroded. An era in which Christian intellectuals like Reinhold Niebuhr could assume that their voices would receive a wider hearing in the wider culture has given way to a time where mainline Protestants represent a component of a larger cacophony of religious perspectives.

Yet as a spate of recent surveys on American religion points out, Christianity in early twenty-first-century America is alive and well. While the majority of Americans identify themselves as "Christian," the majority of that number identify themselves with evangelical Protestantism, translating into a total population of approximately 100 million Americans.[9] Evangelicalism has been a constant feature of American religious history, and despite the tendency of liberal Christianity to assign the movement to the periphery of American life, it could be argued that those who identify themselves as liberals (by definition and/or practice) reside on the true edges of the American religious landscape.

And yet despite all the ways that the tradition has been attacked and seemingly buried, liberal theology still remains a ubiquitous feature of contemporary American society, manifesting itself in a variety of religious and secular movements. Prior to becoming labeled a political pariah during the 2008 presidential campaign, the Rev. Jeremiah Wright served as the chief inspiration for Barack Obama's breakthrough oration at the 2004 Democratic National Convention. While Wright would later become associated among many Americans with an extremist, black nationalist ideology, he echoed sentiments that Obama effectively embraced in his run for the White House. Throughout his political rise, Obama used rhetoric reminiscent of the language of Rauschenbusch, Niebuhr, and King: that despite the social-political obstacles of the present, Americans needed to be hopeful about the future—as individuals and as a nation. This is the essence of what Wright and Obama called "the audacity of hope."

> That was the best of the American spirit, I thought—having the audacity to believe despite all the evidence to the contrary that we could restore a sense of community to a nation torn by conflict; the gall to believe that despite personal setbacks, the loss of a job or illness in the family or a childhood mired in poverty, we had some control—and therefore responsibility—over our own fate.
>
> It was that audacity, I thought, that joined us as one people. It was that pervasive spirit of hope that tied my own family's story to the larger American story, and my own story to those of the voters I sought to represent.[10]

Obama's words extend beyond hyperbole. On one hand, he critiques his historical context and observes the ways that Americans fall short of being a just society. On the other hand, he offers a vision that is rooted in something transcendent, predicated on the ways that diverse individuals are able to live together as one people. While Obama does not pin his vision of America's future upon a specific religious vision, he is clear that any critical engagement over America's political future is inseparable from a critical engagement with religion. As he reflected on his decision to be baptized and join the Rev. Wright's Chicago church, Obama noted that embracing a life of faith "did not require me to suspend critical thinking, disengage from the battle for economic and social justice, or otherwise retreat from the world. . . ."[11] Like many secular and religious leaders in the past, Obama grasps hold of many core themes within the heritage of American theological liberalism: in particular, personal piety, social-political engagement, and critical intellectual inquiry. This example is an important sign that an earlier tradition of theological liberalism is not dead.

This book provides a summary of key historical and theological themes coming out of the heritage of Christian liberalism, arguing for the ongoing importance of the heritage for churches and people of faith in twenty-first-century America. On one hand, I want to accentuate the vital role that theological liberalism has played in the shaping of American Christianity. On the other hand, the book suggests ways for church leaders and Christians (whether or not they identify themselves as liberal) to begin the process of discerning how theological liberalism can still address the ecclesiastical *and* cultural contexts of our time. In large measure, the heritage of liberal theology is inseparable from specific academic movements of the nineteenth and twentieth centuries. However, many of the most enduring aspects of theological liberalism were shaped by faith communities and popular movements that reflect the ongoing appeal and resiliency of certain components of the heritage.

As a spate of recent studies indicates, liberal theology will continue to be a subject of interest for academicians and scholars. However, the question remains whether Christian liberalism can speak in a pastoral and prophetic voice to an era that is often defined as post-liberal (and its accompanying label, as discussed in the next chapter, postmodern). While Christian liberals will face numerous challenges in the upcoming years, I believe the question of liberalism's future rests partly with those who strive to recover certain historical and theological themes of the heritage, not for the purpose of an uncritical enshrinement of the tradition, but for creating a basis for the renewal of the tradition within twenty-first-century Christianity.

Defining and Describing Theological Liberalism: Again!

Providing any concise definition of theological liberalism is extremely problematic, due to the fact that liberalism, like every theological tradition or movement, is far from monolithic.[12] Like every theological heritage, liberalism is represented by countless schools of thought, and often these liberal movements have stood in opposition to one another (this is illustrated especially by the heritage of figures like Reinhold and H. Richard Niebuhr, who in the 1930s identified themselves as liberal critics, yet who by the standards of later commentators have become associated with the liberal heritage).[13] By the same token, I believe it is possible to offer a general definition of theological liberalism as an orientation for the reader: *Theological liberalism is a historical movement born in the nineteenth century that supports critical intellectual engagement with both Christian traditions and contemporary intellectual resources. As opposed to more traditional forms of Christian theology, liberalism has been characterized by an affirmation of personal and collective experience, systemic social analysis, and open theological inquiry.* This book makes no attempt to do a comprehensive analysis of theological liberalism, as that work has already been done exceedingly well. However, the book focuses upon those aspects of liberal theology that have displayed ongoing resiliency within Christian thought since the inception of liberalism as a discernible theological heritage in the early nineteenth century. Consequently, while the book will make note of contemporary movements of liberal theology, my focus will be on more classical forms of liberalism arising out of the nineteenth and twentieth centuries that have not just intentionally identified themselves as outgrowths of Christianity, but have been intentional about maintaining a dialogue and an interface with earlier forms of Christian tradition.

Within the parameters of this study, I believe it is possible to identify characteristics that link together disparate components of the liberal tradition. First, liberal theology needs to be understood as a heritage that sought to interpret Christianity in the face of an Enlightenment/post-Enlightenment worldview. Gary Dorrien stresses that what differentiates liberal theology from earlier forms of Christian theology is its role as a mediating heritage. It is a heritage that attempts "to reconceptualize the meaning of traditional Christian teaching in the light of modern knowledge and modern ethical values."[14] Perhaps a more colloquial way of expressing Dorrien's sentiment of what characterizes liberal theology is that it is a heritage that takes cultural engagement seriously. Indeed, all forms of liberalism are contingent in one form or another on a continuous interaction with cultural norms, values, and suppositions. This is not to say that earlier forms of Christian theology did not engage in these processes, as various forms of Christian theology were deeply concerned with the question of how Christians should interact with the wider society (in particular, various incarnations of Calvinist theology are noteworthy for the way they view a major part of the church's role to be the moral conscience of the secular world). However, most theological traditions formulated up to the early nineteenth century were contingent upon a worldview in which the theology of a particular tradition (whether Catholic, Reformed, or Anabaptist) embodied doctrinal truths in which all believers had to abide. Liberalism swung the pendulum both ways. Not only did Christian communities see themselves as responsible for the shaping of the culture, but liberals were receptive toward receiving wisdom and insight from the culture.[15] Critics of liberal theology since the early nineteenth century have responded that such a theological orientation is inherently flawed because it compromises the doctrinal integrity of Christianity (and the point is often made by conservatives that liberalism embraces a "humanistic" gospel, as opposed to the truth of the Bible). However, this positive orientation toward culture has given to liberalism a remarkable elasticity, both in the ways that the culture has informed theological growth and innovation and in how liberal ideals have engaged in repeatedly reassessing various heritages of Christian doctrine.

This intentional engagement with culture is especially evident in the fact that theological liberalism emerged out of a time in the nineteenth century when developments in modern science served as a direct challenge to centuries of Christian tradition. If modern science was saying that the world was millions, if not billions, of years old, how does this fact square with the creation narrative in the book of Genesis that speaks of God creating the world in seven days? What does one do with New Testament genealogies that trace Jesus' lineage all the way back to Adam? And most problematic, how does one confront the challenge from people like Charles Darwin who argue that humans evolved from earlier primates? For many Christians in the nineteenth century, and for sizable groups of Christians today, the response to these and other questions was solved by appealing to and defending scriptural authority over scientific inquiry. However, liberal Christianity made the effort, and is still making the effort, to find ways of reconciling the modern scientific world with the narratives of Scripture and the teachings of Christian tradition. There is no question that at times this enterprise has led liberal movements, as H. Richard Niebuhr judged in *The Kingdom of God in America*, to an uncritical embrace of culture. Yet this engagement has also led to an amazing theological resiliency within the liberal movement, in which the heritage has been able to critically examine itself amidst changing historical circumstances.

The way liberal theology has served to bridge the gap between faith and culture is reflected in a second contribution of the movement: *its extensive and diverse intellectual heritage*. Even though on the surface the two movements appear not to be connected, American liberal theology partly emerged in the early nineteenth century from the matrix of one of the most orthodox theological traditions in America: New England Calvinism.[16] What connects these two seemingly disparate heritages is a shared passion for how Christianity should intellectually interpret the source that has always been at the center for Protestantism: the Bible. Nineteenth-century liberalism moved a great distance from the biblical hermeneutics of New England divines like John Winthrop, Anne Hutchinson, and Cotton Mather. Yet liberalism took hold in Western Christianity largely through its ability to reinterpret Scripture in the face of an emerging scientific and social-scientific worldview. This approach to doing theology has likewise been critiqued for the ways it is perceived to devalue Scripture. Yet in contrast to historical and contemporary movements of biblical literalism (in particular, the apocalyptic themes inherent in many fundamentalist and conservative-oriented traditions), liberal theology has enabled individuals to recognize that being a person of faith is not incompatible with raising questions about the faith. In juxtaposition to literalistic interpretations of Scripture, liberal theology spawned creative movements in theology, as well as biblical interpretation, epitomized by numerous traditions of biblical criticism and textual analysis that are widely embraced today.

By the same token, theological liberalism as an institutional phenomenon has largely been confined to those churches and denominations historically connected to the so-called Protestant mainline, that is, churches and denominations with historical roots that extend deeply into America's past.[17] Even though in recent years these churches have lost significant ground numerically and culturally to churches identified with evangelical theology, today approximately one-quarter of all Americans identify themselves with this tradition.[18] Yet even within these traditions, which have historically been characterized by the influence of liberal theology, liberalism's impact within denominations and individual congregations has been quite uneven, as few congregations today would self-consciously define themselves as liberal.

A constant dilemma confronted by liberal theology has been that much of its primary base has resided within specific academic centers, emerging from a select number of theological seminaries and divinity schools. Schools such as Union (New York), Andover, Yale, Harvard, the University of Chicago, Boston University, and Claremont Theological Seminary, among others, represent some of the chief citadels at the center of liberalism's development over the past 150 years.[19] Yet American liberalism emerged in the nineteenth century as a tradition whose primary spokespersons were not professional theologians, but ministers of local churches; this tradition includes such prominent names as William Ellery Channing, Horace Bushnell, Henry Ward Beecher, Theodore Munger, George Gordon, Phillips Brooks, Newman Smyth, Washington Gladden, Walter Rauschenbusch, and perhaps the most prominent figure of the twentieth-century liberal Protestant pulpit, Harry Emerson Fosdick.[20] In many ways, the real failure of liberalism is not that it is not still a vibrant intellectual heritage; *its failure is that its base for the most part is no longer associated with congregations.* This does not suggest that there are no longer any churches that are self-consciously "liberal" in theological orientation, but it does suggest that components of contemporary liberal theology have largely forgotten that its historical genesis came through individuals who were concerned with making the heritage relevant to grassroots audiences, not just intellectuals.

Liberalism is a movement that has *historically stressed a balance between personal* and *collective experience.* Most liberal detractors emphasize that, far too often, liberal movements elevate personal experiences over the weight of centuries of Christian tradition. Yet subjectivism is problematic in *all* theological traditions, especially in the Protestant heritage that elevates Scripture as the chief criterion of truth, above any particular form of tradition. However, liberal theologies, as disparate as the late nineteenth-century evangelical liberalism of William Newton Clarke, the mid-twentieth-century Christian realism of Reinhold Niebuhr, and the late twentieth-century liberation theologies of James Cone and Rosemary Ruether,[21] are united in a belief that what makes Christianity transformative is that it extends *beyond* individuals to speak in behalf of a faith community that bears witness to the presence and power of God.[22] William Newton Clarke, one of the most influential liberal theologians in the late nineteenth century, succinctly expressed this conviction when he noted that "human experience in religion bears witness to the good God, and affords in fact the most practical evidence that [God] exists."[23]

A frequent criticism made against liberal theology since the early nineteenth century was that liberalism placed human experience above any other criterion of theology, ultimately negating the importance of classical theological themes pertaining to original sin and human evil. Overwhelmingly, representatives of liberalism in the nineteenth and twentieth centuries never questioned the reality of sin or denied the existence of evil in the world. However, their views of human sinfulness were counterbalanced by beliefs that human actions, indeed human nature itself, were not inherently corrupted by original sin. These liberal beliefs in human goodness set the stage for the emergence of new theological traditions that revised how Christian faith communities viewed humanity's relationship to the world, as well as the very nature of salvation itself.

Perhaps the most well-known liberal movement to emerge in the late nineteenth and early twentieth centuries was the social gospel. The social gospel popularized the concept of "social salvation"; that is, the belief that a major goal of Christianity was to respond to the collective nature of human experience, by addressing social-economic problems. Most leaders of the social gospel, such as Walter Rauschenbusch, never discounted more traditional evangelical notions of individual conversion. However, these experiences needed to be seen in relationship to larger movements to transform the collective behavior of American society. Specifically, the legacy of the social gospel has perhaps played the single most important role in shaping the worldview that central to Christianity's purpose is to work for social justice in relation to a range of political, economic, and (more recently) cultural issues. The identification of Christian liberalism with specific social-political positions has been a bone of contention for some. However, the imperative for Christians to work for the creation of a just world through the achievement of *systemic* social-political change not only represents one of the major contributions of liberal theology, but displays liberalism's continuity with earlier movements of nineteenth-century evangelical theology.[24]

While there is a tendency to use the terms "liberal" and "social gospel" interchangeably, many proponents of liberal theology at any given historical time have not identified themselves with the social gospel. Just as important as liberalism's stress on "social salvation" was how the tradition placed great importance on the sacred worth of the individual. One of the forgotten aspects about liberalism is that it opened up to Western Christianity an entirely new way to look at an individual's relationship to God. Historically, Catholicism defined the individual primarily around the rhythms of the church. An individual who strayed from the church (in particular, the seven sacraments of the church) was literally putting his or her soul at risk.[25] While Protestant ecclesiologies never stressed the same type of certitude about the infallibility of the church (although some seventeenth-century Calvinist churches and contemporary fundamentalist churches have come close), they put a tremendous onus on the individual believer. The good news for most Protestants up to the nineteenth century was that they came out of traditions that took the Reformation ideals of justification by faith and the priesthood of all believers seriously. Instead of salvation through the church, you were saved by virtue of faith in Christ, a faith that was not dependent on the work of priests, ministers, or fidelity to any specific institutional incarnation of the church.[26]

The bad news was that regardless of whether you were Catholic or Protestant, you still bore the weight of thousands of years of Christian tradition that stressed that humanity was steeped in sin, a reality that made any act of human volition inconsequential to one's salvation. Part of the appeal of liberal theology was that it not only viewed the world as inherently good, but also helped individuals see themselves as beings of sacred worth. This theme has had an enormous impact on the development of pastoral ministry in North America, both in terms of therapeutic models of ministry that emerged at the end of the nineteenth century and more recent manifestations of pastoral care "systems theory" analysis that appeared by the end of the twentieth century.[27] Various therapeutic pastoral models have not been without controversy, as these movements have sometimes been judged part of a secular accommodation to Christianity. Perhaps the most frequent assertion made against liberal theology is that the heritage places too much emphasis on human goodness at the expense of an adequate view of human sin. While many have debunked this notion, this assertion remains a point of necessary engagement, in which this book will lend its voice.

The question of how "good" individuals can be and how far communities can achieve any sort of realization of a just social order represents one of the age-old questions of Christian theology. One of the difficulties of some aspects of liberalism, including some movements associated with the social gospel (or, to use the more generic term, "social Christianity"), has been a tendency to equate the kingdom of God with specific social-political remedies. While at times this emphasis on faith and politics has led liberal Christianity to neglect spiritual discernment, at its best the liberal tradition has fueled an awareness that one cannot separate questions of faith from sustained reflection on social problems such as racism, economic justice, and gender equality. The best of the liberal Christian heritage reflects this balance between personal piety and social transformation.

Finally, liberal theologies are significant in terms of how they have *connected God to the events of human history.* On the surface this assertion seems hardly novel, as many movements of Western theology have repeatedly stressed the idea of God's providence leading a chosen people to a better future. While many forms of liberal Christianity have hung onto this notion, liberalism has been characterized by its insistence that God directly becomes part of historical processes and events. While the first governor of colonial Massachusetts, John Winthrop, could identify with the idea that God had a hand in bringing a group of Puritan dissenters from England to North America, his conception of God was of a sovereign deity who stood apart from the events of the world. The God of liberalism, however, was *directly* involved in the events of history. Part of this involvement can be characterized by the doctrine of God's immanence, a belief that God is present and acts through individuals and groups living in history. Simply put, liberal theology has stressed the centrality that God not only acts in history, but that individuals and

communities have the power to change history.[28] This foundational principle to liberal theology was articulated in the mid-twentieth century by
Daniel Day Williams, who noted,

> The liberal vision sees God working in human history for a progressive
> achievement of a higher order of life for mankind. The culmination
> of His work will be the establishment of a universal brotherhood of
> justice and love. The historical process taken in its overall course is
> thus essentially, if not wholly, the story of God's success with man.
> In the liberal perspective, we understand the meaning of our human
> existence when we see our place in this mighty drama of God's creative
> achievement.[29]

The way that liberalism views the importance of history, and in particular the study of history, reveals another unique dimension of how
liberalism swings the "Christ and culture" pendulum *both ways.* Historically, Catholics and Protestants talked about transformation of society
through the ministrations of the Christian church. In Catholic theology
the affairs of the world were secondary to those within the context of the
faith community. In Reformation and post-Reformation Protestantism,
Christian communities affirmed a degree of toleration in the ways that
individuals might explore the contours of the culture and the so-called
modern world. However, most Protestant theologians tended to see
God's hand at the center of all activity and change. History was important primarily in the way that it served as an arena to display God's power
at work (and, increasingly in American theology, this activity took on an
apocalyptic nature). As the nineteenth century progressed, liberal Christianity began to chip away at this dynamic, not only through embracing emerging secular social-scientific rationales surrounding history as an
academic discourse, but also in the ways that liberals reinterpreted earlier
arguments related to God's providence. By making God a direct partici-
pant in historical events, liberals came to the conclusion that the failures
of history (whether ecclesiastical, political, or cultural) were not caused
or willed by God. *They were a consequence of humanity's inability to carry
out what they were supposed to do in the first place.*

There is no doubt that the majority of liberal theologies have har-
bored, in one form or another, this progressive orientation toward history.
However, in the main, liberals have never believed in what Martin Luther
King Jr. called a "cult of inevitable progress."[30] As liberal Christianity
came of age in America by the end of the nineteenth century, it coincided
with an era where men and women believed that they had the intellectual
and practical tools to change society. Liberal Christianity not only rode
this wave of optimism, but contributed to it mightily. By the same token,

this optimism was counterbalanced with one of crisis. As will become evident in the pages that follow, the best of the liberal tradition has never shied away from the belief that God judges those who are responsible for sin and evil, while hanging onto the hope expressed by Walter Rauschenbusch, Reinhold Niebuhr, and Martin Luther King Jr. that change, in the individual and in the larger culture, is always possible.

Connecting the Past to the Future

I need to make clear to the reader that I write this book from the perspective of a professor who teaches at a seminary that historically has been identified with the heritage of theological liberalism. Also, I am someone who has spent years in parish ministry, and coming out of this background, I believe that there is much in the liberal tradition that is critical to the future of American Christianity, at the same time that the tradition is in need of critique. To begin a book that has as a primary objective a "recovery" of the liberal heritage entails a sense of balance, accentuating not only the positive contributions of liberalism but taking a serious look at why liberal Christianity appears, at least on the surface, to be in retreat. Yet central to the premise of this book is the assertion made by Gary Dorrien at the conclusion of his third volume on *American Liberal Theology*. "Throughout its history, liberal theology has broken beyond its academic base only when it speaks with spiritual conviction about God's holy and gracious presence, the way of Christ, and the transformative mission of Christianity."[31] I hope that readers of this book will keep this assertion in the forefront of their thoughts as they read this book. In examining the history of American liberal theology, one sees many aspects of the tradition that have not been particularly successful. By the same token, one also sees how certain themes coming out of the history of American liberal theology might contribute to the tradition's renewal in the future.

Chapter 1 wrestles with a question that resides at the surface of life in early twenty-first-century America, mainly, why liberalism, in general, has become a target of public ridicule. The so-called backlash against political liberalism has its equivalent within the arena of contemporary American Christianity. For several decades theological liberalism has been singled out as one of the major problems facing American churches; in particular, the tradition has been blamed, by church leaders and scholars, for the membership decline of mainline denominations since the mid-1960s. Liberal theology (like comparable traditions of American political liberalism) has been assaulted not just based upon the tradition's theological premises (such as denying the role of the supernatural), but also because it is an elitist phenomenon that does not care about "average" Americans. While conceding that the elitist label attached to movements of theological liberalism remains problematic, the chapter suggests that the tradition remains embedded in the historical and contemporary contours of American Christianity—a history that needs to be rediscovered by faith communities in our era.

Chapters 2 through 4 reconstruct some of the significant historical and theological currents in American Christian liberalism. Unlike more detailed scholarship into the history of liberal Christianity, my intent is not to present a description of every genre of theological liberalism, but to point out those aspects of the heritage that reflect the strengths of liberalism's evangelical and modern dimensions identified by Dorrien. Chapter 2 highlights liberalism's origins and accentuates the ways liberal theology played an indispensable role in the development of nineteenth-century American theology. Although liberalism cannot be understood outside of its moorings within certain traditions of eighteenth- and nineteenth-century German philosophy and biblical scholarship, its rise in America was largely connected to specific congregations and ministers, a pattern that would shape much of liberalism's development through the early twentieth century. Many scholars see the "golden age" of theological liberalism as extending through the first quarter of the twentieth century, especially embodied in the tradition of the social gospel. Chapter 3 examines some of the chief contours of this important heritage of American Christianity, including the ways it bequeathed to contemporary Christianity a heritage that was rooted in prophetic action, spiritual discernment, and pastoral praxis.

Most survey texts of American Christianity tend to see liberalism fading in influence after World War I.[32] However, contemporary scholarship indicates that liberalism, far from dying out, transitioned into numerous religious and secular movements that played a critical role in the development of American religious and secular thought. From the prophetic realism of Reinhold Niebuhr, the mysticism of Howard Thurman, the Christian existentialism of Paul Tillich, and the social activism of Martin Luther King Jr., liberalism played a formative role in changing the contours of churches and the larger culture. Liberalism was at the center of an emerging mid-twentieth-century worldview that has been referred to as "the Protestant establishment," a time when many leaders of American denominations saw themselves at the center of the American religious, political, and cultural landscape.[33] Yet even as Protestant leaders saw the success of their causes through the rise of the ecumenical movement, or their ability to meet with national political leaders, other segments of an earlier liberal coalition grew disillusioned with Christianity's perceived institutional failings, disseminating their beliefs through a number of parachurch and secular organizations. Chapter 4 traces some of these disparate streams taken by liberalism in the twentieth century, showing the vitality of liberal theology but also ways that liberalism began to move away from its earlier context within congregations.

Chapters 2 through 4 not only summarize important thematic emphases in the history of Christian liberalism, but allow the reader to understand liberalism's indebtedness to larger developments in American religious history, especially its connection to American evangelicalism. Historically, Protestant churches have long viewed themselves as the moral caretakers of the nation, and the mind-set of many twentieth-century liberals affirmed this historical posture. However, historically liberal Christianity has often been unequipped to engage the language of evangelical populism. Chapter 5 hones in on one of liberal Christianity's great failures: an inability to sustain popular movements to counter the ongoing historical appeal of American popular evangelicalism. Institutionally, liberalism won control of most of the so-called mainline Protestant churches, and by the 1930s numerous evangelicals left these churches behind to create an emerging subculture of churches and parachurches. As this chapter points out, at a time when liberal theology was thriving institutionally and academically, it largely remained aloof from larger movements of popular evangelicalism that flourished throughout the twentieth century. Even as many scholars today are paying close attention to what has become known as global Christianity, the indigenous rise of Christian movements in the countries of Latin America, Africa, and Asia frequently has more to do with the influence of conservative evangelical movements, as opposed to any global engagement with liberalism.[34] As Chapter 5 asserts, if liberalism is to continue as a distinctive heritage, not only must it come to terms with its inability to become a grassroots movement, but with how the heritage must begin the process of clarifying its own Christian beliefs, in order to offer a compelling alternative to the apocalyptic scenarios employed by many contemporary evangelical and fundamentalist churches.

Chapter 6 offers insight on how liberals can use their unique heritage to begin a process that may lead to a recovery of liberalism's mission for twenty-first-century American Christianity. While liberalism is a tradition with deep roots in various movements of philosophical idealism, the chapter asserts that any sort of future revival of liberal theology needs to be rooted not simply in academic centers; it needs to reconnect with the one institution central to American liberalism's development in the nineteenth century: the church. Glenn Miller points out that part of what characterized liberalism's rise in the late nineteenth century was that its principal adherents did theology "on the fly," reflecting an ability to provide theological insight that addressed the immediate societal crises of the time.[35] The chapter discusses how liberal Christianity may take this theme from the late nineteenth century and apply it to some of the pressing theological and social issues of the early twenty-first century. While Christian liberalism faces many challenges in the present, our context also provides some indications as to the directions it may follow in the upcoming years.

At points, this book comes down hard on the liberal tradition; however, it ends with a word of hope. Chapter 7 concludes by offering a final assessment of liberalism's future in twenty-first-century American Christianity. In many ways the central question for liberal Christianity at the beginning of the twenty-first century is a question that is central to every Christian movement throughout history: what is Christian liberalism's mission? Chapter 7 argues that the future of American theological liberalism is not predicated on the size of churches or the specific positions churches take on social-political issues. The question is to what extent liberal Christianity can return to the themes that historically have given shape and vitality to the movement: mainly, an earnest theological questioning, a passion for justice, and a faith centered upon the importance of ongoing spiritual discernment.

I make no attempt in this book to construct a specific incarnation of twenty-first-century liberal theology. My hope, however, is that this work can aid those who are interested in beginning a conversation that will lead to new forms of Christian liberalism attentive to the best parts of its historical tradition. Christian liberalism cannot easily be put into a cookie cutter, as earlier studies of the movement show. However, there are plenty of signs that the tradition still can offer contemporary persons of faith a way to look to the future with a critical eye and (to use the words of John Wesley) "a heart strangely warmed."

Many readers of this book, whether or not they identify themselves with liberalism, will likely find bones to pick with me. However, my hope is that this book can serve as a point of departure for many persons who are concerned about the future of Christianity in America to engage in something that has been, and should always be, a cornerstone of any liberal movement: asking tough questions about the past, in hopes of building for the future. My own conviction as a Christian who is deeply influenced by liberal theology is not that we will see the emergence of any sort of Christian utopia (a goal categorically dismissed by liberals like Rauschenbusch, Niebuhr, and King). Rather, my hope is that our questions will serve us well as we form faith communities that speak with conviction and authenticity to our society.

It is easy with historical hindsight to see how many of the liberals discussed in this book were guilty of making pronouncements that have been proven false by subsequent historical events (as is true of *most* figures in history). However, these individuals show us that even as some of their dreams for the future turned out to be illusions (such as the wide-ranging hope of making America a Christian Protestant nation), the deeper teachings of many Christian liberals on theological questions of life, death, hope, justice, and salvation remain vibrant in our time.

Not long after the tragic events of September 11, 2001, a colleague of mine shared with me a passage from Reinhold Niebuhr that reflects upon the uncertainty of our times, yet also holds out the possibilities that the God of history has not forsaken us.

> Nothing worth doing is completed in our lifetime; therefore, we must be saved by hope. Nothing true or beautiful or good makes complete sense in any immediate context of history; therefore, we must be saved by faith. Nothing we do, however virtuous, can be accomplished alone; therefore, we are saved by love.[36]

Niebuhr's words serve as a reminder of one key theme characteristic of many of the classic representatives of the liberal heritage. For all the ways that liberal theology can engage Christian tradition and the wider cultural landscape with a critical eye, faith in the future of humanity and our planet must be grounded in something beyond reason. As long as churches carry some vestige of Niebuhr's vision, there is indeed a future for Christian liberalism that moves beyond the abandoned illusions of the past.

One

Why Do Americans Distrust Liberals?

Despite its impact upon the religious and cultural landscape for almost two centuries, liberalism has become a sort of scarlet-letter term in contemporary America. During the 1988 presidential campaign between George Herbert Walker Bush and Michael Dukakis, then-Vice President Bush succeeded in hanging the liberal label upon his opponent, seeing this designation as the ultimate sign of weakness. While the early twenty-first century may be a time when Americans say that they have transcended using terms like "liberal" and "conservative" to describe their religious and political convictions, the word "liberal" has become a generic concept filled with negative connotations. On one hand, Bush's branding of Dukakis as a liberal represented the image of someone who was tied too closely with a heritage of secular liberal thought, associated with the government welfare initiatives of the 1930s New Deal administration of President Franklin Roosevelt. Yet beyond the way the term became synonymous with someone who politically favors an active role for the federal government in promoting social and economic equality, Bush's chastisement of Dukakis represented something far more sinister in the public's mind: a liberal was someone who was outside the values of mainstream America and, worse still, someone who lacked any religious faith. Bush's branding of Dukakis as a liberal appealed to factors that went beyond any sort of rationalism, a fact that Dukakis himself failed to recognize.[1] However, it also reflects on an important theme that should carry over into contemporary conversations about theological liberalism: mainly, the ways liberalism has been seen as a popular scapegoat for many of the problems facing American Christianity in the early twenty-first century.

As a term, liberalism has overwhelmingly negative connotations. In his examination of the so-called culture wars, Thomas Frank notes that the use of the term "liberal" is not simply a descriptive designation related to one's politics (or, by extension, to one's religious beliefs). It has become a term synonymous with an attitude that promotes a cultural elitism whereby a small number of arrogant, self-righteous cadres castigate the "common person" in American life. Not only is liberalism "evil" because of how it promotes a dangerous political agenda (predicated on government usurping of individual freedom), but it is dangerous because it promotes an ideology that falls way outside the mainstream of what "ordinary" Americans believe.[2] The political and cultural dimensions of liberalism discussed by Frank carry over into conversations on theological liberalism.

The public castigation of the Rev. Jeremiah Wright represents a perfect example of the alleged sins of liberalism.[3] Thanks to YouTube, millions of Americans were able to hear Wright in countless sermons (usually downloadable in short sound bites) condemn America for its racist past, its militarism, and its dehumanizing economic practices. The same individual who helped Barack Obama craft a persuasive public rhetoric of political and cultural inclusion was transformed in the public's mind into an individual associated with the "evils" of liberalism: mainly, its lack of patriotism and its desire to tear down "traditional" American institutions, including its churches.

In part, the Jeremiah Wright controversy reveals the lack of public knowledge of the history of American religion (and in Wright's case, the unique historical and theological circumstances that shaped the black church in America). But it also accentuates the range of arguments used by political and cultural conservatives who associate a "liberal" as someone who is out of touch with the values of "common folk" in America.[4]

This perceived lack of concern for the common person (or the "person in the pew") has been picked up by many mainline commentators who castigate what they perceive as an elitist culture at work within mainline Protestant institutions. Numerous church renewal books that began to appear during the 1980s chided mainline churches for the fact that they were more interested in preserving denominational structures than engaging people in transformative ministries.[5] Many of these books, even though several were written by authors who could be classified as theologically liberal, nevertheless crafted a worldview that saw liberalism, in the institutional forms of mainline denominationalism, as out of touch with the struggles of regular churchgoing people.[6] Yet for all the ways that many of these mainline commentators often unfairly caricature liberalism, there are some sobering realities that liberal Christianity has been reluctant to face. Despite Gary Dorrien's assertion that liberalism's future rests with the gospel-centered tradition embodied by persons like Walter Rauschenbusch who were focused on issues of church renewal, the vast majority of figures he discusses in his three volumes were men and women whose careers were defined not primarily by congregational ministry, but as scholars in seminaries and university divinity schools.[7] Dorrien's study also reflects upon another contemporary development: mainly, the fact that identifying clearly delineated schools of liberal theology in recent years has become more difficult.

This factor not only reflects the diffuse nature of liberal theology over the course of the twentieth century, but also the fact that many contemporary theologians, who by Dorrien's definition fall into the liberal category, resist being identified as such. This reluctance is borne out in the Baylor survey that asked respondents how they would label their religious affiliations. While 26.1 percent used the label "Mainline Christian" to identify themselves, only 13.8 percent described themselves as "Theologically Liberal."[8] Even the recent emergence of a number of ecumenical and interfaith associations that court a decidedly liberal theological (and political) agenda balk at using the word "liberal" to describe their missions, opting instead for the label "progressive." Recent works on "Progressive Christianity," such as those by theologian Delwin Brown, echo this desire to distance themselves from liberalism, arguing that progressive Christianity is "not liberal Christianity in disguise."[9] While Brown rightly castigates liberalism for an overreliance on philosophy and an uncritical embrace of a modern scientific worldview, his generalizations do not apply to all, nor the majority, of liberals in American religious history. In fact, the bulk of Brown's vision of progressive Christianity relies *mostly* on key aspects of Christian liberalism, including the social gospel, open theological inquiry, *and* its affinity with earlier views of Christian evangelicalism. My point is not to castigate Brown or others who follow the banner of Christian progressivism, for I believe they seek to invigorate an important Christian tradition. The problem is that they often do so at the expense of *naming* the very tradition they seek to revive.[10]

Despite the fact that even those who, by the criteria that I laid out in the introduction, fit the description of being a liberal, few Americans in churches today embrace that identity. As I argue later on, the common accusation that theological liberalism is elitist is accurate, in the sense that it has never had the same type of grassroots support, compared to numerous varieties of evangelical theology. Paradoxically, even a cursory sample of scholarship on American religion can leave one with the impression that liberalism "won out" in terms of popular influence.

Liberalism and the Writing of American Religious History

Since the mid-nineteenth century, a great deal of scholarly writing on American religious history reflected what historian R. Laurence Moore called a "historiography of desire" (that is, a reflection of how the past should be interpreted, as opposed to what the past actually tells us).[11] Many of the early historians of American religion, such as Philip Schaff, embodied a theme that would be championed by later liberal scholars in the twentieth century: mainly, a belief that the story of American religion was one of political and cultural progress, manifested in the "triumph" of more "liberal" denominations over their sectarian "evangelical" counterparts.

Since the 1960s, the dominant theme in the writing of American religious history highlights the pluralistic character of America, whereby a country that was rooted in the suppositions of various Protestant faith communities developed by the end of the twentieth century into the most religiously pluralistic nation on earth.[12] While these studies concede the importance of the American Protestant past, the earlier heritages need to be viewed as one component of a larger religious landscape that includes a variety of *Christianities* (Protestants and Catholics), as well as non-Christian religions. For all the ways that recent studies on American religious pluralism break new ground, they are largely the heirs of an earlier tradition of historiography that was a direct outgrowth of an earlier twentieth-century liberal Protestant ethos. In the middle of the century, historians such as Winthrop Hudson, Sidney Mead, and Sydney Ahlstrom saw the story of American religion as essentially one of how a diverse number of nineteenth-century religious movements (chiefly emerging out of various traditions of New England Calvinism and evangelical Protestant revivalism) were able to put aside their differences and forge a shared spirit of religious and national unity. These historians did much to accentuate what Winthrop Hudson labeled "the great tradition of the American churches," emphasizing the ways that America stressed a heritage of religious freedom.[13] For many of these historians, the glory of America's Protestant past was that it was opening the doors to a more inclusive type of religious spirit, predicated on a respect for democratic institutions, political toleration, and religious pluralism. These narratives saw this transformation through a liberal lens, whereby evangelical movements were able to jettison their sectarian and exclusive characteristics in favor of a "liberal," tolerant form of religion that was adaptable to a post-Protestant environment.

I do not want to disparage the contributions made by past and contemporary scholars who cite pluralism as the defining theme of the American religious experience. Indeed, any understanding of American religion without an understanding of religious pluralism would be incomprehensible. The issue is not whether religious pluralism exists. The issue is: how does one interpret the reality of religious pluralism? Should one see pluralism primarily thtough a lens of religious toleration and unequivocal acceptance of religious "others," or is pluralism more a consequence of intense competition between dominant and subordinate religious groups?[14] The former angle is largely indebted to the legacy coming out of an institutional vision grounded in theological liberalism; the latter reflects the realities of sectarian religious groups where, in the case of American Christianity, the dominant movements emerged from groups often invisible to liberal historians and church leaders: popular evangelicalism.

While it is easy to chide an earlier generation of religion scholars for not noticing the massive tide of evangelical Christianity, much of the public religion they saw came from liberal churches within mainline Protestantism that vigorously championed the ideals of religious tolerance and pluralism. From approximately 1945 to 1965, the so-called Protestant establishment was in its heyday. Mainline Protestant church attendance boomed throughout the country, especially within growing suburban communities. Additionally, the ecumenical movement, largely an outgrowth of twentieth-century liberal Protestant initiatives, had reached its apex in terms of influence. Prominent leaders of the ecumenical movement such as Reinhold Niebuhr, John Bennett, Henry Van Dusen, and G. Bromley Oxnam relished their perceived influence in the wider cultural marketplace and their belief that they spoke on behalf of a unified Protestant theological consensus. They could count on the fact that their public pronouncements on religious and political matters would gain a semblance of attention from the news media, as well as invitations to meet with American presidents and other prominent political leaders.[15] Many of the denominations influenced by theological liberalism increasingly saw their mission in terms of interdenominational unity, culminating in the push of Protestant churches toward mergers. The pinnacle of these religious trends can be seen in the Second Vatican Council of 1962–1965, which led to numerous reforms introducing liberal innovations into Catholic liturgy, doctrine, and, in particular, Catholic engagement on matters pertaining to ecumenical and interfaith dialogue, as well as engagement with wider cultural movements. When historians looked at the American religious landscape during the 1950s and early 1960s, they were not just crafting a vision predicated on wishful thinking. They were responding to visible signs that the latter half of the twentieth century was going to be a time when ecumenical and interreligious unity would increase, as the nation's churches got larger and larger.[16]

Yet much scholarship that stresses religious pluralism has been reluctant to acknowledge what many contemporary surveys of American religion confirm: Americans overwhelmingly identify themselves as Christian, and the dominant "flavor" of Christianity comes from the historical reservoirs of American evangelicalism. A great deal of historical scholarship over the past generation emphasizes the uniquely sectarian nature of American religion, especially its evangelical heritage. As opposed to seeing America as a place where diverse religious groups find ways to cooperate with one another, these scholars emphasize the recurring theme of religious competition, in which a diverse range of sects and churches stress the exclusiveness of their beliefs, as well as the false teachings of other religious groups. Today, the religious diversity of the United States is an indisputable fact. Yet the vast majority of the country's population still identifies itself as Christian, with approximately one-third of Americans, 100 million people, identifying themselves as evangelical Protestant.[17]

Despite the steady growth of more liberal denominations for a good part of the twentieth century, recent historians point out that the vast majority of growing churches tend to have traditional theological bents. Nathan Hatch's groundbreaking study, *The Democratization of American Christianity*, argued that the history of American revivalism was not predicated on "liberal" models of cooperation, but on competition that accentuated religious differences, encouraged entrepreneurial models of religious leadership, and celebrated a culture of popular Christianity that challenged and overturned the claims of preexistent colonial religious elites.[18] In a controversial book from the early 1990s, sociologists Roger Finke and Rodney Stark stated bluntly that the history of American religion was essentially one in which the more ecumenically minded, liberal churches were doomed to failure. They note, "the churching of America was accomplished by aggressive churches committed to vivid otherworldliness."[19]

The historical focus on popular religion has led some scholars to conclude that if one is looking to identify a quintessential American religious tradition, it would not come from the churches associated with Christian liberalism, but churches associated with pentecostalism. A religious movement that emerged at the end of the nineteenth century and burst on the public scene in the early twentieth century, pentecostalism represents a diverse array of mostly theologically conservative sects and churches that stress personal conversion through the direct intercession of the Holy Spirit (manifested in many cases by the ability of persons to speak in tongues), and a theology that has increasingly veered in the direction of an apocalyptic otherworldliness stressing Jesus' Second Coming. By the end of the twentieth century, pentecostalism not only represented the fastest growing religious movement in America; it now serves as a vanguard of emerging Christian communities in Africa, parts of Asia, and even within historically Catholic countries in Latin America.[20]

Like many "old light" ministers during the great awakenings of the eighteenth and nineteenth centuries who opposed the improvisational measures of revivalism, today many liberal church leaders ridicule the dominating role of popular evangelicalism by asserting that it is unkempt in its means and simplistic in its message. Historically, this view only fuels the argument made by evangelicals that their critics were essentially apostates who were ignoring the biblical truths of the faith. Sadly, often when liberals attack evangelicals for the simpleness of their faith and the misguidedness of their beliefs, they are only supporting the assertion that liberals are out of touch with the simple virtues of the gospel and what it means to plain folk.

Liberalism and Postmodernity

The widely discussed upsurge in conservative evangelicalism since the 1960s has also paralleled the struggle of mainline liberalism to make sense of what is commonly referred to as postmodernity. A term largely associated with existentialist philosophical movements that emerged after World War II (as well as an emerging tradition of architectural design), postmodernity described a growing skepticism toward the absolute truth of scientific and social scientific knowledge and discounted earlier liberal notions that history was moving in the direction of a desired outcome or end point. In the aftermath of the social and cultural revolutions of the 1960s, the concept of postmodernity was embraced by many church leaders to describe the collapse of a Christian worldview in the West, accentuated by arguments that churches could no longer take for granted that Americans would understand, or care about, the meaning of inherited traditions coming from churches and denominations.[21]

Debates on postmodernity point to a central feature of why many church leaders today distrust the use of the term "liberal": the perception that liberalism not only contributes to a culture of unbelief through its uncritical embrace of the so-called modern world, but that its institutional structures are incapable of dialoguing with the emerging worldviews of postmodernity. The theme of doing theology in a postmodern context has triggered a range of responses by American church leaders. Since the 1980s, a tradition of post-liberal theology has emerged, represented by disparate figures like George Lindbeck and Stanley Hauerwas. While Lindbeck and Hauerwas come from different theological epistemologies, they unite in a belief that liberal theology historically accommodated the truths of the gospel to the demands of supporting a decaying culture of modernity.

For post-liberal theologians like Lindbeck and Hauerwas, liberalism predicated its truth claims more on an enlightenment gospel of reason, as opposed to the unique truth claims of Christianity, in which liberalism, in effect, enslaved Christianity to the whims of a secular world that in itself is unsure of its own moorings in the "modern" world. In a highly influential book from the early 1990s, Hauerwas and William Willimon castigated the liberal church for the ways that it transformed the gospel of Christ into an uncritical embrace of American culture that had drained mainline Protestantism of its vitality. The authors use an argument accentuated by other scholars and church leaders since the late 1980s, mainly, that liberal mainline churches are essentially living out of a Christendom model. Referring to the fact that Christianity since the early fourth century became the institutionalized faith in the West (epitomized by the Roman Emperor Constantine's actions to make Christianity the state religion of the Roman Empire), the church suffered the consequence of losing its theological zeal in exchange for a culturally dominant role. Seeing much of mainline Christianity as "the dull exponent of conventional secular political ideas with a vaguely religious tint," Hauerwas and Willimon use the metaphor of "resident aliens" to describe Christian churches living in a post-liberal, post-Constantinian world. Instead of the liberal church's insistence on attempting to engage and transform the secular culture, they see Christianity's future as the domain of faithful churches that live intentionally as faith communities in ways that are counter to the culturally embracing paradigms of liberalism.[22]

The "resident alien" label has become a popular metaphor for many mainline churches that have struggled with questions of theological identity and institutional mission, paralleling the explosion of popular "church-growth" literature that has flooded religious bookstores throughout the country. These books and manuals emphasize the fact (often with justification) that contemporary Americans are largely alienated from the practices of Christendom (in particular, challenging earlier taken-for-granted assumptions that the Christian message can be conveyed through the construction of grand theological narratives). Consequently, congregations need to reorient their entire approach to ministry in ways that can communicate the message of Christianity to those in the culture who no longer understand the "code words" of Christianity. This theme is particularly evident in how many mainline churches over the last two decades have followed the lead of nondenominational, evangelical congregations by emphasizing "seeker" services, predicated on user-friendly liturgies, congregational participation, and lively contemporary music.[23]

I do not have a problem with the use of the term "postmodernity" as a general description of how there has been an erosion of an earlier Christian worldview in the West, and some components of the liberal intellectual heritage have at points stressed the all-encompassing faith in human reason to perfect the world. My chief problem with many who embrace the rhetoric of postmodernity is that it can create a highly simplistic view of history, in which the erosion of religious meaning is seen primarily as a development of the twentieth century (specifically the 1960s). Those influenced by Christian postmodernity also tend to see the early church as a type of rarified Christian community that was theologically and liturgically attuned, and was a unified, trouble-free body (and a serious reading of the Apostle Paul should quickly end that historical fiction!).[24] Part of what is troubling about these "golden age" histories is that they create the impression that once upon a time in America, people were theologically literate, they always read their Bibles, they understood their traditions perfectly, the meaning of traditions never changed, and religious leaders (i.e., clergy) spoke with unequivocal authority. There is no doubt that Americans for much of the nineteenth century and for part of the twentieth century were probably better versed in various aspects of their faith,[25] but America has always been an open marketplace for individuals to choose their religious commitments. Additionally, while it can be argued that clergy have lost some of their luster as public figures in America, clerical authority has always been a malleable commodity, in some respects always circumscribed by a variety of cultural and ecclesiastical factors (and this even includes the age most seen as the pinnacle of clerical authority, seventeenth-century Puritanism, where ministers often lamented over two themes that are still heard by clergy today: poor salaries and the fact that their congregations were not listening to their sermons).[26]

It is also forgotten by many who jump on the postmodern bandwagon that liberalism's ascendancy in American Christianity occurred at a time when many Americans were questioning their faith. Liberalism emerged at a time when more traditional patterns of Christian belief were being challenged by numerous historical factors. In the nineteenth century, America was shifting from a rural to an urban society, and emerging movements in science and technology were chipping away at traditional models of intellectual inquiry, including centuries of taken-for-granted assumptions about the timeless doctrinal truths of Christianity. Despite the controversy surrounding it, liberalism gave to many people a basis by which they could have faith, not just in an emerging "modern" world, but in the God who reveals God's self through the person of Jesus Christ.

The fact that many traditions of liberalism attempted to hang onto themes of historical Christianity has largely been forgotten by many critics of liberal theology. At the heart of George Herbert Walker Bush's castigation of Michael Dukakis was a well-worn caricature that liberals were individuals outside the cultural mainstream of America, identified specifically with social and political causes on the so-called Left. In contemporary denominational circles, liberalism is identified with a variety of social-political issues such as support of feminism, multiculturalism, gay and lesbian rights, a pro-choice stance on abortion, and a tendency to support an activist role of the government in addressing social-political questions. Many conservative critics of liberalism in general identify it as a pariah movement that has been responsible for ushering in a secular worldview. For persons who watch CNN, FOX, or any major media outlet, stories on religion tend to be framed around the dichotomies of conservative politics as synonymous with the virtues of Christianity's central role in defining American greatness, and liberal politics being connected to secularism (this fact has always haunted a liberal politician like Hillary Clinton, even though she has been a lifelong United Methodist, and has often spoken candidly of the influence of her faith on her public life). What sticks out in the minds of many Americans is that liberalism is not just an ineffective strategy of theological and political engagement, but it is a godless movement that is out to destroy America's Christian heritage.

To be a Christian liberal in the early twenty-first century is to find oneself an easy target. On one hand, you are held suspect by those who perceive your religious, cultural, and political values as out-of-bounds with the so-called "mainstream." On the other hand, you are attacked by many within your own religious family who perceive that you represent an obsolete heritage that is irrelevant to the complexities of our era and is slowly dying on its deathbed.

Christianity and Secular Liberalism

For much of the twentieth century, many church leaders in the liberal camp sought a voice that would speak to Americans beyond the institutional parameters of their denominations. Today, liberal Christians find themselves frozen out of the media not only by evangelicals, but increasingly by many secular liberals. One of the ironies of American liberalism's history is that Walter Rauschenbusch's grandson turned out to be one of the major architects of a major tradition of contemporary secular liberalism: Richard Rorty. Not long before his death in 2007, Rorty commented on the work of his grandfather. While applauding Rauschenbusch's idealism, Rorty saw his grandfather as representing a movement of liberal Christianity that had run its course. While Rorty once represented a dominant trend in American philosophy that saw religious influence declining in the West, he now affirmed that religion was not likely to die out in America. The trouble was that it was the wrong form of religion, represented not by the liberal churches of the social gospel, but by conservative, otherworldly Christianity. As he surmised, "The likelihood that religion will play a significant role in the struggle for justice seems smaller now than at any time since *Christianity and the Social Crisis* was published."[27] Rorty's assessment is positive when compared to recent books by secular liberals (and proud atheists) such as Christopher Hitchens, who assert that all forms of religion are aberrant to the goal of a just society (in which Hitchens, for example, blames religion for virtually every manifestation of evil that has held back human progress).[28]

Interestingly, many critics of religious liberalism assert that it does have one thing in common with more traditional forms of Christianity: a dogmatic spirit. Traditionally, liberal theology was born out of a desire for theological innovation and an ability (at least in theory) to hear disparate viewpoints. By the same token, many Christians who do identify themselves as liberals have been slow, indeed stubborn, to acknowledge that the character of American religion has changed, and that they occupy a universe where liberal mainline churches no longer sit at the center of the culture. In short, liberal Christianity has been reluctant to do what all good liberals have done at other moments in history: adjust one's interpretation of the faith amidst changing historical circumstances.

The Past and the Future

One scholar has noted that the majority of conversations among church leaders in American mainline churches revolve around "a rhetoric of crisis,"

predicated on the belief of an impending collapse of the mainline.[29] This
rhetoric largely ignores the fact that despite all of their problems, mainline
congregations are still a major component of the American religious landscape, even amidst the staggering number of religious options unknown
a half century ago, including nondenominational megachurches and the
recent growth of what has been called "the Emergent Church" movement
(the former centered within congregations of several thousand persons,
the latter reflected through reviving the early church model of "house"
churches).[30] Recent studies by sociologists Nancy Ammerman and Diana
Butler Bass corroborate the theme that even amidst all the religious diversity in the country, there are plenty of examples of liberal congregations
that are growing and engaging in vigorous ministries.[31]

By the same token, persons who feel called to invest their time and
talents in the ministries of mainline congregations will likely encounter
obstacles that might make "growing" a mainline church more difficult
than those in megachurches or house churches. Years ago, I attended
a clergy gathering conducted by a well-intended facilitator who spoke
about the need for clergy to be more innovative and receptive to emerging
paradigms of "postmodern" Christianity. His words made a lot of sense,
as he cited a half-dozen or so recent books on church growth. But the
individual's bubble was burst when a colleague of mine asked the facilitator a perceptive question: "It's fine to talk about creating new-paradigm
congregations, and reinterpreting Christianity for a new generation. But
what are we supposed to tell the individuals in our congregations who
are over the age of sixty-five, who historically support this Christendom
model of the church? Are we supposed to tell them that everything they
believed in and supported throughout their lives was wrong?"

In microcosm, this question sums up the dilemma of liberal mainline
congregations today. Many church-growth enthusiasts that see Christianity's future through the lens of many nondenominational megachurches
or small house churches assume a clean slate when talking about their
mission. They work out of a model that one can target one's ministry
toward a particular market, frequently determined by factors of class and
generational identity.[32] Liberal mainline churches don't work this way.
Throughout America today, faithful pastors and laity find themselves
working and laboring in churches made up of congregants of diverse
ages, ethnic backgrounds, lifestyles, theological beliefs, and at times
incompatible missions, worshiping in buildings sometimes in excess of
a hundred years old (whose ornate sanctuaries and architectural makeup
fit perfectly the congregation's vision of an earlier time, but are often
a financial impediment to mission in our time). These churches share

one common denominator that transcends their denominational traditions: a scarcity of resources within congregations (and denominations)
that often don't share a clear consensus over mission. While other leaders may speak for the need for drastic changes in the ways that churches
operate (advocating any one of several church-growth gurus as a guide),
they often don't recognize that the vanguard of most mainline churches
consists of older generations that in all likelihood are guided by earlier
models of a church that many in America, both inside and outside of the
liberal mainline, pronounce as dead.

Walter Rauschenbusch frequently made the assertion that Americans
had little use for understanding history, opting instead to see the past
through a myopic lens. I think he was essentially right, and part of the
appeal of many popular evangelical movements historically is that they
are predicated on a belief that through reading the Bible in a certain way,
or encouraging certain types of behavior or worship, one would be able
to replicate conditions of the early church. Part of the problem mainline
churches have today is that they carry lots of historical baggage, whether
related to architectural design of churches (think of the difficulties of
doing contemporary worship in a gothic sanctuary), inherited cultural
customs, or institutional organization. I believe that one reason many
mainline churches flock to church-growth literature is that these works
can present a compelling vision of change, in which congregations are
called to let go of all the baggage of the past. Yet part of what is often
missing from these calls to change is an ability to look critically at the
past, assessing the past not only for its weaknesses, but for what it can
offer to congregations in the future.

Many liberal mainline Christian churches today are tempted to
embrace a vocabulary of popular evangelism that speaks of embracing
change and the hope that congregations will "burn for Jesus." There is
nothing wrong with this motivation, but the deeper question with which
churches need to wrestle is, does the mantra for church renewal represent
a willingness to enter the twenty-first century, using the past as a resource
to build a new future, or is it merely an attempt to reclaim a vision of a
lost past? (And, I would argue, to embrace a vision of the past that never
existed in the first place.)

Perhaps the one thing that unites those in most mainline churches
today is not so much accepting the concept of change. The question is, *to
what end* is that change to be directed? In the context of the institutional
uncertainty that confronts those who are brave enough to acknowledge
their identity as liberal Christians (and even for those who shun this
identity), there are resources within American theological liberalism that

reflect upon the possibility of reviving a larger holistic tradition of American Christianity that is faithful to the *past* heritage of the church, while looking with hope to the *future*. Like any other tradition of Christian theology, the history of American liberalism does not lead us to a new heaven on earth. But it does reflect upon the ways that certain leaders and communities were able to use tradition, while also engaging historical currents of momentous cultural and religious change. If liberal Christianity is to move into the future, it needs to take seriously something that has never come easy for Americans: examine the past. The next three chapters show that Christian liberalism is far more than an obsolete caricature but, like every movement of theology, is a living tradition that has reflected and responded to changing historical contexts.

Two

Evangelical and Modern
Christian Liberalism in the Nineteenth Century

P art of the difficulty of telling the story of Christian liberalism is that it
lacks a clear point of historical origin. Unlike many Protestant denominations who look with reverence to particular founding figures such as Martin Luther, John Calvin, and John Wesley (or more recent outgrowths of
American religious history, such as Joseph Smith and the Mormons or Mary
Baker Eddy and the Christian Scientists), there is no single individual who
stands out as a "founder" of liberalism. Yet liberal theology arose because
of a unique interface between emerging religious and secular currents that
over a period of time created centers where liberalism flourished, both in
academic institutions and, to a lesser extent, on a popular level in Europe
and North America.

One of the most common assertions against liberalism is that it is a theology welded to the precepts of the dominant cultural traditions of the West.[1]
Yet liberal theology emerged at a time when centuries of scientific, political,
and theological values were in a state of flux. Those who associate liberal
theology only with a vision of social progress often ignore that many of the
major figures of this tradition in Europe and North America lived during
times of tumultuous historical change. The Enlightenment in the eighteenth
century, followed by the ascendancy of liberal theology in the nineteenth century, were eras marked by scientific discovery, economic change, and political
revolution (epitomized by numerous popular democratic uprisings in France,
Germany, Italy, and the United States). Even though many of the principal
figures associated with the origins of liberal theology came out of Enlightenment and post-Enlightenment traditions of European philosophy, liberalism's
formative years in America emerged out of churches and denominations that

in various forms wrestled with a historical context of rapid social change. While American liberalism was indebted to several European antecedents, especially traditions of German philosophical and theological thought, it soon developed along lines that were in dialogue with distinctive currents of theology emerging in nineteenth-century America.

Reason and Experience: Liberalism's European Origins

Discerning a precise starting point for theological liberalism is difficult due to the numerous historical currents that fed its evolution. In the aftermath of the Protestant reformations in the sixteenth and seventeenth centuries, a number of anti-Trinitarian movements emerged that foreshadowed the development of Unitarianism in Europe and North America. These groups made an appeal to Scripture for justifying their beliefs that the doctrine of the Trinity was a fabrication of the early church, and not directly sanctioned by the Bible (the most radical being Socinianism, a movement that arose in Eastern Europe in the seventeenth century that denied the divinity of Christ). Yet these movements were also characterized by a growing tendency to stress a theme that would become critical to later movements of liberalism: *an appeal to human reason*. In the early eighteenth century, a movement in the Church of England, pejoratively referred to as Latitudinarianism, stressed the importance not only of reason, but of theological toleration. In the aftermath of the English Civil War in the mid-seventeenth century, many Anglicans were troubled by the divisive role of Puritanism in leading to religious and civil strive. Latitudinarianism's rise in England coincided with the emergence of the European Enlightenment, in particular the writing of John Locke. Locke stressed the primacy of reason in intellectual discernment, seeing this as the ultimate means to discern religious knowledge. Although emerging evangelical movements of the eighteenth century rejected many aspects of Lockean philosophy (especially the deistic tendencies of Locke's thought), increasingly evangelical movements ranging from the Calvinist-oriented Protestant communities in New England to the free-grace revivalist sects embodied by John Wesley's Methodists examined their theology in light of Locke.[2] While evangelicals like Wesley rejected Locke's tendency to deny the supernatural, they embraced Locke's emphasis that claims of divine revelation needed to withstand the test of intellectual scrutiny.

While John Locke's writings at the end of the seventeenth century signaled the ascendancy of later traditions of liberalism associated with the Enlightenment, the major intellectual spokespersons for what would become identified with theological liberalism in the nineteenth century

came from Germany. Foundational to many future traditions of theological liberalism was the work of two philosophers: Immanuel Kant and
Georg Hegel. Kant's work has been seen as striking a counterpoint to the
work of Enlightenment figures like Voltaire, who tended to see moral and
religious truth as subjectively formed. For Kant, however, reason was the
sine qua non of human existence and the primary resource to discern religious meaning. Reason was not only a means by which humanity could
ascertain the values and standards of predetermined moral and ethical
norms for human behavior, it was the means by which individuals could
actually know that the universe was in the hands of a just God. In direct
challenge to centuries of Christian tradition that stressed the sinfulness
of humanity, Kant affirmed that the essence of human nature was to will
and do that which was good, and the foundation for this goodness was
grounded in a world created by a just God.[3]

While Kant's idealism contributed greatly to future developments
in liberal theology, the work of Georg Hegel served as a critical bridge
between German philosophical idealism and emerging traditions of theological liberalism in Europe and later in North America. Hegel's work
is often associated with his views of a dialectical tension between two
opposing ideas "whereby the conflict of thesis and antithesis is resolved in
a higher synthesis."[4] Besides becoming foundational to the work of nineteenth-century political theory (most notably, the later work of Friedrich
Engels and Karl Marx), Hegel's work had a critical impact on Christian
theology due to his insistence that human experience was not something
stagnant, but actively engaged the world in the quest to discern the nature
and character of God's being. While Kant and Hegel saw the pursuit of
reason as the highest form of knowledge, Hegel stressed the dynamic character of human experience in the pursuit of reason, and as humans sought
to ascertain religious and moral truth. Unlike Kant, the God that Hegel
sought was not merely a timely monument to reason, but a being actively
engaging and willing to be engaged by humans. As Peter Hodgson notes,
Hegel saw God as a living spirit, "in the sense of energy, movement, life,
mind, manifestation, . . ."[5] This concept of God's lively and purposeful
engagement with humanity would become one of the major themes of
numerous liberal theologies to take root in North America in the nineteenth and twentieth centuries.

Kant and Hegel's work was a bedrock for many traditions of Christian liberalism for two reasons. First, it helped provide later liberals with
a theological foundation for justifying their belief in human goodness
(much like the way many Western European Christians in the late medieval era appealed to the philosophy of Aristotle to justify their doctrinal

beliefs). Their ethics became for many liberals an escape from an unappealing rationality associated with another religious outgrowth of the Enlightenment: deism. While never a unified movement, deism was not so much an organized religion as it was a philosophy that saw God as a benevolent deity who had no direct bearing on historical events. For most deists, Christianity represented a religion predicated on ethics and morals, drained of any clear foundation in Christian doctrine and tradition.

While Kant and Hegel's stress on the primacy of reason had tremendous ramifications for later traditions of ethics, their work led to many later incarnations of theology centered upon human experience. As opposed to centuries of Christian tradition that dismissed human experience as sinful, increasingly experience was to be trusted as a guide for discerning the nature of God's purpose in the world. Second, Kant and Hegel provided future liberal theology with a grounding in one of its fundamental concepts: that God was not solely a transcendent and immutable being. Hegel's theology, in particular, stressed that human experience can access and, in some manner, "know" God, and that God was immanent and personal in the sense of being ascertainable by human experiences *and* through historical processes.

The work of Kant and Hegel set the tone for the reinterpretation of Christian doctrine in nineteenth-century German theology. No figure embodies these changes more than Friedrich Schleiermacher. It is impossible to overstate Schleiermacher's importance to the development of liberal theology (and Christian theology generally) in Europe and North America. Along with Hegel, he was one of the principal founders of the University of Berlin, and over several years Schleiermacher trained not only individuals who would later be identified with liberal theology, but more orthodox scholars who helped forge in Germany emerging movements in theology, biblical studies, and church history.[6] While Schleiermacher embraced Kant's view of reason as a means to justify the existence of God, like Hegel, he sought to avoid a stagnant view of God by stressing the role of divine revelation within the realm of human history. In many ways, Schleiermacher remained firmly rooted in the precepts of traditional Protestant Reformation thought. However, he signaled the way that many later nineteenth-century theologians began to reinterpret Christian doctrine through a decidedly liberal lens.

One example of how Schleiermacher impacted the emerging movement of liberal theology was how he rethought classical Christian doctrines, such as the atonement. Historically, the doctrine of the atonement mostly emphasized various substitutionary theologies. In this view, which became prominent in Western Christianity by the Middle Ages,

Christ's death was seen as a form of redemptive sacrifice that saved humans from the "biological" perils of original sin. Schleiermacher and later nineteenth-century German liberals moved more in the direction of another medieval tradition of atonement theology called "moral influence" theology. In this view, Christ's death was not a means of being cleansed, or pardoned, from the travails of sin, but a means to fully grasp and understand the mind of Christ, in order to embody the teachings of Christ in the church and the world.

Part of the major significance of liberalism's embrace of a "moral influence" doctrine of the atonement was that it signaled how liberal theology was shifting in its view of human nature. Historically, atonement theology viewed human beings as hopelessly sinful and in need of forgiveness that could come only from God. Emerging movements of European and North American liberal theology, however, stressed that the true essence of Christianity was predicated not on various classical doctrines of human depravity, but on how human experience could enable persons to act in accordance with the divine will. As the nineteenth century progressed, a variety of theologians and church leaders increasingly saw their task not simply to proclaim that Jesus forgave sinners through his death and resurrection, but to lead believers in the process of discovering the true nature of Jesus' ministry to the world. Many components of nineteenth-century American liberal theology showed a passion not only to rethink questions of Christian doctrine, but increasingly to wrestle with how Christian teachings could be lived out in the world. What is interesting about the development of American liberal theology is that many of its major proponents, well into the twentieth century, came not out of the universities, as was the case in Germany, but from ministers of strategic American pulpits.

American Christianity in the Early Nineteenth Century

American Christianity during the first few decades of the nineteenth century revealed a paradox. On one hand, the country was overwhelmingly Protestant, with little numerical competition from Roman Catholic and non-Christian traditions. On the other hand, America as a nation displayed a range of religious diversity that made the country, as one historian put it, a "spiritual hothouse."[7] For the Protestant churches that had dominated the religious terrain before the American Revolution, the early nineteenth century was a difficult adjustment. Deprived of direct government support by the disestablishment clause of the First Amendment to the U.S. Constitution, colonial churches such as

Congregationalist, Presbyterian, and Anglican now found themselves in a nation where several upstart evangelical churches led by the Methodists and Baptists were growing exponentially, in particular in the emerging "frontier" regions of the West and South. The first third of the nineteenth century witnessed a torrent of popular revivalism that radically rewrote the religious map of the country. By the 1830s, these groups, led by the Methodists, far outstripped in size those churches that had been at the vanguard of colonial religion.[8]

Despite the ways that these older colonial-era churches suffered numerically, they continued to play a dominant role in the shaping of American theology, especially the Congregational and Presbyterian churches historically linked with the Reformed heritage associated with sixteenth-century reformer John Calvin.[9] Although many of the nation's Congregational and Presbyterian churches were losing numerical ground to a variety of evangelical movements, the theological orientation of these traditions played a major role in shaping American Protestant theology prior to the Civil War. These churches were firmly rooted in the suppositions of an earlier Calvinist worldview stressing the sovereignty of God, the fallen nature of humanity, and, for the most part, beliefs in limited atonement (the belief that Christ died for those whom God had "elected" for salvation). One of the ironies of American religious history is that for all the ways liberal theology stood in contrast to these classic Calvinist doctrines, its primary point of emergence in the early nineteenth century came out of the churches associated with the cradle of American Calvinism: New England. At the same time that many New England Calvinists sought to reaffirm their fidelity to the Reformed heritage, others coming out of that same heritage attacked its basic tenets, setting the stage for the rise of liberal theology.

On the other hand, the emergence of American theological liberalism also dovetailed with the rise of popular evangelicalism prior to the Civil War. In an early nineteenth-century theological context where many evangelicals affirmed a message of free grace, in which all persons were offered the potential of salvation through faith in Jesus Christ, many American Protestants took up the banner of making America a society that would be filled with personal *and* social righteousness that ultimately would set the stage for the return of Christ. Many of the pioneers of American liberal theology sought to avoid what the movement saw as the theological excesses of evangelical revivalism, as well as the dim view of humanity predicated by the Calvinists. Yet the majority of these nineteenth-century liberals never questioned the fact that they were part of a larger network of Protestants who sought to bring the saving message of Jesus to the masses. For much of the nineteenth century, the vast majority of liberalism's major spokespersons were represented by ministers who desired to propagate this new form of Christianity not just through preaching and a growing number of popular lecture venues, but through a variety of scholarly *and* popular publications.

"What Would Jesus Do?": Liberalism's Emerging American Accent

In 1897 a congregational minister in Topeka, Kansas, gave birth to an expression that would be embraced by future generations of American Christians. This minister, Charles Sheldon, in addition to his pastoral responsibilities, loved to write stories that he used in a variety of adult education classes in his church. By the early 1890s, Sheldon had already written fiction that was loosely based upon his parish experiences. As he wrote the manuscript that would later become known by the title *In His Steps*, Sheldon not only produced a novel that would sell millions of copies and go through numerous editions, he created a book that helped popularize many themes that reflected larger developments within nineteenth-century liberal theology.

The book tells the story of a group of parishioners in the First Church of Raymond (a church and city that sounds a great deal like Sheldon's own ministerial context), who find their world turned upside down by an impoverished man who interrupts a Sunday morning worship service. After this "tramp" tells the church his hard-luck story of how his life has been destroyed by the circumstances of modern industrial life, he brings his "sermon" to a climax before he collapses and dies.

> I have heard some people singing at a church prayer-meeting the other night:
>
>> All for Jesus, all for Jesus;
>> All my being's ransomed powers;
>> All my thoughts and all my doings,
>> All my days and all my hours;
>
> and I kept wondering as I sat on the steps outside just what they meant by it. It seems to me there's an awful lot of trouble in the world that somehow wouldn't exist if all the people who sang such songs went and lived them out. I supposed I don't understand. But what would Jesus do?[10]

In the aftermath of the man's death, the pastor makes a covenant with a group of church members to judge every action they do over the next year through the lens of the dead man's question, "What would Jesus do?" The novel highlights the subsequent actions of the various characters who seek to live out Jesus' teachings, and concludes by suggesting that the spark ignited in Raymond has touched off a national renewal of Christianity.

In His Steps is a novel that accentuates many of the cultural suppositions of late nineteenth-century white middle-class America. Even though the book is frequently cited as a harbinger for the social gospel movement, Sheldon reflected upon many classic themes that connected to a late nineteenth-century evangelical Protestant worldview (especially in regard to gender, in which one of the book's characters, an aspiring singer, serves as a paragon of womanly Victorian virtue that compels others to accept Christ). In some ways, the book has a conservative view toward social reform, seeing societal change through individual conversion and acceptance of "the Golden Rule" of Christ (Sheldon goes out of his way to debunk one of the political movements that would be embraced by some liberals in the early twentieth century: socialism). No doubt, the book's ongoing popularity among Christians of many theological persuasions was a reflection of the fact that it spoke to a context associated with middle-class American Protestantism.[11] Yet the book serves as a microcosm into an emerging American liberal theological worldview that the rest of the chapter will flesh out.

If one had to categorize what separated the growth of nineteenth-century liberal theology from earlier forms of Christian theology that emerged out of the sixteenth-century Protestant Reformation heritage, it would be the ways liberalism engaged in a sustained reinterpretation of the nature of Jesus Christ. Conservative Christianities have long critiqued liberals for the ways they watered down Christology, robbing Christianity of its ability to offer the saving faith of Christ to repentant sinners. However, the argument could easily be made that one of the major contributions of liberal theology was how the movement reinterpreted the Christological significance of Jesus, beginning with Unitarianism.

While Unitarianism's roots lay within a range of anti-Trinitarian European Protestant sects that emerged after the Reformation, the movement largely rose in the late eighteenth and early nineteenth centuries as a protest against New England Calvinism.[12] Unitarianism shared with orthodox Congregationalist churches a penchant for two themes. First, early Unitarianism tended to place stress on the model of a learned clergy, emphasizing the role of ordained ministry at the center of ordering the life of local churches (although, like their more orthodox counterparts, Unitarian churches shared a Congregationalist policy in which the local church had the ability to hire and fire their ministers). Second, early

Unitarianism was not to be outdone in seeking truth through the study of Scripture, and like all Protestants, the Bible was the source of authority by which one discerned God's will for humanity.

By the same token, American Unitarianism differed tremendously from its Calvinist cousins on how the Bible should be interpreted, and the most influential figure in charting the direction of the movement in the early nineteenth century was William Ellery Channing. Channing came of age right at a historical moment when Unitarianism was separating itself from the theological orthodoxy of New England Calvinism. As minister of the Federal Street (later Arlington Street) Church in Boston, Channing built a platform as a church leader and theologian who helped set the direction for future movements of nineteenth-century liberalism. Channing reiterated arguments long used by European Socinian apologists that the New Testament does not support the doctrine of the Trinity. Like many early Unitarians, Channing did not dispute the idea of Christ's divinity.[13] However, the idea of Christ's connection with the Godhead in Trinitarian theology created what Channing and other Unitarians saw as a dualism between the human and divine qualities in Jesus' nature. More important to Channing than attacking the doctrine of the Trinity, however, was the way he reinterpreted Jesus' significance to human history.

In examining the nature of Jesus' ministry, Channing signaled directions that would spread far beyond Unitarianism. In challenging traditional substitutionary theories of the atonement, he argued that Jesus' death on the cross was not paying a debt for human sin; it was a means of showing the extent to which Jesus would go to do the will of his heavenly Father, symbolizing God's love for the world. Jesus' life and death also pointed out the fact that Channing believed that God's eternal nature was different from orthodox Calvinism. "We cannot bow before a being, however great and powerful, who governs tyrannically," Channing observed. "We venerate not the loftiness of God's throne, but the equity and goodness in which it is established."[14] Channing and other early Unitarian leaders were familiar with developments in German theology, including the work of Schleiermacher, and they asserted that the nature of humanity was prone not to evil, but through the example of Christ, toward virtue and goodness.

As the nineteenth century progressed, Unitarianism began to move away from its Christocentric moorings; however, what connected the evangelical ethos of Channing to the later post-Christian expressions of the Unitarianism of Ralph Waldo Emerson and Theodore Parker was an idealism that rejected the biblical literalism of Genesis: that human beings were steeped in original sin.[15] American Unitarianism helped foster new ways of looking at the significance of Christ, not just in terms of his death and resurrection, but for people like Charles Sheldon, in how the nature and purpose of Jesus' life gave people a blueprint for living out their lives.

Horace Bushnell and the Rise of "the New Theology"

After Channing's death in 1842, liberal theology was well into a new process of development, not only in Unitarianism, but within more "orthodox" Protestant churches. The one figure at the center of this next phase of liberalism's development was a Hartford, Connecticut, clergyman: Horace Bushnell. One of the ironies surrounding Bushnell's life is that his major influence upon American theology really did not occur until after his death in 1876. While frequently cited as one of the "fathers" of American liberal theology, others have argued that the designation of Bushnell as a liberal is anachronistic and not a true description of how Bushnell or his contemporaries viewed his work. Bushnell biographer Robert Bruce Mullin calls Bushnell a "theological tinkerer," an individual who grew up in the heart of Calvinist New England and sought to find ways to adapt this tradition to the changing realities of the nineteenth century.[16] Yet Bushnell serves as an important bridge connecting the early American Unitarianism of Channing to traditions of liberal theology that emerged in several Protestant churches in the final decades of the nineteenth century—a tradition that contemporaries initially called "the new theology."[17]

From his longtime pulpit at the North Congregational Church of Hartford, Connecticut, Bushnell spent a long career as a parish minister and a respected civic leader in Hartford. (One of Bushnell's legacies is that he was an early advocate for the creation of public parks in the United States. Bushnell Park in Hartford, one of the first public parks in the country, is named after him.) Beyond considerable time spent as a minister and civic leader, Bushnell was a prolific author whose writings stoked the imaginations of many young ministers in the mid- and late nineteenth century, even as he suffered chastisement at the hands of his critics.

Bushnell was an individual who looked at the religious landscape of his time and didn't like what he saw. In his native New England, he was caught in the crossfire between Unitarians and Congregationalists, seeing the former as a perversion of historical Christianity and the latter as a heritage that had lost much of its theological verve. Of equal concern for Bushnell was the rapid proliferation of evangelical revivalism that had become commonplace in American Christianity. Since the mid-eighteenth century, American Christianity had gone through what historians have referred to as "great awakenings," characterized by periods of popular revivalism. The first third of the nineteenth century had been an especially vigorous time of revivalism, in which Methodist and Baptist churches and scores of smaller sectarian movements were successful in staging mass revivals (often through the medium of the camp meeting), and emphasizing the centrality of an emotionally charged conversion experience.

Bushnell was certainly no friend of revivalism, and he frequently attacked Protestant revivalism for the ways that it placed the heart over the mind. Yet he also was deeply influenced by many of the same intellectual currents that impacted Unitarianism, especially a view toward humanity that tended to stress human virtue over innate human sinfulness. Unlike Unitarian leaders like Theodore Parker, who moved beyond the moorings of traditional Christian language, Bushnell castigated Unitarianism for its departure from Christian tradition and the way Unitarianism had in his mind become a relativistic religion centered solely on human subjectivity. However, like Parker, Bushnell was heavily influenced by currents in the wider culture that increasingly stressed the importance of the experiential. In particular, Bushnell shared with many Unitarians an interest in the tradition of Romantic literature represented by English writers such as William Wordsworth and Samuel Taylor Coleridge. The writings of Coleridge were especially important in galvanizing the movement known in the 1830s and 1840s as Transcendentalism, an offshoot of Unitarianism that signaled a critical shift away from an exclusive emphasis upon Christian doctrine, stressing that God was embodied mostly through human experience and the natural world. While Bushnell rejected the post-Christian theology of Transcendentalism associated with Parker and Ralph Waldo Emerson, he did share their fascination with the natural world, and in particular the Transcendentalist tendency to seek out distinctive metaphors to speak of God's being.

Part of the decidedly "liberal" turn in Bushnell was that he laid a basis for the defense of Christian orthodoxy upon the metaphorical nature of language. For Bushnell, to speak metaphorically of God as "Father, Son, and Holy Spirit" was not to question the truth behind the doctrine of the Trinity, but to lay a basis for understanding what for him was an indisputable fact: the power of Christianity as a *historical religion*. To speak about faith as metaphor was not to diminish God's power; rather, it was to use the imprecise qualities of human language to approximate what was infinite.[18]

A second major contribution of Bushnell to the future of Christian liberalism was the emphasis that he placed on what he referred to as "Christian nurture." Part of Bushnell's critique against revivalism was that it elevated conversion experiences above the wisdom accumulated over centuries of collective Christian experience. Bushnell never discounted the importance of individual conversion; however, he sought to place conversion within the context of the larger Christian tradition. In this regard, Bushnell shared a Unitarian optimism about human potential, and he applied this to his views on Christian nurture. As individuals matured, they grew not only in their knowledge and wisdom of the world, but also in their understanding of the nature and purpose of God in the world. Comparing the process of nurture to the role of parents enabling their children to reach healthy adult maturity, faith needed to be taught with an eye to the needs of the child. This understanding of faith as a developmental process was especially critical for how Bushnell looked at the church's education of young people. As opposed to the need to inculcate youth with doctrine, young minds needed to be cultivated in such a way that they could be opened up to "the more difficult views of Christian doctrine and experience."[19] In effect, Bushnell advocated a progressive model of education that had as a goal an ability for young Christians to match their life experiences with particular doctrinal teachings.

Later critics of Bushnell assert that he helped contribute to a legacy of religious illiteracy, in which religious feeling supplanted doctrinal truth. Yet Bushnell's discussion on Christian nurture had a profound impact in American Protestantism in the final quarter of the nineteenth century, especially in terms of emerging theories of Christian education. His influence was critical to the rise of the modern Sunday school movement, predicated on training children and young adults in the rudiments of the Christian tradition.[20]

Later in his career, Bushnell's theology also picked up on emerging liberal theologies of the atonement, arguing against substitutionary (or "ransom") theologies, whereby Christ's death had been seen as serving as a form of biological pardon of human sin. Yet he also wanted to make sure that Christianity did not lose its theological grounding in the uniqueness of Christ, and make the mistake of the Unitarians by moving solely in the direction of seeing Jesus only as a moral-ethical figure. Bushnell split the difference by arguing for an atonement theology of "vicarious sacrifice." As Jesus embodied the highest example of obedience to God, it required him to sacrifice his life. What made Jesus unique in human history was the extent of his obedience to God, even to the point of laying down his life. "It is only when the GREAT HEALER dies, that we look to find his cross a deed of power."[21]

Much of Bushnell's atonement theology was formulated around the time of the Civil War, where he strongly identified the war's carnage as part of a redemptive sacrifice that would cleanse America of its evil. Like many ministers of his generation, the war was not just a political and military conflict. It reflected a divine struggle between the forces of good and evil, and to sacrifice one's life for your country (whether Union or Confederate) was not only the highest act of patriotism, but an act of divine import. The ideas promoted by Bushnell during the Civil War not only reflected an emerging liberal theology of atonement, but helped lay the cornerstones of what scholars have called "a civil religion," whereby the attributes of the American nation are directly associated with beliefs of a divinely sanctioned purpose on earth.[22] While these notions later became associated with the emergence of the so-called Christian Right in the 1980s, these ideas have deep-seated roots in American history, and many liberal movements of the late nineteenth century were some of the strongest supporters of these ideals.[23]

Bushnell left a blueprint that would be amplified by liberal theologians well into the twentieth century. To follow Christ meant devoting your entire life to serving him, even to the point where one might be called upon to suffer death, as Christ died for us. The idea that Christian theology needed to examine and reclaim the ramifications of Jesus' death became a recurrent theme in numerous genres of liberalism that took root in the years after Bushnell's death, and influenced the rise of a liberal strain of thought that contributed to Charles Sheldon's worldview when he raised the question in 1897, "What would Jesus do?" For many late nineteenth-century Christians, Jesus suffered to the point that in dying, humanity could "reawaken" to the possibilities of new life in Christ. William Newton Clarke expressed this sentiment when he noted that Christ's own suffering needed to awaken within people a sense of connection with the world's sins. Only when people could do this were they truly disciples of Christ. "The new humanity is one that joins with God in sin-bearing. Like him it seeks to save, and is willing to work and wait and suffer, that the great end may be gained. Union with Christ delivers a man from that selfish isolation in which the sins and burdens of his human brothers are nothing to him, and brings him into the fellowship of saviourhood."[24]

This new Christocentric emphasis on Jesus' death became one of the major cornerstones of liberal theology by the end of the nineteenth century. However, to fully understand this emerging worldview, one has to examine how liberalism sought to redefine the place of Christianity in the face of a rapidly changing world, especially related to how liberalism reinterpreted the nature and meaning of Scripture.

Liberalism, the Bible, and the Protestant Pulpit

By the end of the Civil War, American Protestantism found itself at a crossroads. On one hand, numerous movements of evangelical revivalism were still strong within many traditions, and the mantle of that movement was being donned by figures such as Phoebe Palmer and Charles Finney before the Civil War, and Dwight L. Moody after the war. Yet America as a society was going through numerous transitions that for some raised questions about sustaining earlier models of evangelical theology. Even before the Civil War, the country was being flooded by immigrants. In the 1840s and 1850s, the country's population swelled as Irish and German immigrants poured into the country, especially into cities such as New York, Boston, Philadelphia, and Chicago. After the war this immigration continued, spiked this time by arrivals from Italy and Eastern Europe. Increases in immigration not only caused population explosions in several American cities; it brought droves of Catholic immigrants to America, leading to the Roman Catholic Church becoming the largest religious body in the United States by 1870.[25]

Despite these changes, many Protestant churches still saw themselves as the moral caretakers of the country. Organizations such as the Evangelical Alliance were formed prior to the Civil War in hopes of not only promoting interdenominational unity, but also creating an organized Protestant movement in the face of Catholic gains (and Horace Bushnell himself was a major supporter of the Alliance). By the same token, even as many denominations were speaking in one voice about the need for unity and the shared mission of churches to "Christianize" America (and, by extension, the world), noticeable theological fault lines were opening up within many churches.

Theological liberalism had a slow and uneven acceptance outside of Unitarianism. Many Protestants worried that there was too much in liberal theology that reflected the excesses of German scholarship, and feared that liberalism might lead to religious skepticism and unbelief (and for many nineteenth-century Protestants, the emergence of figures like Theodore Parker gave pause to think carefully about these scholarly innovations). However, even as many Protestant ministers stayed away from the fine points of German liberalism, they took seriously the idea that clergy were facing congregations that increasingly were having doubts about how Christianity fit into an emerging scientific worldview—in particular the theories of evolution first put forth by Charles Darwin in the 1860s. By the early 1870s, small pockets of upper- and middle-class congregations began to emerge who, in one way or another, addressed this growing anxiety. By far the most famous of these congregations was Plymouth Congregational Church in Brooklyn, New York, pastored by the charismatic, and controversial, Henry Ward Beecher.

Beecher was the final child of the famous New England Calvinist revivalist Lyman Beecher. While the elder Beecher became known for his promotion of evangelical revivalism in the early nineteenth century, the younger Beecher largely rejected his father's faith in favor of a positive assessment of human nature and the need to preach a gospel predicated on Christ's love for humanity. Like his famous sister, Harriet Beecher Stowe, Henry Ward Beecher was a staunch abolitionist and, after the Civil War, he became an enthusiastic supporter for women's suffrage. In the 1870s, Beecher endured a highly publicized libel trial brought forth by his former friend and colleague Theodore Tilton. The public controversy brought to light questionable aspects of Beecher's character, not the least being that he not only had an affair with Tilton's wife, Elizabeth, but also that his pastoral concern for several women in his congregation extended beyond the platonic.[26]

Despite the scandal generated by the trial, Beecher's reputation remained strong in American Protestantism until his death in 1887. Moreover, Beecher served as the model for an emerging generation of liberal Protestant "pulpiteers" who rose to prominence between 1865 and 1900. Among them were Phillips Brooks, rector of Trinity Episcopal Church, in Boston; his clergy neighbor George Gordon, at Old South Church; Washington Gladden, pastor of the First Congregational Church in Columbus, Ohio; and David Swing, pastor of the Fourth Presbyterian Church in Chicago.

While largely a forgotten figure, it was Swing who articulated many themes that defined the future of liberal theology in American Protestantism. Swing had served as a professor of classics at Miami University in Ohio before becoming, in 1866, pastor of the Westminster (now Fourth) Presbyterian Church in Chicago. While lacking spellbinding skills as an orator, contemporaries saw him as an individual who possessed exceptional skills as a communicator, and in particular, an ability to relate Christianity to an emerging "modernist" view of the faith. Washington Gladden reflected on his influence when he noted that Swing "treated the dogmas of the church with great freedom, yet he sought to present the essential truths of religion in a manner so untechnical that they should commend themselves to the common sense of men." Gladden further asserted that many individuals who "had been repelled from the traditional statements of religious truth, were led back to respect and reverence" through Swing's influence.[27] Gladden's comment helps one understand the assertion made by historian William R. Hutchison that Swing was the first theological modernist to emerge within nineteenth-century American Protestantism.[28]

Modernism and "the New Theology"

The term "modernism" has frequently been used by religion scholars in one of two ways. For many, modernism has been used interchangeably with liberalism to reflect how theology assimilated knowledge emerging from the intellectual conditions of the contemporary (or modern) world. The term has also come to designate a specific movement within liberal theology that was mainly grounded in "modern" intellectual movements emerging from the sciences and social sciences. As Kenneth Cauthen noted, the modernist Christian judged the truths of Christianity through "the presuppositions of modern science, philosophy, psychology, and social thought. Nothing was to be believed simply because it was to be found in the Bible or Christian tradition."[29] Yet part of what fed this emerging theological ethos within liberalism was how some liberals embraced theories of biblical higher criticism. Reflecting another aspect of the traditions of theological scholarship coming out of Germany, biblical criticism was a reflection both of nineteenth-century archaeological discoveries and an appropriation of social scientific methodologies related to the study of Scripture. The majority of discussions surrounding biblical scholarship in the late nineteenth century revolved around Old Testament studies, and the publication of several works, most notably Julius Wellhausen's 1878 classic, *History of Israel*, led to reinterpretations of the Old Testament canon, especially challenging age-old notions about the authorship and dating of specific biblical works.[30] In many ways, David Swing was a precursor for the kinds of questions that would divide orthodox and liberal Protestants over the next several decades, questions not only surrounding the historical accuracy of Scripture, but to what extent Scripture speaks with authority on matters spiritual and temporal.

Swing's contention was not that the Bible or church tradition wasn't true. Rather, these needed to be interpreted in light of modern intellectual trends. Echoing sentiments similar to Horace Bushnell, Swing cited human language as an imprecise means of grasping something that was perfect. For Swing, the point of the Bible was not that every word in Scripture was somehow infallible, but that the Bible pointed toward the perfection of God. This led Swing to question the validity of many historical creeds, because they stifled not only religious imagination, but denied what Swing and other late nineteenth-century liberals came to believe was the crux of Christianity—that it was a religion primarily about a way of life, rather than dogma. As William Hutchison argues, "the crux of Swing's deviation from orthodoxy lay in his insistence that all religious expressions are dependent upon the culture within which they are formulated, and that they cannot be understood apart from that culture."[31] Swing's perspectives were not well received by many of his colleagues in the northern Presbyterian Church, and in 1874 he was put on trial for heresy. Although Swing was exonerated, he left Westminster Church to form a nondenominational church in Chicago, where he remained until his death in 1894.

Swing's trial represented the first public battle between Christian traditionalists and liberals that erupted within many denominations for over a half century from the 1870s through the 1920s. These battles amplified many of the issues coming out of the Swing case, and were engaged over a variety of issues pertaining to biblical inerrancy, doctrinal interpretation, and the relationship of science and religion (especially the impact of Darwin). In the years after Swing's trial, tensions mounted among many northern Protestant denominations, resulting in numerous heresy trials of high-profile liberals. Even as most of these traditions were largely dominated by clergy who represented more orthodox theological perspectives, liberal theology was gaining a foothold within many theological seminaries, in addition to gaining the influence of several prominent pulpits. By the mid-1880s, Andover Seminary, which ironically had been founded as an orthodox alternative to the Unitarian leanings of Harvard in 1807, had moved clearly into the liberal camp. Andover Seminary, as well as the writings of major liberal clergy, reflected the vanguard of "the New Theology." In this context, seminary professors like Charles Briggs at Union Seminary, New York, and, in particular, ministers such as Theodore Munger, George Gordon, and Newman Smyth became some of the most articulate spokesmen for what by the end of the nineteenth century was becoming known as liberalism.[32]

Even though "the New Theology" was largely identified with clergy and seminaries on the East Coast, the 1890s witnessed the birth of an institution that would influence liberalism's future well into the twentieth century: the University of Chicago. From the time of its founding in 1892, the University of Chicago Divinity School became one of the major centers of American liberalism, whose faculty became international leaders in the fields of religious history, theology, ethics, and biblical studies. The figure who symbolizes the nascent beginnings of this tradition was Shailer Mathews. For a later generation of Christian realists like Reinhold Niebuhr, Mathews became synonymous with all of the worst sins of liberalism, in particular, an over-optimism in human nature and transforming Christianity from an otherworldly faith into a culture-embracing ideology that only carried vestiges of religious belief. Yet Mathews played a major role at the end of the nineteenth and the beginning of the twentieth centuries in helping to synthesize some of the major themes of German liberalism for a North American audience. Mathews' influence is especially germane in the ways that his work synthesized theories of biblical criticism, sociological theory, and historical analysis, in ways that had a profound impact upon scholars, clergy, and laity of his generation.[33]

One of the major questions that characterized Mathews' work dealt with trying to discern the nature and purpose of Jesus' ministry. Part of the inevitable controversy surrounding German biblical scholarship was that it raised questions not only about the authorship and meaning of the Old Testament, but also the New. In particular, if German biblical scholars were accurate in denying that statements in the Old Testament did not serve as predictions for the coming of Christ (such as numerous verses of the prophet Isaiah), then how should one understand the nature and meaning of Jesus? Increasingly, biblical scholars on both sides of the Atlantic looked at Jesus' significance from the perspective of modern social sciences, seeking, in effect, to better understand the specific historical and religious context of the first-century Middle East. One school of biblical scholarship stressed the apocalyptic content of Jesus' message. Another tradition, embodied by Mathews, reinterpreted Jesus' message in ways that are still carried on today by the controversial Jesus Seminar and well-known academics and church leaders like John Dominic Crossen, Marcus Borg, and John Shelby Spong.[34]

Liberalism and the Kingdom of God in America

Despite the fact that liberalism emerged as an alternative to various forms of Protestant orthodoxy by the end of the nineteenth century, outside of specific urban congregations it was far from a grassroots movement. Yet increasingly, themes within liberal theology—its accommodation to science (especially the teachings of Darwin), its questioning of historical doctrines, and, in particular, its understanding of Jesus' mission—became the major topics of conversation within a variety of church periodicals and assemblies. A central theme of debate within many Protestant churches, and a key theme within emerging traditions of liberal theology, centered on interpreting the meaning of Jesus' teachings on the kingdom of God.

The term "kingdom of God" has always carried imprecise meaning, and its ultimate meaning depends on how one defines it. However, the term applies to a belief that the teachings of Christianity, as revealed in Scripture and through the witness of the church, lead to a final culmination of history. In Scripture Jesus made reference to the kingdom of God in his preaching, clearly using the term as a means of arousing his followers to the idea that God would bring about some sort of ultimate outcome to humanity's destiny. Yet throughout church history the precise nature of this final destiny has always been open to debate. In medieval Catholic theology, the idea of the kingdom of God was seen mostly as a vague, futuristic goal. What was most important in Western medieval Christianity was the role of the church in bringing people into the fold and saving their souls from the power of sin. In the aftermath of the Reformation, emerging Protestant churches began to reexamine the doctrine of the kingdom of God with greater scrutiny. For some, the kingdom of God was synonymous with the Second Coming of Christ, whereby Jesus in his bodily return to earth would bring an end to human history and inaugurate a heavenly realm on earth. While the association of the kingdom of God with an apocalyptic interpretation carried on in popularity through the nineteenth and twentieth centuries,[35] an alternative model for the kingdom of God emerged out of Germany that had a strong impact on the development of liberal theology. The most famous architect of this viewpoint was a German theologian and historian, Albrecht Ritschl.

Even though his is a name that few in the laity today would recognize, Ritschl's legacy has influenced just about every theological tradition to emerge in the West since the late nineteenth century. Ritschl followed the tradition of Schleiermacher by stressing the importance of religious experience in discerning the truth of Christianity. Yet Ritschl became focused on identifying what he considered to be the theological forces that historically united Christian movements. It was one thing to discuss the nature of Jesus' ministry, as well as interpret the meaning of his life, death, and resurrection. But how did the historical event of Jesus relate to the ongoing significance of Christianity in history? For Ritschl, and for legions of theologians who followed him, that connective tissue historically was the doctrine of the kingdom of God. For many liberals in the Ritschlian tradition, the kingdom of God was not centered upon an apocalyptic end of history. It was defined by how Jesus' teachings embodied the power of God *in* history. Jesus' coming into history represented a significant moment for Israel, whereby in his ministry Jesus was calling forth a new religious vision, one that dramatically represented the precepts of a divine society on earth (embodied by many generations of liberals through Jesus' words in Matthew 20, "the last shall be first, and the first shall be last"). While theologians influenced by Ritschl debated the extent to which Jesus' statements on the kingdom should be interpreted apocalyptically, they were united in an insistence that the primary significance of Jesus' theology needed to be understood in terms of the concrete historical realities of the first century.

Part of Ritschl's influence was that he contributed to a legacy that increasingly relied on the study of church history and in the interpretation of Scripture and Christian doctrine. In the early nineteenth century, most standard accounts of church history written in Europe and North America tended to emphasize a providential angle, whereby churches were usually guided by the hand of God (a style of writing that conversely was quick to identify those churches that were not of God). By the middle part of the nineteenth century, historical writing increasingly examined the ways in which religious movements were interconnected and how churches and individuals worked with God in the shaping of that history.[36] Adolf von Harnack, a German historian who taught at Berlin in the generation following Ritschl, took this concept even further by emphasizing that, while much of church history chronicles human mistakes, it also reveals times, especially in the history of the early church, when the followers of Jesus were able to latch onto "kernels" of truth that represented the essence of Jesus' teachings on the kingdom.

One of the frequent criticisms of liberals like Ritschl and von Harnack is that their work could be prone to romantic interpretations of church history. Many individuals who later came out of the social gospel movement tended to idealize the tradition of the Synoptic Gospels (Matthew, Mark, and Luke), due to their emphasis on how Jesus' teaching reclaimed the utterances of the Old Testament prophets (in particular, Isaiah, Jeremiah, and Amos). Conversely, these liberals tended to shy away from the perceived otherworldly themes of the gospel of John and, in particular, the Pauline Epistles (the latter being central to the reform ministries of Martin Luther and other Protestant leaders in the sixteenth century). Not only did it lead to a tendency to romanticize the early church, but it also fed into a pervasive spirit of anti-Catholicism, seeing Catholicism's ceremonialism as a priestly faith that impeded the true message of Jesus to change society. However, the historical stress on the kingdom-of-God ideal became critical to synthesizing a lively expression of Christianity that moved beyond the rationalism of certain traditions within Unitarianism, yet avoided the supernaturalism of more orthodox forms of Christianity. History was not just a stage set for God to act; it was the stage in which righteous individuals *and* churches could discern and follow God's will. Simply put, the theme of the kingdom of God helped solidify within future movements of liberal theology the belief that Christian communities could change the course of history.

For liberals like Shailer Mathews, the key to understanding the contemporary significance of Jesus hinged on the extent to which one understood Jesus as a historical figure. In 1897 Mathews published his first major book, *The Social Teaching of Jesus*. For many, this book served to validate the claim made by Albert Schweitzer in 1905 that the quest for the historical Jesus was a vain pursuit of a historical figure who didn't exist (reflected in Schweitzer's assertion that what one finds in this quest is the mere reflection of the self).[37] Yet Mathews helped pioneer a tradition of critical biblical scholarship in America that has largely been overlooked. In many ways, he helped give scholarly credence to a view that had long been advocated by many liberal ministers: that the importance of Jesus cannot be discerned by his otherworldliness, but by how he lived his life. In juxtaposition to an anti-Ritschlian movement of biblical scholarship fueled by the work of Johannes Weiss in Germany, Mathews sought to interpret Jesus along the lines of what he called "Christian sociology," whereby one could recover "the social philosophy and teachings of the historical person Jesus the Christ."[38] Mathews believed that "Jesus thought of the kingdom as a concrete reality rather than an idea" that could evolve in the context of history. "The kingdom of God for Jesus meant an ideal (though progressively approximated) social order in which the relation of men to God is that of sons, and (therefore) to each other, that of brothers."[39] For Mathews, Jesus was not embodying a religion that looked beyond the realm of this world, but represented a religion that addressed the social realities of this world. Mathews stopped short of identifying Jesus' teaching with specific social-political institutions. However, he clearly left the door open for future interpreters who saw the kingdom in the context of Jesus' struggles to bring about a vision of justice upon the earth. The question that remained wide-open for many liberals by the turn of the nineteenth century was the extent to which Jesus' teachings on the kingdom could be utilized in order to achieve a vision of social-political change. Charles Sheldon represented only one voice that raised the simple question, "What would Jesus do?" Increasingly, a number of influential church leaders engaged in a full-blown effort to see how

Jesus' teachings from the first century could be made relevant in American culture at the dawn of the twentieth.

Liberalism at a Crossroads

By the early twentieth century, liberal theology was beginning to splinter in numerous directions. On one hand, those who adhered to a more "modernist" perspective began to explore the complexities of religion in ways that moved beyond Christian traditions. For some academicians and church leaders, it became difficult, if not impossible, to hold in tension the claims of Scripture and those of the modern world. This was especially evident with Mathews' University of Chicago colleague George Burman Foster, whose work on the philosophy of religion pushed beyond the parameters of Christian theology.[40]

Yet another component of liberal theology was determined to hold in tension the claims of evangelical faith and the modern world. For many young ministers who came of age in the late nineteenth century there remained a strong fidelity to the evangelicalism of their parents, yet also a skepticism that this heritage on its own was adequate to the challenges of an increasingly industrial and urbanized world.[41] This combination of deeply felt piety and skepticism toward inherited traditions helped forge one of the most significant legacies to emerge from the heritage of theological liberalism: the social gospel.

Three

Christian Liberalism
and the Social Gospel Heritage

Most historians tend to see the social gospel's origins[1] around 1880 and cresting at the end of World War I in 1918.[2] However, the movement's genesis began long before 1880, and extended well beyond 1918. The classic definition for the social gospel came in the early 1920s from Shailer Mathews, who referred to it as "the application of the teachings of Jesus and the total message of the Christian salvation to society, the economic life, and social institutions, . . . as well as to individuals."[3] Mathews' wording could easily apply to a larger heritage of nineteenth-century American evangelicalism that carried a belief that individual conversion would transform America into a righteous nation. Susan Lindley provides a helpful nuance to Mathews' earlier definition when she notes that the social gospel "moved beyond traditional Christian charity in its recognition of corporate identity, corporate and structural sin, and social salvation, along with concern for individual sin, faith, and responsibility."[4] What is critical to both the definitions of Mathews and Lindley is that they reflect how the social gospel was closely tied to emergent themes in liberal theology. What characterized the social gospel as a distinctive genre of liberalism was its belief that social reform could lead to concrete signs of the kingdom of God in contemporary social institutions, whether in families, businesses, or governments.

The social gospel has been called the most original theological heritage to come out of the United States, and the influence of the tradition remains much discussed in the twenty-first century. While sharing a diverse range of political commitments, what tended to unify the representatives of the social gospel was a critical engagement with Charles Sheldon's question, "What would Jesus do?" The effort to discern how Jesus' social teachings could be applied to emerging problems associated with urbanization, immigration, and, in particular, the wealth disparities exacerbated by late nineteenth-century capitalism were central to the social gospel agenda, and forged numerous efforts to synthesize theology with specific arguments for economic and political reform. While the thrust of the social gospel may have run its course in the years following World War I, its legacy continued throughout the twentieth century in a number of religious and secular movements.

For some Christians, the social gospel is seen as a movement that saved Christianity from other-worldly futility, but for many conservatives, the tradition represents a decided shift away from theological orthodoxy. Yet many late twentieth-century theological movements, from liberation theology to various expressions of post-liberal thought to emergent traditions of American evangelicalism, claim some affinity with the movement.

The social gospel had many protagonists in the early twentieth century. A few, like Shailer Mathews, served as its academic apologists, who helped provide intellectual grounding for the movement. The vast majority of social gospel proponents, however, as with many representative leaders of late nineteenth-century liberal theology, came out of churches. In the 1880s and 1890s, Washington Gladden, pastor of the First Congregationalist Church in Columbus, Ohio, represented a mainstay of a movement that at the end of the nineteenth century was originally called "social Christianity." Gladden would be joined by other prominent ministers as spokesmen for this distinctive type of liberal theology, which sought to apply the precepts of evangelical and liberal theologies to the conditions of modern society. However, the person who eclipsed them all in terms of influence, and still remains the individual to whom most turn for an assessment of the social gospel, was a Baptist minister who spent his formative years as a pastor in a small German immigrant church in New York City: Walter Rauschenbusch.

"What Would Jesus Do?" II: The Origins of the Social Gospel

Despite the frequently made assertion that the social gospel began in America, the origins of the social gospel clearly had European as well as North American roots.[5] By the middle of the nineteenth century a number of Anglican ministers, disillusioned with aspects of the Church of England's mission, became well known for their ministries in poor, working-class neighborhoods in cities like London. These clergy, including Frederick W. Robertson, Charles Kingsley, and Frederick Denison Maurice, played a major role in what became popularly known as Christian socialism. Christian socialism was not so much a specific political philosophy as it was a distinctive form of theological idealism. Like early American Unitarians such as William Ellery Channing, Christian socialists tended to stress the humanity of Jesus and the importance of Jesus' life as a guide for Christian discipleship. These clergy articulated a theme that became central to the later social gospel movement: a belief that the Bible was a book that advocated justice for the poor. As the American Episcopalian W. D. P. Bliss wrote about the leaders of the British Christian socialist movement, "The Bible they considered the poor man's book, the voice of God against tyrants and humbugs. 'Justice from God to those whom men despise,' was to them the thought running through the Bible."[6] British Christian socialism had a major impact not only on the Anglican Church, but ultimately upon a number of denominations in North America. By the early 1890s, cadres of Protestant clergy and laity had formed a variety of ad hoc organizations that advocated for various measures of social-economic reform. One such group, the Church Association for the Advancement of Labor, was established by the Episcopal Church in 1887, in order to teach laity about the nature of religion and labor questions. The organization even had a collect for worship that called on persons to work with God and "strive to open to all our brothers and sisters the way to honest labor, and secure to them the fruits of their toil."[7] Similar statements appeared from small groups of clergy and laity throughout the country; however, their voices reflected a minority view within Protestant churches.

Like their English counterparts, many Americans who embraced the identity of "Christian socialists" were not necessarily interested in enacting models of political socialism. But at the same time, many Americans were becoming aware of wealth disparities between the rich and poor in the nation's major cities. Church leaders were concerned about the lack of government regulations to protect workers from abuse in sweatshops, extensive work hours with no benefits, and the absence of child labor laws. There was also a growing concern that the nation's churches had grown too complacent in the face of the injustices committed against the growing numbers of Americans (especially new immigrants) who lived in poverty in the tenements of New York, Chicago, and other major cities. Even among many Christians who worried about the radicalism of political socialism, there was a sense that churches had to do something to address the problems of poverty and labor unrest that increasingly characterized the realities of city life. Consequently, many American Protestants who embraced the social gospel saw themselves acting out of a deeply rooted heritage of American evangelicalism.[8]

Too often, the history of American evangelicalism has been depicted through caricatures of narrow-minded ministers who preached only the importance of accepting Christ and getting into heaven. No doubt, a large part of evangelical theology was predicated on the necessity of personal salvation; however, the scope of the evangelical tradition in America, especially in the aftermath of the Second Great Awakening, is notable for the fact that it saw personal conversion as a means to achieve social reform. Many early nineteenth-century evangelicals were tireless reformers. They advocated not only for temperance reform (drinking for much of the nineteenth century was criticized not only because of the intrinsic sin of alcohol, but because of the economic consequences of intemperance upon the plight of the poor), but causes as varied as educational reform, women's rights, economic justice, and, in particular, the abolition of slavery.[9] While the Bible was a proof text for some evangelicals in justifying slavery, for others, the Bible pointed to a message that saw the practice of slaveholding as an abomination against God and neighbor. In the years immediately following the Civil War, these abolitionist visions coming out of evangelical Protestantism were actualized in the founding of numerous African American colleges spearheaded by a variety of missionary organizations.[10] These earlier evangelical initiatives, especially the belief that it was possible to make the world a righteous place through social reform, dovetailed directly into the efforts of numerous proponents of the later social gospel.

What tended to unite many disparate evangelicals in the antebellum period was a shared *millennial vision*. Specifically, the term refers to faith in Christ's Second Coming, related to a thousand-year period of peace mentioned in Revelation 20. More generally, millennialism is a term used to describe the hope in a final historical consummation, in which Christ's Second Coming is seen as the crowning of a final reign of divine righteousness (or, as Revelation 21 affirms, "Then I saw a new heaven and a new earth, for the former things had passed away"). For several American Protestants, from the seventeenth-century Puritans to early nineteenth-century revivalists, the Second Coming would occur only if righteous behavior increased on earth. By the early nineteenth century, this evangelical zeal had in many ways become fused with a faith in the power of American democracy. The American experiment in popular democracy had taken root in several evangelical groups, and many evangelical leaders saw conversion as a means to make America more democratic through the infusion of Christian values and virtues.[11] Regardless of the theological bent of its adherents, American Christianity has been filled with movements in its history that see American democratic institutions as instruments of kingdom building. The social gospel, however, represented an acceleration of larger institutional efforts among American Protestant churches to create concrete structures in churches and in society that would lead to the realization of a better world.

As will be discussed in chapter 5, this millennial spirit went through some dramatic shifts after the Civil War. However, most prominent leaders of the social gospel carried on this tradition (although not sharing earlier Protestant fixations with a literal Second Coming). Yet their passion to make America a righteous nation increasingly spoke through the lens of a liberal theology, reflected in part by church leaders who picked up with greater intellectual rigor Charles Sheldon's plea, "What would Jesus do?"

While leaders associated with the social gospel addressed a wide range of issues, the vast majority originally focused on the nation's economic woes. When social gospel advocates examined the state of American society in the face of late nineteenth-century immigration, industrialization, and urbanization, they were alarmed at the extent to which the rise of business monopolies were increasingly controlling the policies affecting the poor and working class in American cities. Although many social gospelers did provide social-political remedies for these social problems, a larger number of the key representatives of the movement were more concerned about raising public awareness about the plight of the nation's poor, and seeking to stir churches to act, in concert with business and government leaders, to address these social ills.

The Rise of the American Social Gospel

Gary Dorrien notes that the belief that Christianity has a mission "to transform the structures of society is distinctively modern."[12] For all the different emphases that characterized the major representatives of the social gospel, they all shared in some fashion a belief that Christianity's mission was not just to change a person's heart, but to change the structural makeup of society. As the social gospeler Washington Gladden noted, "the end of Christianity is twofold, a perfect man in a perfect society. . . . These purposes are never separated; they cannot be separated."[13]

As a historical movement, the social gospel can be roughly divided into two phases. Its early phase coincided with the final two decades of the nineteenth century, and the second wave occurred in the years

preceding World War I, when the movement gained a prominent institutional stronghold in several large northern Protestant denominations.[14]
The first wave of social gospelers were men and women who promoted
the movement's cause as writers, journalists, scholars, public speakers,
and ministers. One part of the tradition was manifested by ministers like
Lyman Abbot, who served as the longtime editor of the popular magazine *The Outlook* (in addition to being Henry Ward Beecher's successor
to the pulpit at Plymouth Congregational Church). Another component
of the tradition can be seen through the proliferation of what later historians called "social gospel novels," like Charles Sheldon's work, as well as
a tradition of muckraking journalism that relied heavily on propagating
Christian themes. The most famous of these works was *If Christ Came
to Chicago!* written by the British journalist William Stead. Stead's book
echoed Jacob Riis' highly influential 1890 work, *How the Other Half
Lives*, a study that accentuated the economic disparities between New
York City's upper classes and its burgeoning tenements. Stead's analysis
provided a similar contrast in Chicago, but stressed the provocative argument that Jesus would be appalled if he could see the conditions of urban
squalor in this great American metropolis. Stead hammered away at an
argument that became central to just about every major representative
of the social gospel in the late nineteenth and early twentieth centuries:
the failure of churches to mobilize their moral resources to address the
nation's social problems. "The old forms having served their turn and
done their work are passing away. They hinder where they ought to help,
and fail to interpret the full orbed revelation of the will of God toward
us in all its bearings upon the social, political and national life of man."[15]
In many ways, Stead not only laid out a blueprint for the likes of Charles
Sheldon (and some suggest that Sheldon's book was a fictionalized version of Stead's); he raised deeply ethical questions that integrated earlier
evangelical passions for social reform and a liberal theological emphasis
that Jesus' teachings on wealth and on the primacy of the poor had ramifications upon late nineteenth-century society.

Even before Stead and Sheldon's work appeared, groups within
American Protestantism were organizing their resources to address the
needs of inner cities. By the early 1890s, manifestations of the social
gospel could be seen through various women's organizations that supported "home" missions in the country's major cities. These groups, or
deaconess societies, flourished in the late nineteenth century, and while
these women often spoke of their mission in very traditional evangelical
terms, many attended "training schools" that equipped these women to
understand the social-economic realities of urban poverty. Within these

training schools, women frequently did course work in emerging liberal disciplines such as sociology and ethics, and at a time when women were barred from ordination in most Protestant churches, a career as a home missionary, or deaconess, was an attractive path for many young, single women. These women's groups played a major role not only in staffing inner city schools and hospitals, but forging what would become known as "institutional churches" that provided educational and recreational opportunities for poor immigrant communities. Several women's home mission societies also contributed to the growth of the settlement house movement of the late nineteenth century, associated mostly with Jane Addams' Hull House in Chicago.[16]

The most politically radical social gospel leader of the late nineteenth century was a congregational minister, George Herron, who for a few years in the 1890s became a national sensation for his advocacy of political socialism tied to a liberal theology. Thanks in part to the support of a wealthy patron, but also due to his passion and charisma, Herron asserted that Christianity was not a religion for the rich, that Jesus advocated for the poor, and that, in order for America to be a truly Christian country, it had to renounce its wealth. It was up to all true Christian disciples to apply "Christ's Golden Rule and Law of Love to all the business and affairs of life." For Herron, applying the Golden Rule meant that one needed to embrace various forms of political socialism. Compared to the message of Jesus, Herron noted, "even figures like Karl Marx come across as dogged conservatives."[17]

Despite the flurry of interest around Herron, his political ideology was way beyond the mainstream of most social gospelers.[18] By the early 1900s, he had largely moved away from interest in Christianity, and turned his attention to more active engagement with political socialism. (At the height of his popularity, Herron was embroiled in a highly publicized scandal when he became involved in an affair with his patron's daughter, causing him to spend most of his remaining years in Europe.) The 1890s was a time period when other religious leaders like Herron enjoyed short-term popularity. Richard Ely, a prominent economist at the University of Wisconsin, wrote several books that translated the ideals of Jesus into the context of American industrialization. An Episcopalian layman, Ely echoed aspects of the earlier tradition of British Christian socialism, but went further by integrating aspects of liberal theology (related to Jesus' social teachings) to modern economic theory. While Ely's work in integrating religion and the social sciences influenced many social gospelers in the early twentieth century, like Herron, his interests ultimately turned to more secular models of political-economic reform. However, the one social gospel leader who defined the first wave of the movement, and continued to influence the movement well into the twentieth century, was Washington Gladden.

In the span of his lifetime (1836–1918), Gladden could lay claim to knowing just about everyone of religious, economic, and political importance in the United States. After years of seeking to find his calling, first as a congregational minister in New York and New England, then as an editor for the magazine *The Independent*, Gladden became the minister of the First Congregational Church in Columbus, Ohio, in 1882, where he remained until his retirement in 1914. Gladden had some success as an advocate for social reform before going to Columbus, but after he went to First Church he found the public platform that had eluded him earlier in his career.[19] Gladden served as a prototype for many liberal social gospel ministers who rose to public prominence during the first third of the twentieth century—in particular, Harry Emerson Fosdick, the founding pastor of Riverside Church in New York. As the senior minister of a large upper-middle-class congregation, Gladden fit the mold of other prominent liberal "pulpiteers" of his generation, and enjoyed a wide public following through the publication of several books (many of them adaptations of his sermons). However, he went beyond liberal contemporaries like Phillips Brooks in that he intentionally centered a good part of his ministry on teaching his congregation the importance of addressing social issues. Gladden has been identified on the conservative spectrum of the social gospel movement and, compared to Herron, his social-economic remedies were far more mainstream.[20] While supportive of labor unions and a strong advocate for the rights of labor, he was critical of socialism and tended to see social reform in gradualist steps that over time would ameliorate the excesses of capitalism.[21]

It is easy to criticize Gladden for some of his theological simplicity, especially the way that he expressed a tremendous confidence in the role of the church to teach "the Golden Rule" of Jesus as the primary means to transform the hearts and minds of those who are responsible for creating the conditions of social misery (e.g., business leaders and politicians). Yet one of Gladden's major contributions was his ability to speak to a wide middle-class audience on the importance of connecting Christian faith to social-political questions. In his years in Columbus, Gladden usually devoted his morning worship service to matters of "personal religion." However, for his Sunday evening services, he engaged topics dealing with social questions (what he referred to as "issues of life and character") that affected the men and women in his congregation.

As a theologian and church leader, Gladden maintained friendships with many persons associated with more traditional forms of evangelicalism (including the famed revivalist Dwight Moody). Yet part of what characterized his ministry was his concern that Christianity's emphasis on personal salvation did not take into account the changing contexts in which the church found itself in the late nineteenth century. "Systems of theology have their uses, but they are always provisional, always tentative," he noted in an 1883 sermon. "Finality is no more possible in them than it is possible to make final statement of the number and size and form of the branches and leaves on a growing tree."[22]

Gladden's theology reflected the classic liberal emphasis on the idea that theological doctrines needed to be updated to address the context of a particular historical moment. At the same time, a great deal of Gladden's theology emerged out of a pastoral identity that was deeply concerned with individual spiritual renewal. His hymn "O Master, Let Me Walk with Thee" was one of many popular hymns written during the social gospel era that reflected the hope that personal regeneration would lead to a just society.

> Teach me thy patience; still with thee
> in closer, dearer company,
> in work that keeps faith sweet and strong,
> in trust that triumphs over wrong.[23]

Washington Gladden became identified as the "father" of the social gospel, and he served as an influence and inspiration for a younger generation of clergy leaders who rose to prominence in the early twentieth century. Among those young ministers was Walter Rauschenbusch, who did more than any other figure in popularizing the social gospel in America, and left behind the most sustained theological legacy coming out of that tradition. Not only was Rauschenbusch's life critical toward understanding the social gospel, but he remains perhaps the classic representative of American Christian liberalism.

Walter Rauschenbusch and the Staying Power of the Social Gospel

Rauschenbusch was brought up in a German American household, where his father was a prominent Baptist minister and educator. After finishing college and seminary (which included several years of study in a German gymnasium school), Rauschenbusch became pastor of a small German immigrant church in the "Hell's Kitchen" section of New York City in

1886. The eleven years that he spent in New York galvanized his interest in addressing social questions, where he absorbed the social critiques of writers such as Gladden, Richard Ely, and the municipal reformer Henry George. In 1897 he returned to his hometown of Rochester, New York, and became a professor at the Rochester Theological Seminary, where he remained until his death in 1918. While Rauschenbusch began to write on social issues in the late 1880s, it wasn't until the publication of his first book, *Christianity and the Social Crisis*, that he achieved national and international fame. *Christianity and the Social Crisis* remains one of the classic testaments in the field of Christian social ethics. While the book expressed a range of ideas that had been articulated by earlier social gospelers, Rauschenbusch fully developed a historical-theological rationale for the social gospel that served as a blueprint for later movements of twentieth-century theology and ethics. Like other social gospelers, Rauschenbusch shared a passion for the Old Testament prophets, seeing them as a precursor to Jesus' ministry in the first century. Like Shailer Mathews, Rauschenbusch viewed Jesus as the embodiment of a prophetic message of the kingdom of God that had direct ramifications for how Christians needed to confront the problems of early twentieth-century industrialization. For Rauschenbusch, fidelity to the kingdom "is not a matter of getting individuals to heaven, but in transforming the life on earth into the harmony of heaven."[24] As Casey Nelson Blake summarized, "Rauschenbusch tore down the wall that separated faith from the public world and called on the church to address the suffering and degradation that accompanied the rapid industrialization of the United States."[25] Blake's assertion represents an important aspect for later incarnations of the social gospel legacy—an ability to remind persons that questions of politics are, at their core, deeply seated questions of faith.

After *Christianity and the Social Crisis*, Rauschenbusch became a sought-after public speaker and wrote several other books that helped define the contours of the social gospel movement for his generation and the next. It was during the ascendancy of Rauschenbusch that Americans began to use the term "social gospel" with regularity, and part of Rauschenbusch's interest in the final years of his life was fleshing out the theological significance of the social gospel for a wider American audience. His final book, *A Theology for the Social Gospel*, published in 1917, was called by Daniel Day Williams "the classic expression" of liberal theology in America.[26]

Why has Rauschenbusch's theology captivated so many within and beyond the liberal tradition of American theology? In many respects, interest in Rauschenbusch has stayed high because he anticipated ideas that were important not only to the social gospel movement in his life-time, but also to future developments in American Christianity. An earlier tradition of scholarship on the social gospel saw the movement chiefly as a reaction to late nineteenth-century industrialization. Yet more recent scholarship has begun to examine the theological legacy of the social gospel as unique in its own right.[27] One of the reasons it is difficult to assess the social gospel as a theological movement is that it imbibed the wider societal optimism of the Progressive Era. Many of the social gospel leaders were closely allied with "secular" social reformers who were committed to making America a country that could eliminate the social-economic problems associated with capitalism. Yet as the social gospel developed, it also took seriously the idea that it had to grow theologically, relating itself to the conditions of the present era. Rauschenbusch expressed this fundamental principle in the opening of *A Theology for the Social Gospel*. "We have a social gospel. We need a systematic theology large enough to match it and vital enough to back it."[28] As the next chapter will point out, part of the social gospel heritage moved in a direction that largely baptized specific social-political institutions with religious meaning. Yet one reason Rauschenbusch remains an important figure for the larger heritage of lib-eral theology is the way that his optimism was balanced by a sense that society was under divine judgment. What is often forgotten by those who love to cite H. Richard Niebuhr's diatribe against theological liberalism from *The Kingdom of God in America* is that Niebuhr identified Rauschen-busch (along with Washington Gladden) as part of the liberal tradition that had stayed rooted in more classical traditions of Protestant theol-ogy. "In Rauschenbusch especially the revolutionary element remained pronounced; the reign of Christ required conversion and the coming kingdom was crisis, judgment as well as promise."[29] While many social Christians in the late 1890s saw social reform merely in terms of applying "the Golden Rule" to the conditions of modern society, Rauschenbusch had no such illusions. Societal change could not occur only through ideal-ism; it would happen through the labors of men and women who made personal sacrifices on behalf of the kingdom of God.

There is no doubt that Rauschenbusch had some serious blind spots in the way he envisioned the kingdom doctrine. While he was largely pluralistic in his views of other religious traditions, and helped forge an ethos that shaped the Protestant ecumenical movement in the early twen-tieth century, he also was prone to an earlier nineteenth-century world-view that saw the nation's Protestant churches as the moral caretakers of the nation. For all of Rauschenbusch's "liberal" agenda on social-political questions, he was not unlike a component of early twenty-first century evangelicalism that today links the success of evangelical Christianity with the moral character of the nation. (It is also important to remember that Rauschenbusch, like other liberals of his generation and many who would follow him, had no problem with prayer in public schools, as school prayer was seen as a necessary component to teaching young people morality and the virtues of living in a democratic and "Christianized" society.)[30]

Yet Rauschenbusch saw Christianity not just through a lens of Americanization; it was the essence of Jesus' teachings on the kingdom that necessitated the imperative that Christians work on behalf of these teachings. While Rauschenbusch was more radical than Gladden, in his support for political socialism he stopped short of joining the American Socialist Party, and by and large he supported an ethic of liberal capitalism, as opposed to a socialist belief in blanket public ownership and control of the private sector. However, a major part of Rauschenbusch's public influence, like Gladden's, was in his efforts to relate what he considered to be the truths of Christianity to a mass audience. Stanley Hauerwas summarized Rauschenbusch's mission well by noting that "[he] was engaged in a continuous camp meeting designed to reclaim the 'sinner,' America, for the kingdom of God."[31]

These qualities point to another contribution of Rauschenbusch, a legacy of which some later liberals would lose track: *the interconnection between spirituality and social action*. For all of his emphasis on the ideal of social salvation, Rauschenbusch never abandoned his belief that Christian faith needed to touch people where they lived. "We do not want to substitute social activities for religion," he wrote in 1912. "If the Church comes to lean on social preachings and doings as a crutch because its religion has become paralytic, may the Lord have mercy on us all!"[32] One of Rauschenbusch's best-selling works in his lifetime was a book of prayers that sought to remind his audience that social action always had to be God-centered in its orientation. As he noted in 1910: "And if the effect of our prayers goes beyond our own personality; if there is a center of the spiritual universe in whom our spirits join and have their being; and if the mysterious call of our souls somehow reaches and moves God, so that our longings come back from him in a wave of divine assent which assures their ultimate fulfillment—then it may mean more than any man knows to set Christendom praying on our social problems."[33] For Rauschenbusch, prayer was not just a means of the individual communion with God; it was the collective striving of the church to discern signs of the kingdom of God in human history.

Rauschenbusch's Christian vision embodied a central theme that characterized the ascendancy of the social gospel in America: a belief that the disciple who embraced Christ's love for humanity might be called upon to surrender one's life. "Love demands sacrifice, and sacrifice seems the denial and surrender of life," Rauschenbusch noted in 1914. "By seeking life selfishly, we lose it; when we lose it for love we gain it. We are far more active and self-assertive when we impart than when we receive. It is literally true that 'it is more blessed to give than to receive.'"[34] Rauschenbusch practiced what he preached. He became a vigorous critic of World War I, and worked tirelessly to preserve American neutrality, a fact that caused him to lose the support from many influential allies within churches and society at large. As he lay dying of cancer in the spring of 1918, Rauschenbusch wrote a poem that reflected both his intense spirituality and his own sense that the war was a reflection of the tragic consequences of those who failed to recognize the Spirit of God acting in history.

> In the castle of my soul
> Is a little postern gate,
> Whereat, when I enter,
> I am in the presence of God.
> In a moment, in the turning of a thought,
> I am where God is.
> This is a fact.
>
> ....
>
> Is it strange that I love God?
> And when I come back through the gate,
> Do you wonder that I carry memories with me,
> And my eyes are hot with unshed tears for what I see,
> And I feel like a stranger and a homeless man
> Where the poor are wasted for gain,
> Where rivers run red,
> And where God's sunlight is darkened by lies?[35]

The themes of personal piety and social action were key components to Rauschenbusch's unequivocal evangelical-liberal theology that forever altered the character of theology in the West. When Martin Luther King Jr. noted the influences on his thought, one of the chief figures he cited was Walter Rauschenbusch. "It has been my conviction ever since reading Rauschenbusch that any religion which professes to be concerned about the souls of men and is not concerned about the social and economic conditions that scar the soul, is a spiritually moribund religion only waiting for the day to be buried."[36] As Stanley Hauerwas added, "After Rauschenbusch, there is no gospel that is not 'the social gospel.'"[37]

Liberalism and the Theological Legacy of the Social Gospel

As an enduring movement in American theology, the social gospel can be commended for many strengths, as well as assessed for its weaknesses. One of the most frequent critiques of the social gospel is that it stressed a doctrine of love without a concurrent theology of sin and evil. Despite the polemical attacks of later twentieth-century theologians, in particular Reinhold Niebuhr, the majority of social gospelers never discounted the reality of sin. Yet their understanding of sin tended to be tied directly to their positive orientation of history, in particular, the way that the social gospelers picked up on earlier liberal theological notions concerning the kingdom of God. Central to the worldview of social gospel leaders like Rauschenbusch was their heightened sense of the kingdom's role in understanding Christianity's significance in history.

This theme had always been central to various schools of liberal theology in the nineteenth century, in particular, the schools of German liberalism that emerged from Albrecht Ritschl, Adolf von Harnack, and Ernst Troeltsch. These German scholars carried a fondness for sociological analysis, a penchant that Rauschenbusch and other American social gospelers shared. However, where the German school tended to look at theoretical applications of Christianity in history (for example, the way that Ernst Troeltsch, in his epic *The Social Teachings of the Christian Church*, examined the themes of religious sectarianism), American social gospelers like Rauschenbusch were more interested in practical application. As William McGuire King noted, when people like Rauschenbusch spoke of "social salvation," they were referring to something more than engaging in social action; "it also referred to a personal awareness that one's own salvation rested in the freedom God offers mankind to enter into his atoning activity in history."[38] In this regard, the best of the classic social gospel didn't view love as a cure-all panacea to solve social problems; love was the means by which good people must sacrifice themselves for the sake of a larger vision of justice.

For the social gospelers, history was not just an arena of God's redemptive activity, but also where the forces of goodness would wage battle against what Rauschenbusch called "the kingdom of evil." For Rauschenbusch, there would always be groups that would oppose those forces working on behalf of the kingdom of God. These "super-personal" forces created networks that would always be prone toward sin and evil. "When the social group is evil, evil is over all."[39] Many liberals who followed in the wake of Rauschenbusch kept this tension alive. While some late nineteenth-century liberals spoke hopefully about the evolutionary advance of the kingdom of God in history, Rauschenbusch and subsequent generations of liberals had no such illusions. In fact, Rauschenbusch, and many liberals influenced by his thought, believed that if good people did nothing to stand up against evil, there was no guarantee that justice would ultimately prevail in history. As recent scholars have noted, the social gospel sense of optimism was not "evolutionary," nor was it necessarily "shallow" (nor was it a case that social gospelers, like Rauschenbusch, fell victim to a "cult of inevitable progress," as Martin Luther King Jr. famously noted). Rather, laboring on behalf of the kingdom was predicated on moments of success *and* failure. "Progress took place, but it was episodic. Moments of victory emerged only out of a web of suffering and tragedy."[40] This decided note of pessimism became more prominent within social gospel liberalism after World War I. In fact, some scholars see a decided note of cynicism emerging in the heirs of the social gospel tradition after World War I, a movement that helped spawn the tradition of Christian realism (neo-orthodoxy) in the 1930s.[41]

What most separated social gospel liberals like Rauschenbusch from a later generation of American neo-orthodoxy was the way that the former tended to stress the historicity of Jesus, at the expense of a doctrine of divine transcendence. Like Martin Luther King Jr., Rauschenbusch was heavily influenced by a tradition of liberal theology known as "personalism," an early twentieth-century movement that stressed that the best means to ascertain God's activity in history was through the actions of human persons.[42] Increasingly in his career, Rauschenbusch spoke about the sacred quality of human personality as a means of expressing a belief that as human beings were created in God's image, and Jesus was the supreme manifestation of God's love for humanity, so individuals could model the ethics of Jesus in their daily lives. Building upon the work of prominent liberal philosophers and theologians such as Borden Parker Bowne and Henry Churchill King, Rauschenbusch helped set the stage for the development of a rich tradition of theology and ethics that stressed the idea that "reverence for personality" was the central motif in ethics and in religion.[43]

Like earlier traditions of liberal theology, the social gospel was a culmination of a tradition that connected the social teachings of Jesus to a theology that saw Jesus' death on the cross as a redemptive sacrifice on behalf of humanity. Yet social gospelers like Rauschenbusch tended to ignore any sustained theological engagement with the doctrine of resurrection, or for that matter, aspects of Jesus' teachings that carried apocalyptic, other-worldly overtones. For all the ways he sought to stay current in the field of biblical studies, Rauschenbusch never accepted the idea that Jesus' message had any apocalyptic overtones. Even as liberal biblical scholars like Shirley Jackson Case attempted to persuade Rauschenbusch that part of the significance of Jesus' teaching needed to be seen in an apocalyptic light, Rauschenbusch remained unmoved. Jesus represented a radical voice who pointed out the ways in which contemporary society needed to change direction in order to realize signs of the kingdom's presence. In this respect, Rauschenbusch was probably guilty, like other social gospelers, of putting too much emphasis on the perfectibility of the social order and hence on the role of human beings to change history, over against the type of theology that became prominent in the 1930s, which stressed more of an Augustinian emphasis on original sin.

Another major weakness of the original social gospel, one that was shared by many who embraced neo-orthodoxy in the 1930s, was the lack of a fully formed theology of the church. On one hand, Rauschenbusch was very clear to differentiate the church as a historical entity from the theological ideal of the kingdom of God. Yet, for all the ways that he stressed the importance of spirituality, he did not spend much time attempting to flesh out the nature and role of the church, either sacramentally or as a worshiping community. Rauschenbusch tended to ignore thinkers from more liturgical traditions who were interested in integrating doctrines from the early church with a discernible social praxis. One of Rauschenbusch's closest colleagues was Vida Scudder, an English professor at Wellesley College, who sought to integrate her understanding of Anglican tradition into her theology of the social gospel. "Scudder did not think that freedom from doctrine would necessarily mean freedom for the oppressed. Christian doctrine could provide the gateway to human liberation. The creeds gave Christians a clearer vision of God's liberating activity in the history of social action."[44] Scudder possessed a deep interest in upholding the doctrine of the Trinity as representing "the nature of God's creative life, the highest type of social life," and providing "the norm for social relationships."[45] While Scudder shared Rauschenbusch's concern that the church not be confused with the kingdom of God, she placed more emphasis on the role of the church as a spiritual community that equipped its members to use church tradition as a means of addressing the social problems of the present day. For Scudder, liturgy and worship were indispensable parts of the church's social mission. Elizabeth Hinson-Hasty noted how Scudder engaged patristic creedal sources as a means to justify the church's support of democratic reform.

> As the dramatic center and climax of the Church year, the liturgies . . .
> introduced worshipper to the meaning of divine nature for the current social context. Interpreting the Trinity in light of contemporary

discussions of democracy, Scudder argued that it was 'only today, as democracy comes to its own, that these meanings can be fully perceived.' The symbol of the Trinity 'as found in that glorious Athanasian Hymn of Praise, is the noblest expression of man's best and richest religious thought which has ever yet evolved.' What Athanasius won in his fight for homoousion was a social creed teaching that 'social harmony depends not on differentiation of rank but on diversity of function.' Ancient doctrine still bore the promise to inspire Christians to saturate the world with democracy.[46]

Attention on Vida Scudder often focuses on how she advocated a distinctive genre of Christian socialism (especially how she, unlike Rauschenbusch, ultimately joined the American Socialist Party). What is frequently forgotten is that Scudder's stress on sacramental worship formed the basis for much of her liberal theological worldview. In fact, the legacy of Vida Scudder can be seen in many of the arguments within early twenty-first-century movements that speak of a need to create movements of "radical orthodoxy," reflecting the interconnection between early church liturgies and social action.[47]

For all the ways Rauschenbusch valued Scudder's friendship, he always carried a bias against liturgical traditions that he felt drowned Christianity in priestly excess. This bias was even more acute in his lack of engagement with a tradition of Catholic social teachings, represented by the work of Father John Ryan, that sought to connect a program of economic justice with the doctrinal heritage of Catholicism. Like an earlier generation of Protestants, Rauschenbusch carried a bias against Roman Catholicism, seeing it as a tradition that was counter to the spirit of religious democracy and American religious freedom. The inability of Rauschenbusch and other Protestant contemporaries to probe more fully the doctrine of the church would prove in some ways costly to the future of American liberal Christianity as the twentieth century progressed.

Rauschenbusch was referred to by some of his contemporaries (including Vida Scudder) as a modern mystic, a label that he rejected. Yet his life certainly displayed an affinity with historical movements of Christian mysticism, even though Rauschenbusch denied this association.

If one liberal leader in the twentieth century embodies how social action was tied to a deeply rooted vision of Christian mysticism, it was Howard Thurman. Thurman's life drew on an amazing range of influences.[48] Born to an impoverished African American family in Daytona Beach, Florida, in 1899, Thurman attended Rochester Theological Seminary as one of a small number of African Americans who was admitted into this predominantly white seminary, arriving in Rochester just a few years after Rauschenbusch's death.[49] While indebted to a theological grounding in liberalism at Rochester, his later career as a pastor, writer, and educator was defined by the ways that he integrated liberalism with an interest in Quaker teachings, world religions, and a passion to address issues of racism. As chaplain at Howard University, minister of an interracial and interfaith church in San Francisco, and dean of the chapel at Boston University (where he encountered Martin Luther King Jr. as a graduate student), Thurman emphasized not only a message that Christian faith needed to challenge the conditions of American racism, but also stressed that the Christian quest for justice was inseparable from a deeply committed and disciplined spirituality. Perhaps more than any figure coming out of the liberal Protestant heritage, Thurman integrated a vision of social justice rooted in a range of meditative traditions. In a style rich in poetic metaphor, yet relevant to the struggles of twentieth-century faith communities against racism, militarism, and an uncritical nationalism, Thurman's writing revealed a style of liberal theology that was contextually relevant, yet in its own way transcended his historical era. A meditation on Christ's incarnation from the early 1940s reveals the power of Thurman's theological vision.

> The word—Love.
> The meaning of life, what is it?
> Down through the ages the timeless words ring out—
> "Hear, O Israel, the Lord thy God is one;
> And thou shalt love the Lord thy God
> With all thy heart, mind, soul and strength;
> And thou shalt love thy neighbor as thyself."
>
> And thy neighbor? Any man whose need of thee lays claim—
> Friend and foe alike. Thou must not make division.
> Thy mind, heart, soul and strength must ever search
> To find the way by which the road
> To all men's need of thee must go,
> This is the Highway of the Lord.[50]

Much of the attention of liberalism's impact upon African American Christianity centers upon Martin Luther King Jr. However, Thurman represents a largely forgotten chapter in twentieth-century American theology of someone who both honored his moorings in African American Christianity, and strove to build faith fellowships that transcended race, class, and, in some respects, religious tradition. The conclusion to his autobiography published two years before his death in 1981 echoes aspects of Rauschenbusch's earlier "Little Gate to God."

Failure may remain failure in the context of all our strivings, . . . tragedy may continue to yield its anguish and its pain, spreading havoc in the tight circle of our private lives, the dead weight of guilt may not shift its position to make life even for a brief moment more comfortable and endurable, for any of us—all this may be true. Nevertheless, in all these things there is a secret door which leads into the central place, where the Creator of life and the God of the human heart are one and the same. I take my stand for the future and for the generations who follow over the bridges we already have crossed. It is here that the meaning of the hunger of the heart is unified. The Head and the Heart at last inseparable; they are lost in wonder in the One.[51]

The mystical vision of Howard Thurman remains a critical reminder that the imperative to work for justice must come from a deeply felt spiritual core. Thurman's lifelong search for this authentic spiritual center represents an appealing component to the heritage of twentieth-century liberal theology and, perhaps, for the renewal of twenty-first-century Christian liberalism.

The Social Gospel and the Liberal Pulpit

The concern that leaders such as Rauschenbusch and Thurman displayed for the care of individuals, as they sought to transform society, became a defining characteristic in the development of the Protestant pulpit, leading to an era that crested around 1960. The seeds of this heritage go back into the nineteenth century with well-known preachers like Henry Ward Beecher. Beecher's preaching, in part, carried a therapeutic, self-help component that is still characteristic of segments of the liberal pulpit today. His emphasis on the inherent goodness of humanity led to numerous offshoots of this heritage. Included in this tradition are figures like Norman Vincent Peale and a more contemporary figure not often associated with liberal theology: Robert Schuller. Part of the success of Peale and Schuller is they embodied an updated version of a theological heritage first popularized by Beecher. Mainly, God does not judge people for their sins; rather, he wants them to succeed and is ready to help them in this task. Various ministers who have extended the "self-help" heritage of Henry Ward Beecher are seen by many in the liberal tradition with a degree of embarrassment. Yet the whole "prosperity gospel" heritage has proved enormously popular (and lucrative) for many Protestant preachers past and present (and increasingly has entered the realms of many notable evangelical preachers, such as Joel Osteen and T. D. Jakes).[52]

Besides the self-help tradition of the liberal Protestant pulpit, another dimension of twentieth-century liberalism made a direct connection between pastoral care and prophetic theology. Many clergy who came of age in the heyday of the social gospel often carried a dichotomy in their theological worldview, drawing a sharp dualism between priestly ministry, predicated upon an "aesthetic" stress on worship and self-care, and a prophetic ministry, predicated on social action.[53] By the same token, what characterized the success of liberal ministers like Harry Emerson Fosdick was not only the social gospel liberalism they manifested in their sermons (embodied by a tendency to stress the themes of economic and racial justice, and, in many cases, a support of pacifism), but the ways these ministers embodied a deep concern for the care and nurture of their large upper-middle-class congregations. In the heyday of Protestant influence in the mid-twentieth century, liberal ministers such as Fosdick, George Buttrick, Ralph Sockman, Henry Hitt Crane, and Ernest Fremont Tittle used pastoral care as an effective strategy that strengthened these preachers' status, both within their congregations and within the larger culture. Tittle in particular is reflective of a particularly unique example of this paradigm. Between 1918 and his death in 1949, he was senior minister of the First Methodist Church in Evanston, Illinois, one of the most influential Methodist pulpits in the country (in 1954, First Church would host many sessions for the Second General Assembly of the World Council of Churches—the only general assembly of the Council held in the U.S.).[54] Like Fosdick, Tittle had served on the front lines of France in World War I as a chaplain under the auspices of the YMCA. These experiences pushed Tittle into pacifism, a position that he and many liberals of his generation held for the rest of their lives. Initially inspired by Walter Rauschenbusch, Tittle became one of the most outspoken Protestant representatives of the social gospel heritage between the world wars. Yet many of his church's members came from politically conservative, upper-class constituencies who were at the center of the Chicago corporate world. At a time when newspaper mogul William Randolph Hearst organized an all-out assault against liberal ministers like Tittle (reflected in Hearst's financing of several "Christian businessmen's" caucuses), Tittle's congregation repeatedly defended Tittle against a variety of "patriotic" groups that tried to force him from his pulpit. In 1933, First Church passed a "free pulpit" resolution, a largely forgotten chapter in the history of American Christianity, that amounted to a sort of "bill of rights" not only for Tittle, but for any Christian minister who felt bound by faith to speak from one's conscience. "We stand for a free pulpit and a free church," the resolution asserted. "We hold it peculiarly important in this day that the church should stand apart from all appeals to passion, prejudice, and partisanship, and that our nation should have in the Christian church a clear, strong voice rising above all divisions, speaking in the name of God for justice, mutual understanding, and good will."[55]

The acid test for Tittle, as it was Fosdick and other well-known liberal preachers, was that they practiced what they preached. As liberal theology historically embodied a desire that human nature was good, liberal ministers supported this theme by the way they cared for individuals within their congregations, in some cases making use of extensive visitation, as well as what would come to be known after World War II as pastoral counseling.[56] The most famous story related to Tittle's legacy was recounted years later.

> The wife of a man in this congregation had died. The man was obviously embittered by this experience. Dr. Tittle, it is said, went to his front door and offered assistance, and the man wanted nothing to do with anybody at this point. So Dr. Tittle walked just to the end of the block and waited and watched. . . .
>
> Soon the man came out of his front door and made his way along the shoreline, walking nearly three hours with Dr. Tittle 30, 40, 50 paces behind him, never saying a word. They walked north on the shoreline and then came back to his house. Not intruding on the man's privacy, Dr. Tittle stood a good distance from the man as he made his way to his front door. But before that door was opened, the man turned and said to Dr. Tittle: "Thank you for being with me."[57]

This account goes beyond a sentimental reflection, but embodies how many liberal ministers like Tittle sought to embody Christ-like love for their parishioners. Although their number is shrinking, the heritage of an earlier era of big-steeple liberal Protestantism exists in certain urban and suburban pulpits. While the nature of their ministries has changed with the passing of time, these churches still embody vestiges of this earlier model of liberal establishment Protestantism.[58] The downside of this model, however, was that many preachers worked themselves to death. The price that Tittle paid for his public stature in American Protestantism and his long-term tenure in Evanston was at the cost of his own personal needs, most especially, his health. He suffered through several heart attacks during his thirty-one years in Evanston, the final one claiming his life three days after he preached his final sermon.

Although still a component within some traditions in North America (especially in historical African American churches), the appeal of the Protestant pulpiteer has lost much of its cultural muster in mainline

Protestantism. While relatively recent figures such as William Sloane Coffin stressed in their sermons the interplay between spirituality and social justice,[59] the "big steeple" pulpit has suffered through the changing demographics of mainline denominations (highlighted by the decline and closing of several of these former prominent churches), as well as changing cultural views of ministry that have altered the place of the pulpit in American religious life. Yet the connection in pastoral ministry between a passion for social justice *and* a pastoral concern for individuals represents a vital component within many contemporary churches. It is part of the larger debt of many Christian movements today to the legacy of the social gospel.

The Social Gospel Heritage: Yesterday and Today

The social gospel had a major impact upon the institutional contours of American Protestantism, in large measure thanks to Rauschenbusch's influence, that extends to our time. Between 1907 and 1917, the vast majority of Protestant churches in the North, and a few in the South, began to adopt "social creeds," statements that sought to outline the role of Christianity in addressing pressing social-economic problems. Further, the social gospel played a central role in driving the formation of the ecumenical movement in the United States. The formation of the Federal Council of Churches in Christ in 1908 was largely a response of many Protestant denominations to the question of how churches embodied Jesus' teachings in ways that addressed specific social-economic problems.[60] The way that the twentieth-century ecumenical movement was fueled by a concern that churches needed to promote social justice, not just fleshing out the fine points of doctrine, was a reflection of how social gospel liberalism was transforming the contours of American Christianity. Today a wide variety of Christian churches and denominations regularly pass resolutions on a range of contemporary social questions that reflect the ongoing evidence of the social gospel heritage.

Yet the rise of the larger heritage of social Christianity that represents such a major part of the theological story of twentieth-century American Protestantism has largely been a story about the institutional character of American churches. As historian Sidney Mead noted, the social gospel was a movement that did not lead to the creation of any new churches, and was largely consigned to the corridors of power within preexistent Protestant denominations.[61] The social gospel had a major impact upon the leadership of mainline Protestant churches, especially among clergy. However, the movement's impact upon rank-and-file membership in

American Protestant congregations was not as significant as many later liberals wanted to claim, especially when one considered that the social gospel's rise in the first two decades of the twentieth century paralleled the emergence of perhaps the single most significant grassroots movement in the history of American Christianity: pentecostalism.

Even more troubling is that the original social gospel fixation upon economic reform tended to blind the movement to other issues, in particular, race and gender. On one hand, social gospel leaders like Washington Gladden and Walter Rauschenbusch did speak about the need for racial justice, and both men spent a good deal of time teaching and preaching within African American schools and institutions in the South. Yet both tended to see race as a uniquely southern problem that could be solved through economic means. While Washington Gladden devoted a chapter in his autobiography to what he called "the Negro Problem," he largely framed the issue in terms of betterments in education as the means to end racial inequality in America.[62] Rauschenbusch was harsh in his assessment of Jim Crow segregation; however, he too largely consigned the problem of race to the South, and looked toward a day when racism could be eliminated through education and enlightened public opinion. For all the visionary aspects of their thought, white social gospelers like Walter Rauschenbusch largely ignored an emerging tradition of black religion that was thriving not only in the South, but increasingly in the North. By the early twentieth century, African American ministers like Reverdy Ransom represented an incarnation of the social gospel within African American churches, and shared with Rauschenbusch a concern for working toward a vision of the kingdom of God.[63] Sadly, however, the experience of African American leaders such as Ransom and Nannie Helen Burroughs, leader of the Woman's Convention in the National Baptist Convention of America, never intersected with those of the more traditional social gospel of Rauschenbusch.[64] A similar astigmatism can be seen in terms of the way that social gospelers dealt with issues of gender equality. When one reads male social gospelers like Rauschenbusch, it is impossible to overlook their conservative views toward women, in particular, the argument that women served society primarily through their roles as wives and mothers.[65]

Despite the shortcomings of the tradition, the social gospel left a permanent imprint upon American Christianity. The imperative that Christianity had a responsibility to work for systemic changes in the larger culture has been a theme that many Christians from diverse theological persuasions now fully embrace. Additionally, the social gospel is significant in the fact that it honored one of the central tenets of liberal theology:

to engage in periodic theological readjustment and self-analysis, in order that Christianity can address changing historical contexts. While it is true that the classic social gospel did not engage in sustained analysis of race and gender issues, this was not true of the theological heirs of the social gospel who, with greater regularity in the decades following the so-called demise of the social gospel, picked up the mantle of these causes.[66]

The social gospel's legacy helped shape a distinctive legacy of twentieth-century Christian social action, one that, as Martin Luther King Jr. recognized, sought to connect the theology of spiritual conversion with a praxis that was committed to the reform of society. Yet there is also a dimension to the social gospel's legacy that puts a tremendous stress on human capabilities that at points approaches a "work's righteousness" theology. For some future heirs of the social gospel legacy, social action became the sole means of discerning the success, or failure, of Christianity. As the twentieth century progressed, this tendency was passed on to many movements coming out of American liberal theology. For all the ways that the Niebuhrian response against liberal Protestantism in the 1930s was an attack against liberal views of human goodness, the revolution that theologians like Reinhold and H. Richard Niebuhr signaled was, in its own way, a distinctive phase in liberalism's growth. Yet by the mid-twentieth century, the Niebuhrian movement reflected only one aspect of how liberalism found new theological outlets, both inside and outside of mainline churches.

Four

The Diffusion of Liberal Theology

Throughout the twentieth century, liberal theology went through a number of transformations. The legacy of the social gospel remained a powerful force within many Protestant denominations, influencing traditions as disparate as 1930s neo-orthodoxy and various post-1960s movements of liberation theology. Additionally, movements of liberalism flourished not only within theological seminaries and universities, but carried to the center of "the Protestant Establishment." At mid-century, liberal mainline churches appeared to be growing and, in the aftermath of World War II, most of these denominations had good reason to believe that their future was secure. The liberal-inspired ecumenical movement flourished, as did efforts among Protestants and Catholics to reach out to one another across centuries of division. The Second Vatican Council that took place between 1962 and 1965 opened American Catholics up to numerous currents of liberal theology, contributing to creative theological currents that still influence contemporary theology.[1]

And yet even during a time of Protestant cultural dominance, liberal theology was in a state of flux. In the years after World War I, many individuals disillusioned with that war's outcome left institutional Christianity in favor of expressing their faith within more secular venues. These venues would forge a disparate network of social action movements that would ultimately lead to the direct action movements of the civil rights movement of the 1950s and the anti-Vietnam war movement in the 1960s. When the confident posture of the mid-twentieth-century Protestant establishment gave way to the cultural uncertainties of the 1960s and 1970s, liberalism became an easy scapegoat for the problems of mainline Protestantism, whose churches steadily lost members in the years after 1965. This changing historical landscape served also as a backdrop for the public resurgence for many movements of evangelicalism by the mid-1970s.

The growing fragmentation within twentieth-century liberalism showed how the heritage had moved away from several of the theological and cultural suppositions of the late nineteenth century. In the early twentieth century, the majority of major liberal spokespersons saw themselves addressing a unified church within a nation that they believed was at the forefront of building the kingdom on earth. By the end of the century, while vestiges of that earlier liberal Protestant vision remained, liberal theologies spoke in many voices, but often found themselves struggling to find a popular audience.

Neo-Orthodoxy and Liberalism

Despite the fact that most historians and theologians separate the movement of American theology frequently known as neo-orthodoxy from earlier traditions of liberalism, it is probably more accurate to speak of neo-orthodoxy as one of several streams of liberal theology that developed in twentieth-century theology.[2] As Gary Dorrien notes, while neo-orthodox theologians "blasted liberal theology repeatedly and contributed mightily to its eclipse, their thinking always belonged essentially to it, and they . . . contributed greatly to refashioning it."[3] What frequently gets labeled American neo-orthodoxy certainly carried a strong critique of earlier liberal theologies. Yet for all the ways that studies of American theology see the so-called neo-orthodox turn as a decisive shift away from liberalism, the heritage represented the most public evidence of how liberal theology was entering a new period of critique and self-examination.[4] While neo-orthodoxy reintroduced many theological arguments associated with earlier Protestant traditions (especially emanating from the sixteenth-century magisterial reformations of Luther and Calvin), the movement was essentially liberal in terms of how it understood Christianity's role as a mediating tradition, and for Christianity to stay experientially open to the larger culture.[5] Theologians like Karl Barth might have castigated earlier liberals for their social optimism (especially their progressive view toward history) and what they considered to be their abandonment of classical Christian doctrine; yet theologians who followed in the shadow of Barth never doubted the relationship of their thought to decidedly "modern" views of scriptural interpretation, scientific examination, social reform, and religious experience.[6] Embodied in the U.S., most especially in the legacy of Reinhold and H. Richard Niebuhr, neo-orthodoxy critiqued earlier liberalism while also constructing new theological movements that built upon the ashes of earlier liberal movements like the social gospel.

The influence of the Niebuhr brothers cannot be overstated, and their work still sounds themes made by many contemporary theologians and ethicists. While both brothers had their own emphases (with Reinhold's interests lying mostly in ethics and politics, and Richard's in historical theology and the sociology of religion),[7] their work coalesced around a critique of earlier traditions of theological liberalism. Yet these critiques, as Dorrien suggests, need to be seen as arguments that engaged and strengthened liberalism, as opposed to overturning it. Most importantly, each brother lifted up themes emerging from continental neo-orthodox theologians like Barth who stressed the inherent sinfulness of humanity, predicated on the sixteenth-century reformations' "recovery" of St. Paul and Augustine. This stress represents perhaps the most recurrent theme within the larger tradition of neo-orthodoxy. By placing too much confidence in human beings to change their environment, liberalism generally, and the social gospel in particular, placed too much confidence in humanity to change history. What was needed was a Christian faith strong enough to recognize the classic tenants of its faith as a means for one to root out social injustices. As H. Richard Niebuhr noted in 1936, "repentance for the sins of social life is not enough; there needs to be repentance for the sin, for the false faith, for the idolatry which issues in all these sins. Men will be ready for no radically new life until they have really become aware of the falsity of the faith upon which their old life is based."[8]

The Niebuhrs never questioned that part of what constituted the strength of Christianity was that it critiqued the social-economic problems facing modern society. In the 1920s and 1930s, Reinhold followed in the progression of earlier social gospel liberals like Rauschenbusch by advancing a Christian socialist and anti-capitalist worldview. However, whereas the classic social gospel tended to view social regeneration through an increase in human goodness, the Niebuhrian turn in theology grew increasingly pessimistic about this possibility. While segments of liberal Protestantism in the 1920s accentuated the theme that good people, embodied through the moral power of the church, needed to work to change history,[9] Niebuhr came to articulate a characteristic argument: that the pursuit of justice had less to do with human perfection than it did to the control of human proclivities toward injustice. As he noted in *Moral Man and Immoral Society*, "the sentiments of benevolence and social goodwill will never be so pure or powerful, and the rational capacity to consider the rights and needs of others in fair competition with our own will never be so fully developed as to create the possibility for the anarchistic millennium which is the social utopia, either explicit or implicit, of all intellectual or religious moralists."[10]

Part of what made Reinhold Niebuhr so controversial in the 1930s and 1940s was his challenge to a growing movement of Christian pacifism prominent among liberal church leaders and various Protestant youth organizations. While a pacifist in the 1920s, Niebuhr grew increasingly disillusioned with the pacifist worldview, citing that ethical admonitions alone could not control an irrational humanity. The atrocities of World War II, in particular the horrors of the Holocaust, gave credence to many of Niebuhr's views, supporting his perspective that coercive measures of violence, while on one level abhorrent, are unavoidable toward the construction of a just world. Indeed, one specific illustration that gives practical support to Niebuhr's worldview came from a parishioner of Ernest Fremont Tittle, one of the chief spokespersons of liberal pacifism in the 1930s and 1940s. After receiving counsel from Tittle to become a conscientious objector during World War II, the parishioner, after a great deal of soul searching, enlisted in the army and later was part of an American force that liberated one of the Nazi death camps. In viewing what he witnessed in the concentration camp, and reflecting about the evil that caused it, this individual could only reach one conclusion: Tittle was wrong.[11] This illustration underscores how Niebuhr gave voice within liberal denominations for a larger tradition of "just war." Derived from the teaching of Augustine, just war theory emphasizes the belief that war, while morally reprehensible, can be fought if the cause is deemed just, and the means are just (such as not targeting civilian populations). In the cold war years after World War II, many Protestant leaders like Niebuhr gave voice to this doctrine. During the Vietnam era of the 1960s and 1970s, however, a growing anti-war movement in America challenged many of the precepts of just war doctrine, especially the concept that it was possible in an age of "modern" warfare to make easy distinctions between combatants and noncombatants. Nevertheless, even as Reinhold Niebuhr's work has been justifiably critiqued, the influence of his thought remains embedded within the landscape of contemporary theology.[12]

Many critics of Reinhold Niebuhr have argued that his polemical style led him to make simplistic assertions concerning liberal theology, especially the often-repeated charge that liberalism denied the tragic elements in human nature. The noticeable Augustinian streak in Niebuhr and other neo-orthodox thinkers obscured them to the ways that earlier twentieth-century traditions of liberal idealism did not deny the reality of human sin and evil. Yet part of understanding the differences between Reinhold Niebuhr and Walter Rauschenbusch exceeds how each understood the doctrine of the fall. While each came out of very similar backgrounds (with fathers who were ministers out of German-pietist backgrounds), their theological differences are a manifestation of how each came of age in very different historical eras. Rauschenbusch was a product of an era in which the Progressive-Era stress on human goodness was seen as an essential component toward countering age-old arguments that conditions of poverty were somehow divinely and socially immutable. Niebuhr came of age at a time when this idealism was being tested first by Western disillusionment after World War I, followed by the gripping turmoil of a worldwide economic depression and global warfare.

Yet there is also a natural affinity between Rauschenbusch and Niebuhr that often goes unnoticed. Both men in their work were committed to examining the necessity of Christianity in crafting a "public theology," whereby the resources of Christian theology could be used to examine social-political questions for an audience beyond the church. Even though Niebuhr gave an appearance of being a captive to the interests of dominant cultural and political elites (especially in the years after World War II), he never lost his critical eye to the tragic consequences of American dreams of political and military dominance. Reflecting upon the political circumstances confronting America in the face of the cold war, Niebuhr warned Americans of the military and moral limits of American power: "A nation with an inordinate degree of political power is doubly tempted to exceed the bounds of historical possibilities, if it is informed by an idealism which does not understand the limits of man's wisdom and volition in history."[13] Despite the differences that existed between the two thinkers, both Rauschenbusch and Niebuhr stand out as perhaps the preeminent public theologians in the history of twentieth-century American Protestantism.

While many liberal leaders in the1930s and 1940s reacted negatively to some aspects of neo-orthodoxy (in particular, Karl Barth's emphasis on God's transcendence and separation from history), a large segment of the liberal tradition took seriously the neo-orthodox critique, becoming what the liberal theologian Georgia Harkness called "chastened liberals."[14] In the years of her formative influence in American theology during the 1940s and 1950s, Harkness reflected the ways that the spirit of an earlier liberal tradition, rooted in the social gospel, moved into the middle third of the twentieth century. Harkness was the major advocate for women's ordination in the Methodist Church (leading to that denomination's acceptance of women's ordination in 1956), and became one of the major voices in American Protestantism for women's rights, racial justice, and anti-militarism. While she represented a sizeable component of liberalism that remained weary of a wholesale embrace of neo-orthodoxy, she conceded that some aspects of liberalism "capitulated to science almost to the point of kowtowing before it, and in emphasizing the dignity of man it gave too little recognition to the fact of human sin and the ever present need of divine forgiveness and grace."[15]

Part of Harkness' legacy was that she sought to reconnect liberal theology to its late nineteenth-century moorings within specific faith communities. Many of her formative books, written while she was a faculty member at Garrett Biblical Institute[16] from 1939 to 1951, were designed specifically for laity. Like an earlier generation of evangelical liberalism, Harkness displayed a penchant for writing devotional works, including prayers and hymns. Her hymn, "Hope of the World," was sung at the Second General Assembly of the World Council of Churches in Evanston, Illinois, in 1954 and today remains a staple hymn in Protestant hymnals. While the hymn reflects a confident posture of mid-twentieth-century Protestant triumphalism, it displays the classic social gospel emphasis on personal spiritual renewal and collective discernment and action.

> Hope of the world, thou Christ of great compassion,
> speak to our fearful hearts by conflict rent.
> Save us, thy people, from consuming passion,
> who by our own false hopes and aims are spent.[17]

Like many liberal theologians of her time, Georgia Harkness displayed the tenets associated with the heritage of theological personalism. Yet she also was in dialogue with many of the critiques of liberal theology made by neo-orthodoxy, reflecting further the influence of American theologians like Reinhold Niebuhr on the shaping of American theology.

For all of neo-orthodoxy's influence upon the development of American Christianity, its influence was not universally embraced by all liberal Protestant traditions.[18] Daniel Day Williams noted a common critique: that neo-orthodoxy "has recovered for us a profound analysis of the reality of sin and the need of redemption. But it has not made clear how redemption actually makes any difference in this life in this world."[19] Many later movements of American theological liberalism echoed Williams' assessment that the Niebuhrian stress on sin undercut any basis for Christian social action to change society.[20] And yet, few theological conversations today, nor any conversation related to the ongoing impact of liberalism, can be conducted without engaging this heritage, especially the impact of Reinhold Niebuhr. For all the ways that Niebuhr was a liberal critic, his model of a "Christian public intellectual" helped define the cultural status of the Protestant mainline for much of the twentieth century. While neo-orthodox influence was waning by the 1960s, its impact has never completely disappeared from American theology.

The Rise of Process Theology

The creative tension between neo-orthodox leaders, like the Niebuhrs, and liberal idealists, like Harkness, was not the only development within liberal theology during the middle third of the twentieth century. Increasingly, a variety of liberals could not accept the transcendent God of neo-orthodoxy, and were increasingly critical of the personalist understanding of God that characterized many who carried on the tradition of earlier twentieth-century liberal theology. This emerging school agreed with the personalists that God could not simply be understood as a transcendent being, separated from the realities of history, but also disagreed with them on the question of whether the age-old stress on "human personality" was the only way to discern the activities of God in history. By the 1940s and 1950s, several theologians began to stress that God's being was not only immanent, active in history, and discernible through persons, but that God as Being evolved through natural processes of ongoing change and development.

This heritage, known as "process theology," is an outgrowth not only of earlier movements of liberal theology, but emerging patterns of Western philosophical development in the 1920s and 1930s. Indebted to the writings of Alfred North Whitehead, process theology emerged not so much as a unified school (although it did develop distinctive academic centers, in particular at the University of Chicago and later at the Claremont Graduate School in California), but as a diverse theological heritage that sought to recover certain traditions of eighteenth- and nineteenth-century philosophy on one hand (in particular, like earlier personalists, engaging the idealistic philosophy of Hegel), and the desire to challenge predominant theological assumptions of liberalism on the other.

If there is an idea that helps one to understand the worldview of process theology, it is a belief that God cannot be put in a box. Divine reality is in a constant pattern of change, which in its own way is a reflection of how creation itself is always changing. As an early process theologian, Daniel Day Williams noted in the mid-twentieth century that although it was not possible for humans to imagine a triumph over evil in history, we can be confident that God's goodness will always be manifested. "We believe that not only our present victories but even our failures can be transmuted into good. We believe that good is everlasting in God."[21] John Cobb, perhaps the major representative of process thought since the

1960s, accentuates the idea that a key to understanding process theology not only relates to how individuals can change history, but how the quest for achieving justice has direct bearing on God's being. "God loves us not only in that he actively seeks our good regardless of how we respond to him but in that he empathizes with us and takes our feelings into himself. . . . And because we are loved by God, we can also, in some small but perhaps growing measure, love each other."[22] Earlier liberal traditions, such as personalism, emphasized the centrality of human experience and a progressive orientation toward history. Although process thought did not discount these historical themes of liberalism, key representatives of the tradition, such as Cobb, stressed how an individual's knowledge of God correlated with one's ability to utilize God's grace: "Process theologians hold that, if we understand God's power as it is revealed in Jesus, the goodness of God is clear. God is working in all situations for the good of creatures, calling people to join in this work, and empowering them to do so."[23]

In the second half of the twentieth century, process theology represented one of the dominant heritages in American liberal theology, and emphases within the tradition became embraced by many theologians and ethicists not normally associated with the movement. It has been a creative influence not only in terms of revisioning earlier views of Christian doctrine, but in terms of enlarging the range of social concerns addressed by many North American churches. It had a marked impact on earlier movements of American liberalism and, in one form or another, the tradition has been in dialogue with every major movement of liberal theology that has emerged since World War II.

Perhaps the one theme most stressed by process theologians is to challenge the classical liberal stress on the anthropocentric tendencies of Western theology, which place human experience at the pinnacle of human knowledge and divine revelation. Process theology has challenged more traditional forms of liberalism to develop what the Canadian theologian Douglas John Hall calls "a theology of nature," which sees environmental preservation as a primary responsibility of Christian social witness. Many process theologians enthusiastically embraced dimensions of the earlier social Christian stress on economic and racial justice, yet worried that classical liberalism lacked the ability to dialogue with the excesses of industrial capitalism. As Hall surmises, "Liberalism put the kind of emphasis upon humanity that had in the long run a deleterious effect upon the extrahuman environment, which is . . . necessary to human well-being."[24]

Process theology might very well be the dominant tradition of liberal theology to emerge in North America in the second half of the twentieth century.[25] Yet the ability of process theology to strike beyond its academic base has always been suspect, in part because it relies heavily on a philosophical language that moved away from the more traditional language of Christian theology, and because the movement has defined itself mostly in relationship to academic centers, as opposed to faith communities. Yet process theology represents, and remains, one of the major components of liberalism's heritage; the consequences of this tradition upon liberalism's future will be explored in greater depth in chapter 6.

Christ Transforming Culture: Liberalism Beyond the Pulpit

In 1951 H. Richard Niebuhr's *Christ and Culture*, a book that remains largely discussed and debated in North American theological circles, was published. Niebuhr's analysis presented five paradigms reflecting ways that Christianity historically engaged the larger cultural landscape.[26] His final paradigm, and preferred option for contemporary Christianity, was what he referred to as "Christ the transformer of culture." Niebuhr defined this paradigm along what he called a "conversionist" model, whereby in tracing a Christian tradition that he associated with figures such as Augustine and Calvin (and an important transitional figure in the history of nineteenth-century theological liberalism, F. D. Maurice), Christians were able to dialogue with culture, yet ultimately sway the culture to the church's point of view. These conversionists "believe also that such culture is under God's sovereign rule, and that the Christian must carry on cultural work in obedience to the Lord."[27]

In recent years it has become fashionable to castigate Niebuhr's "Christ transforming culture" model in terms of his highly Western view of culture and the ways his analysis favored traditions representative of the larger magisterial heritage of sixteenth-century Protestantism (in particular, those traditions associated with Reformed theology and the heritage of Calvinism).[28] Yet Niebuhr's analysis did touch upon distinctive historical themes coming out of the heritage of Western Christianity, whereby a chief goal of the church's ministry was defined by its ability to create a moral society, and in the process utilize those aspects of the culture that reflected values in accord with the theological values of the church. Niebuhr largely replicated the common assertion that theological liberalism and figures such as Ritschl were responsible for an uncritical embrace of culture (his "Christ of Culture" paradigm). What he did not mention in his analysis, however, is that by the time he wrote *Christ and Culture*, it was the *liberal* denominations and churches of the West who carried on this earlier historical legacy, picking up the mantle once carried in Christendom by Augustine and Calvin. Through their social creeds and pronouncements on a host of social-political issues, liberalism had assumed the deeply rooted Christian legacy of moral suasion, whereby churches sought to appeal to the larger culture and sway it to the church's point of view.

Niebuhr's analysis is also paradigmatic of how segments of mid-century mainline Protestantism looked to the future with hope, believing that their churches represented the vanguard of a new era for American Christianity. Just as Walter Rauschenbusch had talked about "Christianizing" America in the early twentieth century, by mid-century, Niebuhr, while shedding an earlier Protestant language of Christianizing the country, still spoke a rarefied language of theological triumphalism that became the basis for how many liberal churches sought to redefine their ministries during the second half of the century.

By the 1950s, some of the luster of the liberal pulpiteer model was starting to wear off, and increasingly attention was being paid to emerging models that saw ministry in terms of full-time administrative and pastoral counseling. John Cobb and Joseph Hough note that many clergy after World War II, who were not pastors of "big steeple" churches, and who were concerned about the declining professional status of clergy, embraced what H. Richard Niebuhr called the model of "the pastoral director."[29] This model saw the pastor not only as an administrator, but as a skilled leader who could coordinate from the pastor's study all the complex spiritual issues that plagued the members of his congregation (and the larger community). Functions of clergy increasingly mirrored those of the secular world, whereby ordained ministers were not just trained theologians and preachers, but also skilled administrators and pastoral counselors. While several clergy were drawn to emerging therapeutic models of professional counseling, many were also drawn to a tradition of Christian theology best represented by Paul Tillich.

A native of Germany, Tillich had originally been trained for the Lutheran ministry, and after spending several years as a chaplain in the German army in World War I, he found himself, like his contemporary Karl Barth, questioning the wisdom of his inherited theological outlook. Yet unlike Barth, Tillich's theological response was far more positive toward culture, and much of his work in the 1920s and 1930s reflected the ways that he sought to integrate his views of culture into a Christian worldview. While some of Tillich's optimism faded with time, especially after he was forced by the rise of the Nazi regime to emigrate to the U.S., his career was partly defined by how modern persons could find religious value and meaning amidst a world that seemed to be exploding into chaos.

For all of Tillich's diverse interests, his work often returned to the theme of how "modern" individuals could find signs of theological meaning within the larger culture: "Pictures, poems, and music can become objects of theology . . . from the point of view of their power of expressing some aspects of that which concerns us ultimately."[30] Tillich has frequently been identified as the most prominent representative of a "Christ and culture" school of theology (along with H. Richard Niebuhr). This is not to say that Tillich took an uncritical view toward the secular culture, yet at different phases of his career he viewed culture as carrying forth the symbols of Christian belief. "This whole realm of sacred objects is a treasure of symbols," he noted in 1957. "Holy things are not holy in themselves, but they point beyond themselves to the source of all holiness, that which is of ultimate concern."[31]

It could be argued that Tillich's use of religious symbols had much in common with earlier Protestant theologies (in particular, aspects of Reformed theology whose sacramental theology stressed the manifestation of the holy through ordinary items, such as bread, wine, and water). But part of the unintended consequence of Tillich was how his ideas led to later theological movements, both liberal and non-liberal, that centered on the quest of persons to find divine meaning in a number of cultural symbols, in particular within the arenas of popular culture. A recent development within American Christianity is the extent to which popular culture should serve as a prism for the interpretation of Christian tradition. One of the ironies about these developments is that it has been mainly conservative churches, those that affirm the premise that the Bible is timeless and stands apart from cultural influences, that have most enthusiastically used popular culture as a tool of ministry and evangelicalism. The ways in which popular culture media have been utilized by contemporary evangelical movements, in particular numerous megachurches, reflect how some churches spurn traditional liturgies for contemporary worship emphasizing the symbols and rhetoric of popular culture.[32]

Tillich was hardly a fan of popular culture, and, like many "professional" theologians of his generation, he tended to equate theological meaning solely with what has been defined as "high" culture (in Tillich's case, art). Yet since the 1960s, Western popular culture has become an arena heavily analyzed by religion scholars and cultural commentators in terms of how popular entertainers (such as rock musicians) have replaced public theologians like Rauschenbusch and Reinhold Niebuhr as the chief arbiters of moral and religious meaning in America. What is ironic about the current popularity of certain popular culture icons, like Bono (lead singer of the Irish rock band U2) and Oprah Winfrey, is that they represent figures who use their religious faith in ways that seek to transform the values of a dominant cultural-political ethos. Yet they do it *outside* the foundations of institutional religion. In some ways, they illustrate a unique example of Paul Tillich's views toward the interpenetration of the sacred and the secular. Earlier theologians, like Tillich, were rooted in the supposition that the institutional religion of their generation, defined primarily through inherited churches and denominations, would produce leaders that could speak to and transform the culture of their time.

It could be argued that we live at a time when the public heirs of this earlier liberal theological vision are no longer rooted within institutional Christianity. Yet even during an era in the 1950s, when Niebuhr and Tillich represented the high-water mark of an era of liberalism's institutional influence in American Christianity, there were already signs that liberalism was fast jettisoning its roots in institutional Christianity.

"What Would Jesus Do?" III: Liberalism Beyond the Mainline

In the early twentieth century, theological liberals, while a minority in most denominations, were nevertheless committed to working within the parameters of churches and church-related institutions. By the 1950s and 1960s, aspects of that earlier tradition remained strong; however, some of the most powerful representatives of an earlier liberal heritage were no longer associating themselves with specific faith communities. A significant number of persons, influenced especially by the social gospel, took a hard line toward many forms of institutional Christianity, and amplified a theme that had been key to the earlier social gospel. Mainly, the key to understanding the message of Jesus was centered upon his religious *and* political radicalism.

In the aftermath of World War I, a small number of activists within American Protestantism issued calls for "industrial reconstruction," reflecting a desire to carry forward on some of the more radical tenets of the social gospel, which increasingly viewed industrial capitalism as the major obstacle to kingdom building in America.[33] While leaders like Walter Rauschenbusch echoed aspects of this social radicalism, his vision of reform largely envisioned this movement through the ministrations of institutional Christianity. By the 1920s and 1930s, however, there were clear signs that the most radical components of the social gospel heritage were not coming from figures like Rauschenbusch. Part of the forgotten impact of the social gospel was the way it galvanized a generation of student organizations on a number of American colleges and universities during the 1920s and 1930s. While many institutional churches after World War I sought to distance themselves from some of the more radical components of the social gospel, the political ideals of the social gospel found a hearing on several college campuses. These groups laid a foundation for organizations that fought for the rights of conscientious objectors during World War II, and ultimately laid the groundwork for many grassroots groups associated with the civil rights movement of the 1950s and the anti-Vietnam war movement of the 1960s.[34] Part of the fascinating aspect of these groups is that they were often connected through a variety of networks that included informal training centers in direct action methods (such as the Highlander Folk School, which became a center for many social activists, including Rosa Parks, to learn tactics of nonviolence), more "permanent" institutions (such as the Fellowship of Reconciliation and Congress for Racial Equality), and caucuses that were principally designed for the recruitment of young people in local communities and college campuses (such as the Student Nonviolent Coordinating Committee and Students for a Democratic Society). There is no doubt that the key individual for understanding many of the sweeping social-political changes of the 1950s and 1960s was Martin Luther King Jr. Yet King's success as a national leader never would have occurred without the support (and at times creative opposition) he received from these organizational structures, who helped carry his message nationally *and* locally.[35]

At the same time, many Christian leaders who became associated with what one historian calls "social gospel radicalism" lost interest in keeping a dialogue going with institutional forms of Christianity.[36] Moreover, questions of spiritual discernment, so important to persons like Walter Rauschenbusch and Vida Scudder, were lost. Perhaps the individual who best embodies this transition in American religion was Harry F. Ward. In microcosm, Ward captures the possibilities and pitfalls that confronted liberal theology as it moved through the twentieth century. Born in England in 1873, Ward came to the United States as a teenager and eventually studied at Northwestern and Harvard (his mentor at Northwestern, George Albert Coe, was a prominent liberal clergyman who pioneered developments in the Christian education movement in the early twentieth century). After a brief stint working in a Chicago settlement house, Ward was ordained into the Methodist ministry, where he served poor, working-class congregations near the infamous Chicago stockyards. Like

Rauschenbusch, this experience galvanized Ward's desire to devote his ministry to the needs of the poor, and by 1907, his efforts were central to the drafting of a "social creed" adopted by the Methodist Episcopal Church in 1908 (the first such statement officially sanctioned by a denomination in the U.S. and a major influence on the Federal Council of Churches' social creed, adopted at its founding later that year). After a tenure as a professor of social ethics at Boston University, Ward moved to Union Seminary in 1918, teaching there until his retirement in the early 1940s. While Ward strongly identified himself with Rauschenbusch's theology, he had a deeper track record as a community activist that continued throughout his lengthy career. Besides being the longtime executive secretary of the Methodist Federation for Social Service, a caucus that actively lobbied the Methodist Episcopal Church to embrace a range of social-economic reform measures, Ward's name appeared at the top of the list of many religious and secular organizations that were formed after World War I. He was a founder and longtime board member of the American Civil Liberties Union, and his involvement with the ACLU reflected the passion of several secular and religious leaders in the 1920s and 1930s to defend the civil liberties of unpopular minorities, during a time when America was in the grips of anti-communist, red-scare hysteria. By far, however, the most controversial aspect of Ward's legacy was his growing hostility toward capitalism. As the 1920s progressed, he increasingly moved in the direction of Marxism, causing major rifts between him and several former allies. By the 1930s, Ward found himself at odds with many liberals (including his faculty colleague at Union, Reinhold Niebuhr), as he emphasized that the role of religion in the West was to promote class struggle.[37] By the time of World War II, Ward (while never a member of the Communist Party) had come to embrace a position that viewed the Soviet Union as a sign of the kingdom of God. Even in retirement, Ward found his name near the top of a variety of "Red" lists associated with the House Un-American Activities Committee during its heyday in the 1940s and 1950s. Until his death in 1966, Ward remained an unrepentant radical and an individual who saw in Jesus a pure ethic of justice.[38]

Ward's life accentuates two hazards that later incarnations of liberalism have sometimes failed to recognize. First, his theology increasingly took him to the point where Christianity and ethics became interchangeable. Unlike Rauschenbusch and Scudder, he castigated those who emphasized priestly "aesthetics" related to worship and Christian piety, seeing these as undercutting the power of direct-action political movements. The original social gospel was guilty at times of creating a dichotomy between "priestly" and "prophetic" Christianity, whereby "priestly" religion was predicated upon maintaining status-quo Christianity, as opposed to the transformative witness of prophetic Christianity. While Ward was perhaps an extreme incarnation of the tendency to draw this false dichotomy between spiritual discernment and social justice, he has not been the last in a tradition of Christian liberals who tend to see Christianity through a lens that views political struggle as the primary goal of Christian discipleship.

Second, for all the differences between Ward and his Union colleague Reinhold Niebuhr, both sought to shed the label of being a "liberal," but for very different reasons. Niebuhr's primary contention was that the term was a reflection of the tradition's theological naivete, especially pertaining to the perfectibility of society. Ward approached it from the opposite pole, mainly, that liberalism was not idealistic enough. By the early 1930s, he had become disillusioned with liberalism, seeing it as a tradition that only wanted to preserve the political status quo, as opposed to fostering radical social change.

> Because liberal Christianity is "separated from the rising masses in thinking and feeling," it has no real passion and therefore advocates reform and gradualism. It has "no adequate perception of the revolutionary factor in history, in its own gospel and in the needs of the hour." Christians must take account of economic forces and relinquish their preoccupation with the individual. Otherwise they will fail "to reckon with the nature and power of evil."[39]

For Ward, what was needed was not evolution, but revolution—a dramatic transformation of America's social-economic landscape—and liberalism, instead of being part of the solution, was part of the problem.

Part of the tragedy of Ward's life, as his biographer wryly noted, is that he lived too long.[40] He began his career as a significant dissenting voice within institutional Protestantism who played a major (and largely neglected) role in American Protestantism's institutional embrace of social gospel liberalism. Yet the final third of his life was largely spent on the margins of the Protestant establishment, not taken seriously by many Protestant establishment figures who once viewed him as a great prophet. However, Ward's example points to what can easily happen to liberalism when it loses its moorings in more classical notions of Christian theology. While some lauded Ward's "take no prisoners" style of engagement, he ended up (consistent with Erik Gritsch's metaphor for sixteenth-century radical Thomas Müntzer) "a reformer without a church."[41] This framework has led to the creation of a unique sectarian theological rhetoric that Ward biographer David Nelson Duke refers to as "a holy war dualism."

"Ideologically and existentially Harry Ward saw the world divided into two camps: right and wrong, good and evil."[42] Consistent with this image, Ward was confident that he had discerned God's true intent for humanity, and his solution for dissent was simple: those who did not support you were, quite simply, your enemies.

Yet versions of this dualism between good and evil were not just manifested by radicals like Harry Ward. They became a staple for more temperate liberal traditions, including ministers like Harry Emerson Fosdick and William Sloane Coffin, as well as later traditions of liberation theology. This tension within liberal theology was characterized by what William McGuire King calls a "God of Battles" theology.[43] As Harry Emerson Fosdick noted, this theology asserted that God "undergirds our endeavors for justice in the earth with his power; who fights in and for and with us against the hosts of evil; whose presence is a guarantee of ultimate victory; and whose effect upon us is to send us out to war against ancient human curses, assured that what ought to be done can be done."[44] Fosdick's tone is reflective of a type of liberal jeremiad that, on one hand, identifies God with the oppressed, and that God anoints the church to battle these oppressive forces. Within this framework, God is actively engaging historical processes, providing the basis for individuals to work for justice, and to resist evil. Throughout its history, liberal theology has been clear about the imperative to work for justice, and the hope that the pursuit of justice would lead to a better world. On the other hand, the history of twentieth-century liberal theology has often been unclear, not only about the ends needed to obtain justice, but the means to employ to reach those ends.

In the years after Harry Ward's death, mainline Protestantism struggled over numerous questions of mission, seeking to apply a "God of Battles" rhetoric to a range of emerging social-political causes. Yet some of the problems encountered by Ward have never been fully resolved by these radical voices. In particular, how does "liberal" Christianity speak of "radical" social-political change when, in many cases, these liberals are closely tied to the social-political interests that it wants to overturn?

Liberation Liberalism?

The term "liberation theology" has become a sort of generic term to describe many movements of contemporary theology that seek to move beyond the cultural and political suppositions of earlier liberal theologies. In the United States, liberation theology emerged out of the social and political chaos of the 1960s, reflecting the political issues raised by the civil rights movement, the anti-Vietnam war movement, the women's rights movement, and (ultimately) the gay rights movement. Over the last forty years, the movement has evolved considerably and encompasses a number of theological incarnations related to feminist, African American, womanist, and gay-lesbian ("queer") theologies. For all of their differences, liberation theologies assert that theology needs to be written by and for people who are oppressed. It takes seriously the fact that historically many groups (such as women and African Americans) have not been included in the narratives of more traditional theologies (including earlier forms of liberalism). Liberationists seek to address these imbalances not only by focusing on the plight of the oppressed, but by affirming a belief that God stands in solidarity with the oppressed (and conversely often stands against those who represent the dominant traditions of Western theology).[45]

On one hand, liberation theology carried forward liberalism's stress on the necessity of Christian theology to engage in the quest for justice, seeing the transformation of historical processes as one of its primary goals. The stress on human goodness, the desire to change history, and, in particular, the identity with a "God of Battles" who works for justice represent themes that carry forward in numerous traditions of liberation theology. By the same token, liberation theology has often shown ambivalence, if not hostility, toward liberalism, seeing the latter as an incantation of earlier white, Euro-American middle-class suppositions.[46] Unlike earlier forms of liberal theologies, whose goals often centered upon a renewal of preexistent church/denominational institutions, many liberationists viewed these structures as part of the problem that needed eradication. Traditions of liberation theology on one hand have shared Harry Ward's dissatisfaction with liberalism's sense of status-quo Christianity, while on the other hand, moving beyond Ward's interest in economics to look at issues pertaining to what has become known as "identity politics," they centered upon issues related to racial/ethnic identity, gender, and most recently gay-lesbian issues.[47]

Many conservatives (and some liberals) within the mainline church will stress that the problem with liberal churches is that their theologies are too political. On one hand, sociological data point strongly to the fact that most American congregations, both past and present, have never ranked the pursuit of social justice as an ultimate objective of ministry and mission.[48] As will be discussed in chapters 6 and 7, however, the critical question facing many liberal congregations is not so much whether or not to become involved in social justice ministries (which I argue should be central to liberalism's recovery); it is the ends that one pursues in the quest for justice. One of the characteristics of liberal Protestantism for much of the twentieth century is that it tended to rely on what have been called "middle axioms," whereby ethical pronouncements sought to mediate extreme political viewpoints. This term is largely associated with the pronouncements coming from ecumenical assemblies during the middle third of the twentieth century, and also reflects the posture taken by mainline denominations today in many of their policy state-ments. Increasingly, the liberationist perspective has called into question this worldview, and since the 1960s has challenged mainline churches to embrace a range of specific policy recommendations.

The desire of some liberals to follow Harry Ward's example and embrace very specific political ends has a very uneven history in Christian history, and remains a constant theme of debate within contemporary American Christianity. In the 1960s, ethicist Paul Ramsey, responding to a discernible anti-American tone coming from the World Council of Churches (particularly regarding the condemnation of the Vietnam war), noted that the ecumenical movement was relying on the opinions of elite "experts," as opposed to speaking on behalf of local churches.[49] For many liberals at the time, Ramsey's arguments were seen as an assault on the perceived political and theological radicalism of the National and World Council of Churches, and his analysis has become a frequent target of many today who carry a liberationist perspective. Latin American theo-logian Jose Bonino makes a persuasive counterargument by noting that "the inability of liberal pluralism to deal with system-rejection betrays its limits: it operates within a certain consensus and therefore it cannot accommodate in its plurality options that challenge such consensus."[50]

In many ways, the positions of Ramsey and Bonino point to the difficulty of defining liberalism primarily around specific social policy ends. If churches/denominations choose to follow middle axioms, then they will forever live in a zone of affirming status-quo systems. If on the other hand they embrace "radical" political positions, they will likely find themselves, like Harry Ward, largely alienated from the organiza-tional structures of American Christianity. Part of the appeal of libera-tion theology among many who carry a strong liberal theological bent is its uncompromising rhetoric toward an ethics that stands in solidarity with the oppressed. Liberation theology is unequivocal in its calls for jus-tice, arguing (much like Ward) that the gospel needs to relate to specific social-political interpretations. Yet a difficult question for anyone who sees the future of liberalism predicated on the pursuit of justice from a particular social-political perspective is this: how does one handle dissent? Earlier liberals like Rauschenbusch have been seen by many as precursors to later movements of liberation theology. However, the major difference between the former and the latter is that Rauschenbusch carried an irenic spirit that wanted to embrace in his vision of the kingdom those who opposed him. While it could be argued that Rauschenbusch fell victim to a sort of "middle-class captivity," undercutting the radical thrust of his theology, he nevertheless had an audience that felt compelled and challenged by his words—even as many disagreed with him. While I applaud the important questions that the liberationist perspective has brought to the table of American theology, I remain unconvinced that this perspective has succeeded in garnering a popular audience, especially from the groups on behalf of whom liberationists seek to speak.

Like other incarnations of liberalism, liberation theologies have had a tremendous impact upon the shape of contemporary theological debate and discourse. In many ways, the agendas of all liberation theologies, indeed many varieties of contemporary liberal and post-liberal theology, continue to manifest Harry Ward's goal of "social reconstruction," whereby the ends of theology are chiefly seen through the realization of specific social-political ends. Yet for all the ways that liberation theologies have responded to emergent theological and historical currents since the 1960s, their audience, like the majority of traditions coming out of contemporary liberalism, has by and large been confined to discourses within seminaries and universities. In some respects, Paul Ramsey's question from the mid-1960s will always be a critical one: who speaks for the churches?

Part of the foundation for liberal theology was predicated upon the positive view that liberalism had of history, as well as the optimism liberalism assigned to individuals to be able to change history. Even traditions of American neo-orthodoxy, with their note of pessimism, still largely saw the mission of the church to be measured and realized through changing the values of the culture. However, the difficulty that many traditions of liberalism have had to deal with is this: how does one advocate a theological perspective of radical change, when that message is not universally embraced by churches? It has been easy for disparate traditions of liberal theology to argue the case that theology needed to be centered upon notions of solidarity with the oppressed, the poor, and, especially within recent history, groups that are non-white and non–Euro-American. However, how do middle-class churches go about creating the structures, whether religious and secular, that have the potential to lead to these radical changes?

When one looks at the progression from Walter Rauschenbusch to Harry Ward, one sees a chief dilemma of liberalism in microcosm. The identification of liberal Christianity with a middle-class worldview raises questions about the extent to which American churches in the twenty-first century can truly be transformative in terms of a radical social-political vision. By the same token, if Christianity is reducible to clearly defined ethical and political expressions, then how does it relate to larger questions of theological/ecclesiastical identity and (increasingly) the individual pursuit of personal spirituality that has become one of the defining themes of recent American religion?

In the early twentieth century, liberals like Rauschenbusch spoke about the dangers of capitalism and the need for Christians to focus their ministries upon the plight of the poor. Yet they were also concerned that Christianity focus upon the spiritual welfare of people in the pews. At times in the twentieth century, various liberal movements were able to hold these two goals in tension. While H. Richard Niebuhr's "Christ and Culture" analysis was fraught with problems, he strove to see Christianity in light of a dominant tradition in the West that believed that institutional Christianity needed to transform the world.[51] Niebuhr might very well have been wrong in his outlook, yet he spoke to an audience who largely believed in the truths he was upholding. As liberal churches moved through the social-political changes of the 1960s and 1970s, many still tried to balance Niebuhr's "Christ transforming culture" vision with the growing critique from traditions of liberal and liberationist perspectives related to the specific failures of liberal Christianity. Along the way, however, many liberal leaders had to grapple with the reality that their churches were no longer at the forefront of the American religious landscape. While liberals wrestled with a range of questions pertaining to theology and mission, they started to become aware of the fact that a number of disparate churches spoke in a voice that was theologically at odds with the caretakers of liberal Christianity.

Five

Did Liberalism Win?

The twentieth century represented a time when theological liberalism flourished in America. Far from dying out after World War I, liberalism entered new creative periods of critical reflection and development that gave birth to innovative incarnations of theology. By 1960 liberalism not only was represented by a range of theological traditions, but its influence extended into social movements beyond the parameters of institutional Christianity. At the same time, what often bonded diverse groups of liberals together was not predicated by theological concerns, but a sense that liberalism was at the cultural center of the country, epitomized by the stature of the Protestant mainline.

Yet by the end of the 1960s, these mainline denominations found themselves in chaos. Caught up in the social and cultural upheavals of the decade, many denominations began a membership hemorrhage that has continued into the twenty-first century. At the same time, a number of other Protestant churches associated with anti-liberal theologies *were growing*, setting the stage for what many Americans labeled as a resurgence of evangelical theology.

However, this emergence of what many saw as a "new evangelicalism" was in reality the latest phase in the development of a lengthy historical tradition of popular Christianity in America. For many religion scholars at mid-century, there was widespread belief that conservative evangelicalism would wither away in significance, surviving mostly as part of marginalized subcultures.[1] Increasingly, however, the larger history of twentieth-century American Christianity raises the specter of whether it is liberalism, as opposed to evangelicalism, that is in danger of disappearing in the twenty-first century.

Did the Fundamentalists Win?

In 1922 Harry Emerson Fosdick preached the most well-known, and most controversial, sermon of his career, "Shall the Fundamentalists Win?" The conflicts between conservatives and liberals that began with the David Swing case in the 1870s had now reached what later historians would see as a galvanic battle over the future theological destiny of American Protestantism. Fosdick's journey toward liberalism began at Colgate University, where he had the opportunity to study with one of the pioneers of liberal theology, William Newton Clarke, and later at Union Seminary, New York, where he later spent several decades as a professor of homiletics.[2] Although an ordained Baptist minister, by the early 1920s Fosdick had settled into a successful preaching ministry at the First Presbyterian Church in New York, where he became the target of conservative ire for his liberal-modernist views. When Fosdick preached his sermon against fundamentalism, as he later noted in his autobiography, he hoped it would be received as a plea for theological tolerance.[3] Despite what Fosdick considered to be the irenic tone of the sermon, he left little doubt about his theological loyalties.

> I do not believe for one moment that the Fundamentalists are going to succeed. Nobody's intolerance can contribute anything to the situation which we have described. . . . The present world situation smells to heaven! And now, in the presence of colossal problems, which must be solved in Christ's name and for Christ's sake, the Fundamentalists propose to drive out from Christian churches all the consecrated souls who do not agree with their theory of inspiration. What immeasurable folly.[4]

The tone of the sermon reflected the extent to which American Protestantism had been drawn into two competing camps, "fundamentalists," intent on preserving long-standing tenets of theological orthodoxy, and "modernists," liberals intent on adapting theology to the contours of modern life. In many ways, the use of the terms "fundamentalist"and "modernist" does not reflect the diverse array of theological commitments that characterized the representatives of both groups, nor the way that for many years both groups had found avenues to combine their efforts in ministry and evangelism.[5] Yet these terms do accentuate the fact that, by the 1920s, American Protestantism could no longer hold conservatives and liberals together under a "big tent" of a shared theological canopy.

The usual historical angle toward understanding what happened in the 1920s is that the modernists (i.e., liberals) won a decisive battle in terms of determining the future direction of American Protestantism, and in a sense they did. By the early 1930s, most of the northern denominations at the center of battle in the theological controversies that had been waged in one form or another for several decades (in particular, the Baptists and Presbyterians) had come under control of the liberals. The response of the conservatives was to withdraw into a variety of churches and parachurches that would characterize large cross sections of the evangelical community for at least the next fifty years. The consequences of the liberal victory appeared to signal a new era of Protestant virility in the mid-twentieth century, with figures like Fosdick at the center of a renewed rise in liberal theology. And yet, behind the influence of persons like Fosdick and a host of other liberal preachers, as well as the ascendancy of church leaders associated with mainline Protestantism such as Reinhold Niebuhr (and his colleagues at Union, John Bennett and Henry Van Dusen) and a spate of other figures who reflected the continued creativity and originality of liberal theology, the movement all but ignored the fact that a popular revolution was occurring. The "defeated" forces of the so-called fundamentalist battles of the 1920s were not only organizing on a grass-roots level, they were crafting traditions of popular theology that liberalism largely ignored.

For decades, many conservative Protestant traditions flourished in evangelical subcultures, where a wide range of churches grew exponentially. By the final quarter of the twentieth century, evangelicals seemed to reemerge out of nowhere to make their presence known on the national political scene.[6] Today, when media commentators speak about the impact of Christianity in American public life, usually it is not reflecting on the heritage represented by Rauschenbusch, Niebuhr, or even Martin Luther King Jr. Rather, it is often a heritage stemming from the evangelical traditions that were "defeated" by the liberals in the 1920s.

The common liberal mainline response to many types of modern evangelicalism continues to follow a formula perfected back in the 1920s: ridicule. For many Christians associated with mainline denominations today evangelicals are viewed not only with suspicion but sometimes with outright contempt. Today liberals (or progressives) will talk about the errors of evangelical politics, and bemoan the exclusive claims of evangelical theology. Yet rarely will liberals take time to understand the complexities of evangelical theology, nor engage head-on the theological assertions made by popular evangelicalism against liberalism. While liberals like Fosdick reacted strongly against aspects of evangelical theology, they never forgot that their own beliefs were indebted to these traditions. Amidst what many liberals today consider the misguided emphases of popular evangelicalism, liberal Christianity needs to move away from relying on a rhetoric of ridicule and start responding to some penetrating theological issues coming from evangelical Christianity. This engagement may not sway most evangelicals to the liberal point of view, but it will do something that is desperately needed by various forms of contemporary Christian liberalism: clarify belief.

A Brief History of "Fundamentalism"

The history of American Protestantism during the first third of the twentieth century is usually told through the lens of what Martin Marty called a "public-private" split;[7] the missional unity that had long made it possible for disparate Protestant groups to stay connected was ruptured by the 1920s, splitting Protestantism into two camps: "public" liberals who carried on the heritage of the social gospel, and "private" evangelicals who stressed the importance of personal salvation. Marty's definition is helpful in identifying a general chasm that had opened up during the late nineteenth century and early twentieth century, yet the terms "public" and "private" do not necessarily capture the ways that both currents were giving birth to a variety of new theological phenomena. This is not only true within the various offshoots of theological liberalism that formed in the twentieth century, but also among the churches and leaders commonly lumped under the generic label "fundamentalism."

In the aftermath of the Civil War there was a gradual parting of the ways among many Protestant traditions. Many churches continued to emphasize earlier evangelical efforts at social reform, stressing that personal conversion both in America and in foreign missions would signal a coming kingdom on earth. These traditions not only sprouted into what later became associated with liberal theology, but also a wide range of Protestant evangelicals who kept alive many earlier Protestant hopes of worldwide evangelicalism that grew out of most Protestant churches in the early nineteenth century.[8] Yet increasingly, the fabric of American evangelicalism after the Civil War was becoming more diverse, both theologically and missionally. While evangelicals held to various views of the centrality of Scripture, not all were in agreement of how this fidelity to Scripture was to be lived out. By the end of the nineteenth century, many white and African American holiness churches emerged that gravitated toward ecstatic practices of worship, reviving ancient traditions of speaking in tongues, which became one of the characteristics of the founding of pentecostalism in the early twentieth century.[9] Other groups of evangelicals devalued these ecstatic themes, instead seeing theological truth through a belief that every aspect of a person's life needed to conform to

Scripture. However, what tended to tie together disparate movements of American evangelicalism was *not* just the question of appropriate decorum for worship, but increasingly the challenging of widespread early nineteenth-century beliefs that Christian conversion would lead to a better world. It was this movement toward a literalist interpretation of Scripture, and (increasingly) a growing pessimism toward the inherent goodness of the world, that led to the theological position that became known by the 1920s as fundamentalism.

Today, few within the liberal heritage take time to think about the meaning of the term "fundamentalism." Fundamentalism is best seen as a movement that arose out of ecclesiastical traditions (especially Presbyterians and Baptists) that placed their emphasis upon the Bible as the primary source of religious authority, in particular maintaining faith in the doctrine of biblical inerrancy. For those identified with what became known as fundamentalism after World War I, the chief characteristics were a belief that the Bible presented a unified portrait of God's salvation through Jesus Christ, and that every aspect of the Old and New Testaments was infallible and pointed to a sovereign God who was immutable and unaffected by historical events.[10] On the other hand, the term "evangelicalism" is a more general designation for various historical Protestant movements (including many rooted in the heritage of contemporary mainline Protestantism) that stressed the centrality of Scripture, but often saw the Bible as one aspect of how church tradition could be lived out in the world. Consequently, while evangelicalism can refer to movements associated with conservative interpretations of Scripture, it represents a far more inclusive heritage that encompasses a range of American Protestant traditions.[11] By the late twentieth century, what increasingly led to the interchangeable use of the terms "fundamentalism" and "evangelicalism" was more than just the fact that these movements stressed a gospel of personal salvation. Rather, these disparate heritages, the so-called "losers" of the theological battles in the 1920s, were coming to a consensus not only about the centrality of Scripture, but about how to read the Bible in a way that clarified how Christians needed to define their relationship to the larger culture.

Caricatures of Christian fundamentalism often depict uneducated, rural individuals with no sense of cultural savvy or sophistication. Yet the roots of modern fundamentalism were overwhelmingly urban, and were reflected in academic institutions (such as Princeton Seminary), popular revivalists such as Dwight Moody, and urban pulpits in the Northeast and Midwest. In the years between 1910 and 1915, a series of pamphlets entitled "The Fundamentals" was published that reflected the fact that the chief representatives of this tradition were hardly country bump-kins, nor were they necessarily of one theological viewpoint. In many ways, the intellectual wing of what would later be called fundamentalism emerged from leading academics from Princeton Seminary, centered in the late nineteenth century around the person of Benjamin Warfield. Warfield reflected a distinguished legacy of biblical and theological schol-arship that sought to continue an earlier American tradition of training a learned clergy and defending ideas of biblical inerrancy. What is often forgotten about Warfield, however, was that he not only opposed the rise of liberalism, but attempted to stave off the growing influence of an emerging theological phenomenon taking hold among a cross section of American churches: *dispensationalism.*

The Logic of Dispensationalism

If you mention the term dispensationalism to many liberals, you are bound to get one of two reactions. Either liberals have no idea what the term means, or it is associated with the stupidity of many conservatives who embody an evangelical fixation with the end of the world. I would argue that not only is dispensationalism one of the most significant movements of popular theology to emerge in America, but historically the movement has given a range of evangelical Christians a unified mission.

Dispensationalists represent one of the chief heirs of an evangelical Protestant millennial theology that burst with force upon the American scene in the early nineteenth century. Many nineteenth-century evan-gelicals, and indeed many liberals associated with the later social gospel, held to a theological outlook frequently called *postmillennialism.* Picking up on themes from the book of Revelation, postmillennialists believed in the idea that ultimately the Second Coming of Christ would mark the end of human history and represent the final consummation of God's righteousness on earth. Part of the premise for the postmillennial posi-tion was that social conditions would improve on earth before the final return of Christ (and some Protestants going back into the seventeenth and eighteenth centuries actually believed that they were living in the period of the thousand years mentioned in Revelation 20 that marked the era before the final defeat of Satan on earth). While liberals like Wal-ter Rauschenbusch rejected the literalism of holding to a thousand-year period, his framework, as well as many within the liberal theological heritage, was guided by an earlier evangelical view: that before the end of human history, social righteousness would increase.[12]

By the end of the nineteenth century, however, the spirit of evangelical millennialism also tended to join forces with another theological current: *apocalyptic speculation.* Ever since the Protestant Reformation, the idea that history would end suddenly and violently had become a predominant crosscurrent within many sects and churches to emerge in the Western Protestant world. The popularity of the Millerite movement in the 1830s and 1840s, in which a New England Baptist preacher, William Miller, claimed to have figured out through the study of Scripture the precise date when the world was going to end, signaled a growing fascination with the idea that to read the Bible was not just to be inspired, or to understand what was necessary for your salvation, but to uncover hidden secrets of divine revelation—in particular how the Bible pointed to the Second Coming of Christ *and* to the end of the world. Even though Miller's predictions came to naught, the fascination with studying the Bible as a means to understanding end-time prophesies became a popular fascination among many American evangelicals in the final third of the nineteenth century. In the aftermath of the Civil War, "Bible prophesy" conferences in Great Britain, Canada, and the U.S. stoked the fires of speculation about the end times, and at the center of that speculation was the movement of dispensationalism associated primarily with John Nelson Darby.

Garry Wills notes that John Darby is the most influential religious leader that no one has heard of.[13] Yet it was Darby, originally a minister in the Anglican Church of Ireland, who founded a sectarian movement called the Plymouth Brethren, who took much of the apocalyptic theology of William Miller and constructed a theological system that is still widely adhered to by a cross section of evangelicals today. Unlike Miller, who argued for a precise date for the end of the world, Darby saw the Bible in terms of specific time periods, or "dispensations," that were a reflection of how God was using history toward specific divine ends. While the more positive tradition of postmillennialism placed the Second Coming of Christ at the end of history, Darby understood this theme to be in error. He espoused a perspective known as premillennialism, seeing the Second Coming of Christ occurring before the thousand years of peace spoken of in Revelation 20. At the end of the thousand-year period, there would be a final battle between God and Satan that would result in Satan's final defeat. What is unique about Darby's thought is not so much his premillennial orientation (a tradition that has been around since the time of the early church), but the way he added an interesting wrinkle to its interpretation. Seizing upon two verses from

1 Thessalonians 4:16-17,[14] Darby stressed an idea that has become central to later generations of evangelicals: the rapture. Darby and his followers taught that the world was currently living in the midst of what was called "the church age." Within this period, it was essential for Christians to convert as many persons as possible in advance of the sudden reappearance of Christ, in which suddenly and without warning, true believers in the present and those who had already died would be taken up to heaven to be with Christ.

In dispensationalist thought, the rapture is not the literal Second Coming; rather, it is a precursor to events that signal the final battles between God and Satan on earth. Within dispensationalism, the rapture signals the start of a cosmic clock that leads inevitably to the end of the world. After the rapture, history enters a new dispensation frequently called "the Tribulation," a time when the forces of evil under the anti-Christ rise to take over the world. Ultimately there is a major conflict between the forces of the anti-Christ and those not taken up in the rapture who are able to come finally to an acceptance of Christ's truth. At the end of the tribulation period, Christ's Second Coming marks a return of peace (the thousand years in Revelation 20), followed by the final battle between Christ and Satan at the close of history.[15]

Since its inception as a movement in the late nineteenth century, few liberals have taken dispensationalism seriously. Rather, movements that were initially referred to as "Darbyism" or "Millennarianism" were seen as ridiculous and simplistic schemes that reduced Scripture to a code book and turned theology into unsophisticated speculation. For all the ways dispensationalism was ridiculed by liberals, and resisted by conservatives like Warfield, the movement caught on, and the teaching of Darby became adapted by a number of American evangelists like Moody, influential ministers, and an emerging network of Bible schools and Bible institutes.[16] As the twentieth century progressed, it served as a bridge uniting disparate movements of American evangelicalism. Dispensationalism became a feature of several major urban pulpits, as well as of "sawdust trail" revivalists like Billy Sunday, and by degrees the movement had adherents not only among middle-class Baptist and Presbyterian congregations, who stressed a strict biblical literalism, but also among many pentecostals, who frequently found themselves at odds with the former, but who increasingly embraced the dispensationalist worldview by the 1920s. Representative dispensationalists not only included well-known revivalists like Sunday, but church leaders like Arthur T. Pierson, one of the major Protestant pioneers of foreign mission in the late nineteenth century, and Cyrus Scofield, whose popular reference Bible published in

1909 by Oxford University Press contained several annotations related to major features of dispensationist theology. The Scofield Bible was one of the biggest-selling religious books in the twentieth century.[17]

One of the appeals of dispensationalist theology is that it holds in tension specific biblical texts (especially from the books of Daniel and Revelation) with concrete historical events (without making the error of William Miller of setting exact dates for the rapture/end of the world). Yet the appeal of dispensationalism went way beyond the absence of precise dating or the way that dispensationalist preachers, past and present, apply contemporary events to fit into various doomsday scenarios. What dispensationalism offers is a solid foundation whereby, in good Protestant fashion, God's book (the Bible) defines the nature and purpose of life for God's people (the church). Many liberals who see questions of theology solely along Martin Marty's analysis of personal versus social religion miss the genius of dispensationalism. Obviously, much of the rhetoric of dispensationalism does subscribe to the need for individuals to go through some sort of conversion experience. But the nature of conversion is not simply predicated, as some liberals would argue, upon a selfish impulse of "getting saved." The majority of dispensationalists (past and present) believe passionately that their purpose, like all good Christians, is predicated on selfless mission. The difference is that, while the social gospel heritage believed (in varying degrees) in the task of perfecting the world, dispensationalists largely saw the sharing of the good news of Jesus Christ as a necessary labor of love to rescue as many people as possible from a world, and a creation, that is ultimately doomed.

I. M. Haldeman, longtime pastor of the First Baptist Church of New York, epitomized the growing popularity of dispensationalist teachings in American Protestantism by the early twentieth century. Haldeman left no doubt that the teachings of Scripture indicated that the liberal themes of human goodness and perfectibility were not borne out by Scripture. He also embodied the gradual shift of many evangelicals away from a theology that saw the Second Coming as the crowning achievement of righteousness on earth. He told his congregation that they needed to stay vigilant and on guard amidst the evils of the world, which would snare true believers to embrace a false gospel of human progress.

"And ye shall be hated by all men for my name's sake; but he that endureth to the end shall be saved."

According to this statement of the Christ the world will act towards professed followers like a pack of fierce, bloodthirsty wolves. It will spring at the throat of righteousness and truth. It will hate and persecute and kill, seeking utterly to destroy the Holy Name. In whatever age, and whatever form of manifestation, the spirit of the world in relation to the way and work of Christ will be the spirit of the wolf, the wild beast that seeks to kill.[18]

This theology of pessimism is in stark contrast to the way that most dominant strands of liberal theology look to history and culture as a source of hope for signs of the kingdom. What is ironic is that dispensationalism does share a theme characteristic of many strands of liberalism, in that each sounds a note of crisis and judgment. However, whereas many dispensationalists see repentance in terms of saving as many people as possible before the rapture, liberalism views repentance as an indication that Christians are turning their backs on the world and need to shift course in order to redeem society.

The Popular Appeal of the End Times

For all the ways that liberals (and many evangelicals) have ridiculed and argued against dispensationalism, it has become a staple of American popular religion, manifested today in a range of best-selling books such as Hal Lindsey's *Late Great Planet Earth*, and more recently Tim LaHaye and Jerry Jenkins' immensely prolific and popular *Left Behind* novels and films. One of the reasons dispensationalism remains a key feature in popular religion is that its theological premises are malleable to different historical eras. While crises in history may change, the blueprints for dispensationalist thought remain pretty much the same. One can read the work of I. M. Haldeman in the early twentieth century and Hal Lindsey in the late twentieth, and come away with the same conclusion: Christ is coming, and coming soon!

Part of why it is so difficult for liberals to engage dispensationalists in sustained theological conversation is that one is not just talking about differences in theological beliefs (such as the often-used caricature of personal versus social religion): one is talking about radically different worldviews. Dispensationalism represents a way for many evangelicals to redefine history, putting their interpretation of Scripture at the center of Christian teaching, amidst the majority of the world that rejects this message.[19] One of the classic popular culture treatments of dispensationalism was Donald Thompson's 1972 film, *A Thief in the Night*. Long before the *Left Behind* novels and movies appeared on the scene, Thompson reached a large segment of Christian youth organizations (including some within mainline churches) with his account of the rapture. What this film makes clear is that many people "left behind" after the rapture are not bad people. However, they have never been exposed to the authentic teachings of Scripture that make a saving relationship with Jesus possible. This is especially evident in the main character of the film, Patty, who clearly is a kind and thoughtful person (someone that John Wesley in the eighteenth century would have called "an almost Christian"), who regularly goes to church, prays, and seeks to understand Scripture. As the film makes clear, however, Patty's problem is that she's going to the "wrong" church. Her minister, a wonderful caricature of a liberal preacher, is depicted as someone who speaks of the Bible as great poetry, and a book of great wisdom, but hardly indispensable to salvation. "What really matters," he bellows from his pulpit, "is what we can know about man's relationship to man."[20] All the time this bellicose minister is preaching, you see pictures of a bored congregation, including persons like Patty, who regularly check their watches, hoping for the sermon to end. This atmosphere of "mainline" religion is in contrast to the truth of the dispensationalist church depicted in the film, where the minister explains in straightforward fashion to his wide-awake congregation what Scripture says about the rapture.

It is easy to make fun of the contrived plot (and low-budget atmosphere) of the film, but, as Randall Balmer points out, the film not only gives a straightforward explanation concerning the doctrine of the rapture, but a clear overview of how evangelical Christianity offers the only hope of salvation.[21] Central to the dispensationalist worldview is a profound belief that the Bible speaks with unity and authority as one voice, and to understand its mysteries is to gain access to a worldview that makes possible salvation from "the wrath to come."

One reason liberals need to take dispensationalism seriously is that it represents a logical progression of the classic Protestant notion that all theological truth comes from the Bible. The sentiments of Arthur T. Pierson in the early twentieth century would be echoed by many conservatives today: "All the parts of the Bible are necessary to its completeness. Organic unity is dependent on the existence and co-operations of organs. . . . Not one of the books of the Bible could be lost without maiming the body of truth here contained."[22] Yet along with this perspective is the way that dispensationalists and other conservative evangelicals take seriously the Reformation recovery of Paul, whereby true Christians are those who are "born again" by personal conversion, and whose identity as Christians enables them to live in the world without being corrupted by it.

Despite its otherworldly and sectarian connotations, dispensationalists have not historically been people on the margins of American culture (unlike other apocalyptic sects that have emerged in American religious history). Many dispensationalists in the past, as is the case today, come out of prosperous middle-class congregations, and desire, like many of their counterparts in liberal churches, nothing more than to realize "the American dream," as reflected in a good job, a stable family, and time for leisure. Likewise, unlike more traditional religious groups such as the Amish, the vast majority of dispensationalists are not uniformly renouncing everything in the culture (witnessed in part by the increasing political activism of several dispensationalist Christians). Yet, as Mark Noll observes, the fixation of dispensationalists to describe the relationship of human events to divine prophesy contributed to a heritage that has had "disastrous effects" on the future of American evangelicalism.

> Dispensationalism promoted a kind of supernaturalism that, for all of its virtues in defending the faith, failed to give proper attention to the world. The supernaturalism of dispensationalism, especially in the extreme forms that were easiest to promote among the populace at large, lacked a sufficient place for the natural realm and tended toward a kind of gnosticism in its communication of truth. Adherents were instructed about nature, world events, ethics, and other dimensions of human existence, but almost always without studying these matters head-on. Bible verses were quoted to explain conditions and events in the world, but with very little systematic analysis of the events and conditions themselves.[23]

One of the ironies associated with the rise of recent forms of dispensationalist theology is how beliefs in Bible prophesy have converged with earlier Protestant themes of "Christianizing" the world. While it is true that much apocalyptic theology views history as a means to explain biblical prophesy (such as the fixation that many evangelicals today have with supporting the state of Israel, whose preservation figures so prominently in many end-time scenarios), the last quarter of the twentieth century witnessed a convergence of evangelical millennial movements (including strands of postmillennial evangelicalism) that have picked up on the earlier liberal Protestant goal of "Christianizing" America. For all the ways that contemporary liberals bemoan the influence of evangelical theology, and dismiss its nationalism and several of its political stands (such as its anti-abortion activism and, more recently, its efforts to pass laws prohibiting same-sex marriages), segments of contemporary evangelicalism (whether pre- or postmillennial) are engaging in the same type of "Christ transforming culture ministry" that has been a long-standing quest for many liberal traditions (if not for the vast numbers of Protestant churches historically). In this regard, dispensationalists, like a wide range of Protestants, are heirs of the Reformation, and in particular John Calvin, who stressed the need of the Christian church to hold the civic order accountable to its moral worldview. The difference is that historically many liberals felt called to save the world, while many dispensationalists felt called to save persons from the world.

The Inconvenient Truth

In chapter 1, I noted that much of American religious history has been written from the perspective of historians who believed (or wanted to believe) that liberal religious movements "won out" over conservative ones. If considering American religious history solely as intellectual ideas, one could make a strong argument for the triumph of liberalism. Liberal theology was born at the intersection of intellectual and cultural upheaval, leading to significant theological developments that impacted churches, denominations, ecumenical gatherings, and the larger society. The crowning achievement of liberalism was its legacy of integrating Christian theology into questions of social justice, leading to a number of significant efforts to transform American ecclesiastical, political, and economic institutions. The imperative embraced by many Christians today, that Christianity as a faith is inseparable from the transformation of structures that propagate political, economic, racial, and environmental oppression, would not have occurred without the rise of liberal theology. Historically, the best parts of liberalism were broad enough to assimilate divergent theological critiques, while staying rooted in a theology that was modern and faithful to earlier sources of Christian theology.

However, if one wrote a history of Christianity purely from the standpoint of popular religious movements, then it would be difficult to include liberalism as a central narrative. It is true that liberalism triumphed on an institutional level in the 1920s and 1930s, completing a process that began in earnest with the rise of the social gospel in the early twentieth century. But while forms of late nineteenth- and early twentieth-century liberalism did reach segments of middle-class Protestantism, it has never come as close to reaching the mass audiences as have various forms of evangelicalism.[24] What has characterized the development of liberalism, especially since the 1960s, has been how the tradition is largely centered upon specific academic movements of theology. As the next chapter points out, these traditions of academic liberalism remain strong and vibrant; however, contemporary liberalism has generally held a line that a sustained engagement with popular evangelical theologies like dispensationalism is somehow beneath it.

Even though Fosdick connected with a tradition of liberalism that sought to maintain an irenic posture toward evangelicals, the caricatures that evangelicals were all narrow-minded bigots became embedded in the culture of mainline Christianity. Yet it is often liberals who know little about the nuances of evangelical theology, and many who identify themselves with the liberal (or progressive) tradition still tend to use the terms "evangelical" and "fundamentalist" interchangeably, not recognizing that these are two distinct historical movements. The landscape of American evangelicalism, both in historical and contemporary contexts, reflects a stunning range of beliefs and faith communities. Indeed, as contemporary surveys of American religion point out, the use of the term "evangelical" has theological currency that extends throughout American Protestantism, as do various ideas surrounding the Second Coming and the end of the world.[25] This data gives support to the assertion by recent scholars that various strands of apocalyptic thought reside just beneath the surface of contemporary American life.[26]

With the reemergence of evangelical Christianity into the public square since the elections of Jimmy Carter in 1976 and Ronald Reagan in 1980, the question of evangelical theology's impact on American politics has become a frequent topic of conversation among secular and religious liberals. Yet for all the ways in which religious liberals will talk about conservatives being "wrong" in their social-political worldview, there has been little sustained effort by liberals to try to penetrate the theological worldview that drives many evangelicals toward conservative politics. On one hand, evangelical politics is driven by long-standing Protestant ideals of God's providence in America, an ideology with deep-seated roots in America's colonial past. While many forms of liberalism carried forward on this tradition earlier in the twentieth century, it is segments of American evangelicalism that have now picked up the banner of making sure that America is a "Christian nation," epitomized in the public's mind by support for "pro-family" issues, in particular a staunch opposition to abortion and gay rights.

Many liberals who criticize conservative movements often argue that it is an anti-Enlightenment phenomenon, citing in particular its hostility to modern science (including theories of evolution). Yet as numerous studies point out, what commonly is called "fundamentalism" is a profoundly modern development and cannot be understood outside the historical context of what has been taking place in the West over the past one hundred years.[27] In the context of current debates surrounding the teaching of "creation science" and a desire to interject a "Christian" perspective into American public institutions, there is an overarching belief, not that science is evil or that American institutions are inherently corrupt, but rather that fundamentalists (and related movements of conservative evangelicals) see their mission as making sure that America is a nation that conforms to the precepts of the Bible as a means to interpret the "modern" world. Historically this goal was shared by many liberals; however, the differing worldviews of both heritages crafted very distinctive understandings of how Scripture should be studied and interpreted. Aspects of evangelical theology provide many Americans not only with the security of Scripture, but with the sense that their worldview can withstand the "secularizing" forces in America (epitomized by liberalism) that deny the power of God's word and, as films like *A Thief in the Night* reveal, ostracize and persecute true Bible believers.

In many ways, dispensationalist and other apocalyptic theologies reflect the logical extension of Protestant fidelity to the Bible. The desire not only helps explain the sense of security that many contemporary evangelicals feel about faith in the afterlife, but the passion they feel to prepare the faithful for God's final judgment, predicated on the ways that it enables the faithful to be like the Apostle Paul—to live in the world, yet in some way to stand apart from it. This formula continues to motivate many conservative Christian movements today, and enables many conservatives to differentiate themselves from the "humanistic" gospel of liberalism.[28]

The liberal minister in *A Thief in the Night* reflects what many conservative evangelicals see as the chief problem with liberalism: it says a lot but it doesn't believe in anything pertaining to Scripture. This charge harkens back to the rhetoric used by so-called fundamentalists in the 1920s. The question remains: do liberal Christians today confront these accusations in a manner similar to figures like Fosdick, or ignore them?

Several of the most public leaders of the early fundamentalist movement, in particular J. Gresham Machen, shared a distaste for dispensationalism. However, they challenged liberals to think not only about sources of scriptural and doctrinal authority, but ultimately about the purpose of the church. Machen raised critical questions about liberalism that reflected the sentiments of many early leaders of American fundamentalism. In particular, he raised a central question that harkened back to the sixteenth-century reformations: what must one believe in order to be called a Christian?

Machen drew the ire of many liberals in 1923 with the publication of his book *Christianity and Liberalism*. In the context of the theological battles of the decade, the book was contentious and symbolized the growing divide within American Protestantism. Yet Machen raised penetrating questions concerning the relationship of liberalism to earlier doctrinal heritages: mainly, could one seriously call liberal theology Christian theology? "What the liberal theologian has retained after abandoning to the enemy one Christian doctrine after another is not Christianity at all, but a religion which is so entirely different from Christianity as to belong in a distinct category."[29] In microcosm, Machen presented numerous accusations in the 1920s that have been leveled at liberals ever since.

> The plain fact is that liberalism, whether it be true or false, is no mere "heresy"—no mere divergence at isolated points from Christian teaching. On the contrary it proceeds from a totally different root, and it constitutes, in essentials, a unitary system of its own. . . . It differs from Christianity in its view of God, of man, of the seat of authority and of the way of salvation. And it differs from Christianity not only in theology but in the whole of life. It is indeed sometimes said that there can be communion in feeling where communion in thinking is gone, a communion of the heart as distinguished from a communion of the head. But with respect to the present controversy, such a distinction certainly does not apply. On the contrary, in reading the books and listening to the sermons of recent liberal teachers—so untroubled by the problem of sin, so devoid of all sympathy for guilty humanity, so prone to abuse and ridicule the things dearest to the heart of every Christian man—one can only confess that if liberalism is to return to the Christian communion there must be a change of heart fully as much as a change of mind. God grant that such a change of heart may come! But meanwhile the present situation must not be ignored but faced. Christianity is being attacked from within by a movement which is anti-Christian to the core.[30]

Many of Machen's objections to liberalism were hardly new. Increasingly, the question for many conservatives was centered on how liberals not only deviated from Christian doctrine, but were advocating a religion *very different* from the one taught in the Bible. Yet part of the success of earlier incarnations of liberal theology is that the movement grew as it sought to respond to many of the points being raised by conservatives like Machen. How does one reconcile the reality of sin with the liberal imperative that persons are good? How does one understand Christ's death, if one rejects the doctrine of the substitutionary atonement? How does one reconcile parts of Scripture that appear to speak of the end of the world with the liberal faith that Christianity is meant to reform the world? And perhaps most important, how does one understand the uniqueness of Christ in relationship to the conditions of the modern world?

These questions epitomize the ways that many early liberals wrote and spoke from the posture of apologists, whose beliefs arose in dialogue with earlier understandings of Christian doctrine. As liberalism succeeded on an institutional level, theologically it became more concerned with defining its place within American culture as opposed to engaging in sustained dialogue with the vanquished forces of American evangelicalism.

The Ongoing Challenge of Conservative Evangelicalism

And yet, liberalism has largely failed, not only in its efforts to become a popular theological movement, but by staying aloof from the historical currents that have witnessed the continued vitality of earlier traditions of evangelical theology. The issue I want to pose is not that liberalism should abandon many of its core theological commitments (nor certainly to move in the direction of popular dispensationalism). Rather, the issue becomes: how does liberal theology see itself in relationship to the larger Christian historical and theological heritage—including the heritage of American evangelicalism? Put simply, as the liberal theological heritage moves into the twenty-first century, is it ready and able to respond to the age-old criticisms raised by J. Gresham Machen?

Today the quick and painless response toward conservative Christians like Machen is to castigate them for the errors of their theology. However, the central question that many liberals avoid addressing is *still* the chief challenge presented by Machen: what do liberals believe that makes them Christian? As liberalism enters the twenty-first century, it not only confronts an evangelical landscape that has largely won over a popular audience that liberalism coveted, but struggles to provide answers to Machen's question in ways that will produce compelling and transformative understandings of Christianity.

Six

Does Liberal Theology Still Matter?

The 1960s, 1970s, and 1980s saw many efforts by historians, sociologists, and theologians to reassess the future of mainline Protestantism, especially in response to the cultural upheavals of the 1960s and the numerical gains of conservative Christianity. For some scholars, it was a time to challenge the complacency of middle-class religion, which essentially had chained liberal denominations to a "suburban captivity" mentality, in which mainline denominations were unable to offer a radical theological vision of transformative Christianity.[1] For others, liberalism was a way-station movement that reflected the loss of religious meaning and an impending secularization in the West.[2] Yet the rise of conservative evangelical churches also caused many mainline commentators to wonder why these churches were growing. By the 1970s scholars noted the high demands that evangelicals placed upon members related to their beliefs, as opposed to the lack of doctrinal commitment within liberal churches.[3] In response to these often competing perspectives on American religion, representatives of liberal theology made their case that liberalism's disparate historical and theological heritages still could speak a prophetic word to the changing social-historical contexts of the time.[4] These studies noted many of the strengths of liberalism, especially its mediating heritage between faith and reason, as well as its eye toward theological self-criticism and adjustment. On one hand, liberalism could still point to a vigorous engagement with a variety of ecumenical and, by the early 1970s, interfaith encounters. In addition to the growing dialogue between Catholics and Protestants sparked by Vatican II, the 1960s witnessed an increased interest among many Christians to engage questions of interreligious dialogue and the incorporation of many interfaith voices into liberal theological formulation.[5] On the other hand, as mainline churches continued to lose members to conservative Christianity, some began to raise the issue of how liberal theology defined its core beliefs, especially in the face of a culture that would see the rise of a new metaphor to describe many younger Americans: religious seekers. These seekers, represented initially by the post-World War II "baby boom" generation, revealed demographics that over the years displayed a conflicting range of patterns. While many boomers left organized Christianity altogether, opting to embrace a patchwork quilt of beliefs (often defined around the metaphor of "spirituality"), others were increasingly drawn to a proliferation of nondenominational, evangelical churches that grew rapidly in the U.S. during the 1970s and 1980s.[6] Amidst these emerging patterns, the future of liberal theology looked uncertain.

In the early 1980s, Donald E. Miller wrote an analysis of liberal theology largely aimed at an audience who was sitting on the fence between faith and doubt. He cast liberalism as a logical and appealing alternative for those who were turned off by religious orthodoxy on one extreme and agnosticism on the other. Yet for all of Miller's hopefulness in stating the case for liberal theology, he ends with a warning that is still pertinent in the early twenty-first century.

> My fear is that in the absence of a vital liberal theology, many members of liberal congregations are on their way toward creating a class of formerly religious but now secular humanists. I am not opposed to humanism except when I sense that its proponents know more what they are against than what they are for.[7]

Today, Miller's comments still resonate when one looks at the apparent divide that appears to be widening in the United States between those on the political right, who are tied to conservative Christianity, and those on the left, who increasingly are connected to the label of "secularism." There is no doubt that components of the contemporary news media are prone to simplify the complex character of contemporary American religion. But for anyone who watches CNN, FOX, or MSNBC with any regularity, it is impossible to avoid seeing the faces of Pat Buchanan, Bill Bennett, Ann Coulter, and others who call for Christian morality tying together evangelical rhetoric and conservative politics, and "secular humanists" like Christopher Hitchens who see religion as the root of all societal evil. Given this picture of the early twenty-first-century public square, one wonders whether Miller's feared public marginalization of liberal theology has already happened.

If early twentieth-century liberals like Walter Rauschenbusch were alive today they would be not only heartbroken by what they would see on the current social-political scene, but mystified by how wrong they were about the future of American Christianity. These liberals believed fervently in the hope that America could be a place where progressive politics would flourish, and where the theological and political goals of liberalism would be firmly on the larger public agenda. While liberals like Rauschenbusch might look with approval at the growing nature of religious pluralism, they would be despondent by mainline Protestantism's lack of public influence. More than anything else, I believe that an earlier generation of liberal Christians would be at a loss to understand the continued popularity of segments of American evangelicalism, and to learn that apocalyptic theologies, movements that persons like Rauschenbusch confidently believed would die out in the twentieth century, are alive and well and more popular than ever. Much of liberalism's appeal came historically out of its ability to affirm Christian tradition without necessarily renouncing the truth claims of contemporary culture. Historically, liberalism worked *best* when it proclaimed a message of deep Christian commitment while seeking to enable persons to relate their faith to the social, religious, and cultural contours of a given era. Yet one strains to see signs of any larger popular school of liberal theology on the horizon of early twenty-first-century America reminiscent of persons like Henry Ward Beecher, Washington Gladden, Walter Rauschenbusch, Georgia Harkness, or Harry Emerson Fosdick.

Some voices within contemporary American Christianity seek to define liberalism for a popular audience, and figures such as Marcus Borg and John Shelby Spong pick up on aspects of an earlier liberal tradition predicated on critical inquiry and reason.[8] The popularity of these authors leaves little doubt that they provide helpful guides for some Americans toward understanding a type of Christianity that moves beyond an uncritical reliance on Scripture, ancient creeds, and supernaturalism. Yet for all the ways that Borg and Spong attract some enthusiastic followers within mainline churches, they don't represent the wave of the future for liberal theology. In some ways, the dominant perception surrounding Borg and Spong is that they reflect the concern raised by Donald Miller. Mainly, at times it is easier to identify Borg and Spong by what they don't believe about Christian tradition, as opposed to what they do believe.

The sad truth is that if history is any sort of guide, then liberal theology will never approach the type of popular status enjoyed by various incarnations of evangelical theology. Even at a time period earlier in the twentieth century, liberalism's chief victories resided mostly within the confines of specific upper-middle-class congregations and the institutional contours of American Protestantism. And yet, many liberals (or progressives) still largely see their objective as claiming a popular audience that by and large never existed in the first place, a prospect that looks increasingly gloomy, given the proliferation of nondenominational churches, including numerous megachurches and, in recent years, the so-called Emergent Church phenomenon.[9] I don't believe that liberal theology is in danger of dying out. Yet I am concerned that it runs the risk of being a secondary player in the shaping of twenty-first-century Christianity. Today, many denominations point with pride to the robust nature of their missions: how they embody the qualities of prophetic and transformative ministries that are thriving not only in the U.S., but globally. A cursory glance at denominational websites, as well as the theological schools that support them, will leave one with a strong impression that liberalism is strong and vibrant. Yet these gains not only fail to address the deep anxiety facing many American mainline churches today (as reflected in a ubiquitous array of church renewal movements and literature), but as indicated earlier, how the global reach of Christianity in places such as Africa, Asia, Latin America, and in countries associated with the former Soviet Union are often a reflection of evangelical theologies (in particular, pentecostalism), as opposed to liberal schools of theology related to personalism, process, neo-orthodoxy, or liberationist perspectives. Additionally, as a "generation of seekers" is currently moving through the passages of midlife, how will churches, whether liberal or evangelical, relate to the unique needs of this generation's children, who now enter young adulthood with their own unique concerns about faith and meaning in contemporary America?

While I do not believe that liberalism will die out in American Christianity, it needs to find ways of restating its message related to the changing contours of the twenty-first century. There is no doubt that the theological challenges posed by religious pluralism will play an important role in shaping the future of liberal theology (as it will for every Christian tradition). Yet I am concerned that liberal theology has not paid enough attention to how the tradition might impact the faith practices of churches and congregations in America. Liberal Christianity may never be able to match the popular appeal of many movements of contemporary evangelicalism. However, it can make important strides in addressing the challenges posed by individuals like J. Gresham Machen regarding what makes liberal theology Christian theology, and an important force within twenty-first-century America.

Liberalism as Christian Theology

It is impossible to examine the history of theological liberalism without engaging the philosophical roots of the heritage. Any attempt to understand the history of theological liberalism without discussing the names of Kant, Hegel, Schleiermacher, and Ritschl (and later on, names such as Borden Parker Bowne and Alfred North Whitehead) would be crafting an incomplete history of liberalism. Various traditions of philosophical idealism gave liberalism both an intellectual and, in some cases, a practical theological grounding. By providing a basis to believe in the goodness of humanity, liberal theology dared to assert that the pursuit of justice was predicated on something more than individual conversion, providing a basis for individuals and faith communities to work for the transformation of the world. By seeing God as an active being in history, liberalism challenged Christian communities to rethink critically their relationship with one another and with the planet. By countering aspects of Christian tradition that veered toward apocalypticism, liberalism offered theologies that affirmed the sanctity of life and the importance of working for the preservation of life, including our planet's resources. By reflecting on the complexities of the world, especially during times of rapid social change, liberal theology asserted that there were no easy answers, only that Christianity, in its historical and "modern" forms, was indispensable to the pursuit of truth. Quite simply, without understanding the role of various traditions of philosophical idealism upon the movement (in particular, the legacies of Kant and Hegel), liberalism as we know it never would have emerged as a theological tradition.

And yet, in its formative years as a heritage, proponents of the best aspects of liberal theology identified their work with a consistent engagement with numerous sources associated with Christian theology. As a religion, Christianity has always been influenced by its dialogue with philosophy, and those who castigate liberal theology for its reliance on "non-Christian" philosophies would do well to remember that this engagement has been going on in the church since the time of the Apostle Paul. Yet the heavy reliance of recent traditions of liberal theology upon philosophical sources, while germane to academic discussions of the movement, have stymied the efforts of liberal voices to gain a larger audience. If liberalism is to have any future in America beyond an academic base, as Gary Dorrien suggests, it needs to find ways to balance its philosophical rigor with a goal central to many earlier representatives of liberal theology—an engagement with historical sources of Christian theology.

The sobering reality, one that Dorrien's third volume on American liberal theology makes very clear, is that most schools of contemporary liberalism probably owe more to the intellectual influences of twentieth-century philosophy than to classical categories of Christian theology. This characteristic is especially true of process theology, the tradition that is most heavily represented in Dorrien's concluding volume on liberal theology. Initially birthed out of an interplay between personalist idealism and the philosophy of Albert North Whitehead, the movement has become what Dorrien calls the "only vital school" of American theology since the 1960s.[10] Many of the major liberal theological voices over the past forty years have direct ties to process thought, including Marjorie Suchocki, David Ray Griffin, Schubert Ogden, and most especially John Cobb. Yet few Americans outside the world of theological studies have heard these names, or the names of their many disciples, nor will most take the time to read their writings.

Liberation theology has had a similar problem. Although most liberation theologians condemn the false dichotomy that Western theology has made between "professional" and "practical" theology, stressing that any theology needs to speak to the concrete conditions of oppressed peoples, I'm not convinced that this movement has ever achieved any sort of popular audience. When many of the formative texts of American liberation theology appeared from the late 1960s to the mid-1980s, their authors were largely grappling with the social and political fallout of the 1960s. A generation or so removed from the civil rights and feminist movements, however, the rhetoric of "classical" liberation theology often strikes many of my current students, especially those in their twenties, as obtuse (in part because these younger people were born after the historical context that shaped these seminal American theologians). My classes are unsure of how to respond to what they often perceive as exclusive (and angry) rhetoric, and often fail to recognize the historical contexts of racism and sexism that impacted theologians like James Cone and Rosemary Ruether. As noted in chapter 4, most liberation theologians are quick to distinguish their work from liberalism. However, they share with many liberal traditions a theological abstractness that often makes it easier for a reader to know what they don't believe, as opposed to what they do believe.

I want to be clear that my intent is not to berate these outstanding theologians for their larger contributions to the academic study of theology and to the church,[11] but to comment on the fact that most modern schools of liberal and liberation theologies don't move far from the academy. Historically, Christianity is indebted to those in the church who have taken on the task of writing formal theology; however, one of the reasons Christian communities today still talk about figures such as Augustine, Calvin, and Edwards is not simply that they were "good" theologians, but that subsequent faith communities have been able to apply their theology to specific faith contexts and communities. A large measure of liberalism's success in its formative years in the nineteenth and twentieth centuries occurred, in Glenn Miller's words, "on the fly," whereby liberal leaders were interfacing with their immediate historical contexts, often ignoring the theological implications of their ideas.[12] Later liberal movements did a much more thorough job fleshing out the finer points of their positions, in particular, building more carefully defined traditions of theological liberalism. Just as late medieval scholastic theologians became more interested in dialoguing and debating one another, losing sight of the crises facing many European Catholics on the eve of the sixteenth-century Protestant reformations, liberalism has evolved into a prodigious range of academic voices, but largely lacking popular audiences.

One person within contemporary liberalism who recognizes this dilemma is John Cobb. Cobb is accurate when he notes that one of the major tasks facing contemporary mainline churches is finding ways to get lay people to take theological discernment seriously. Cobb accentuates that one of the failures of modern liberalism (and I would include much of the process and liberationist traditions) has been an inability to engage churches in thinking and reflecting upon a host of theological issues pertaining not just toward questions of social justice, but fundamental historical questions of faith related to sin, salvation, and eschatology. Cobb's point is not that laity are required to obtain the knowledge of professional theologians; "it does require that church people recognize that unless we reflect seriously, as Christians, about who we are and what we are called to be, we continue to drift into decadence."[13]

Cobb correctly perceives that what characterizes much of the history of American liberal theology is a movement *away* from local churches and *into* the institutional matrixes of universities and seminaries. Yet when you look over many of the outstanding exemplars of Christian liberalism presented in this book, the vast majority were *not* trained theologians, nor did they identify themselves as such. While many early liberals may not have been keen systematic theologians, they were deeply concerned with questions of how liberal Christianity had a direct bearing on how individuals lived out their faith within churches and the larger society. It is true that aspects of this model led some liberals to superficial statements (which, it could be argued, is a mark of many contemporary movements of evangelical theology today). But at its best, the liberalism of an earlier time was marked by a desire to make faith communities rethink age-old questions of faith, such as the nature of sin, salvation, the atonement, and the role of the church. I believe that the future of liberal theology will in part rest with those who can follow the path struck by those in the past who have been able to make the complexities of theology understandable to a larger audience. It will not simply come through the work of scholars in universities or seminaries, but through those who occupy pulpits, teach Sunday school classes, lead Bible studies, and head up specific ministries. The role of formal theology will never disappear; however, the question of how liberal theology will carry itself beyond its academic base is the central question for twenty-first-century liberalism. If liberalism is to accomplish this, it needs to make sure that it uses its heritage to engage sources in Christian theology related to Scripture and tradition. It also needs to do something central to the best representatives of the liberal heritage: apply historical sources of Christianity to our contemporary context.

Liberal theology was not just born out of various social and theological crises of the modern world, but also out of denominations that were rooted in the supposition of their own institutional longevity (if not permanence). Part of the crisis that will confront the future of liberal theology is that many of its academic centers, rooted within theological seminaries, are shrinking. If liberalism is to capture some sort of renewed vision for our time, it needs to come to terms with a religious terrain that is far different from when liberals like Fosdick and Niebuhr assumed mainline Christianity's cultural dominance.

As was discussed in chapter 1, liberalism is not a particularly popular term in the lexicon of early twenty-first-century Christianity. By the same token, the contemporary religious landscape might present liberalism new opportunities to use the strengths of its heritage to engage in a critical dialogue with the wider society. In a recent analysis of theological liberalism, Peter Hodgson notes that liberalism needs to be "driven to its roots," using its historical roots to confront the challenges of early twenty-first-century life.[14] While I concur with Hodgson's assessment, this historical recovery should *not* just be based upon a recovery of liberalism's roots in philosophical idealism, but on how the tradition strives to enter into critical dialogue with historical resources of Christian theology and finds meaningful ways to communicate these sources to the unique context of our era.

Religion in America has always moved in ways that defy the organizational methods of philosophers, theologians, and historians. It has been characterized by innovation and improvisation, resulting in a variety of new churches and new religious movements, and these patterns show no sign of ebbing in the new century. This diversity will likely make it even harder for liberal Christianity to find its voice and witness within our current religious marketplace. What follows is a discussion of four areas where liberalism can engage in theological conversations that may help clarify what it is that liberals believe, and how to move forward into the future. The ways that Christian liberalism enters into a critical dialogue with these four themes might push liberalism beyond its professional moorings in seminaries and divinity schools, and serve as channels by which church leaders in the twenty-first century can work to reinvigorate new incarnations of Christian liberalism.

Liberalism and Popular Evangelicalism

After World War II, when many academic traditions of evangelical theology began a serious effort to rethink earlier core beliefs, it was difficult for many liberals to take evangelical theology seriously (regardless of whether or not it was dispensationalist). As one scholar notes, for much of the twentieth century evangelicalism "provided the [Protestant] establishment with a foil against which to define its concerns. It was The Other—first an antiecumenical other and then a spiritually conventional other, a politically reactionary other, and a disappearing unsecular other."[15] Even as the relationship between evangelicals and liberals has shifted over the years, the posture of some liberals toward evangelicalism is scorn, at worst, and benign neglect, at best.

The reemergence of evangelicalism in the 1970s caught many Americans by surprise. However, the groundswell of support for born-again presidents Jimmy Carter, in 1976, and Ronald Reagan, in 1980, was a reflection of the strong grassroots activism that many conservative evangelical churches had been building for several generations. Today, it is impossible to have any serious conversation about the future of American religion without discussing the ongoing significance of evangelical Christianity, especially the ways that modern evangelicalism (unlike liberalism) has succeeded in fostering a high level of tension with the wider culture.

I'm always struck by the inability of many liberals to understand the appeal of conservative evangelicalism (especially dispensationalism). What many don't understand is that the appeal of evangelicalism goes beyond psychological arguments (such as the need for assurance in an afterlife), but represents the fact that many evangelicals know their Bible, and are not afraid to use it as a means to help them order their personal and collective lives (although, I would argue, sometimes in misguided ways). For the majority of evangelicals, the Bible represents not only the primary source for religious authority, but a guide to navigate through a culture that is often perceived as being hostile to those who identify themselves as Christians.

A major challenge for Christian liberalism in upcoming years will be finding ways to reclaim the authority of Scripture without succumbing to the pessimistic and literalistic interpretations of the Bible that characterize some components of evangelical theology. Part of what is forgotten about Walter Rauschenbusch is that much of his theology of the social gospel emerged in dialogue and debate with dispensationalist theology, in the hope that he could present the church of his time with a theological alternative to this movement. While he castigated dispensationalists for their negative views of history, and for negating the role of churches working for the betterment of society, he felt that the contemporary church needed to listen to proponents of dispensationalism (or what he referred to as Millenarianism) for the ways the movement held in tension the radical nature of the church in the present with an age yet to come.

> We have often been taught to look for the mighty manifestations of the Spirit in the past and not in the future. We are led to think that the faith has once for all been delivered to the saints to be guarded like water in a cistern, and not like seed-corn to be scattered on the ground for a richer harvest. It is orthodox to believe that the age of miracles has ceased and that inspiration stopped with the closing of the New Testament canon. Millenarianism has put in its protest against this merely reminiscent attitude of the church, and bids us lift up our eyes and behold the coming Christ.[16]

Liberals are justified in viewing various millennial theologies as a distortion of the biblical message. Yet to simply argue that millennial theology is delusional and irrelevant in contemporary theological discussion is tantamount to believing that conservative theology will disappear merely by wishing it away.

Part of the amazing aspect of the larger history of American evangelicalism in the twentieth century is not only the diverse array of theological traditions that have emerged from the evangelical heritage (including, as discussed in chapters 2 and 3, liberalism), but the way that liberalism has made its way into various aspects of evangelical theology.[17] This interface has moved way beyond questions of ecclesiastical control of churches and denominations. For better or worse, evangelicals and liberals frequently embrace a shared heritage of cultural Christianity, whereby success is defined more by the ability to have one's voice heard on Capitol Hill and in the White House, as opposed to theologies that relate to a shared heritage of personal and social renewal coming out of congregations. Many progressive voices reacted with disdain over Barack Obama's decision to have evangelist Rick Warren give the invocation at Obama's presidential inauguration. Yet the inclusion of Warren is in keeping with a history of presidential inaugurations, in which a high-profile evangelical Christian (in a previous incarnation, Billy Graham) has taken on the role as a sort of American high priest—an extensive tradition of American civil religion that will likely not pass from the scene in the near future (and one can only speculate at the public reaction that would have occurred if Obama had chosen a non-Christian religious leader to give the invocation). Yet Warren's presence at Obama's inauguration also challenges one to rethink common caricatures of labels such as "evangelical" and "liberal" when it comes to questions of religious and political commitment. While many progressives reacted with disdain to Warren's anti-gay rights stand, Warren has also been highly critical of many traditional evangelicals for ignoring problems related to economic justice and support of the poor. Warren's popularity indicates that the historical landscape is changing, and might very well forge an opportunity for greater dialogue between liberal and evangelical congregations over the next several years.

What is ironic about many conservative evangelical political movements is that they claim the moral example of an individual whose legacy falls squarely in the liberal tradition: Martin Luther King Jr. Many pro-life evangelicals appeal to Martin Luther King Jr.'s nonviolent philosophy as justification for their protests of abortion clinics. Yet many evangelicals who appeal to King ignore the liberal underpinnings of his theology and ethics. Typical of this engagement was an article by Fleming Rutledge in the June 2008 issue of *Christianity Today* praising King for his biblical Christianity, which stood up to evil. Yet Rutledge argues that King's example stood in juxtaposition to the values and worldview of theological liberalism. "The belief that an 'experiential,' humanistic perspective on the Christian story is more accessible and appealing is proving not to be the case; several decades of this thin gruel have left us without any transcendent dimension to draw upon, either for social action or for individual regeneration."[18] Rutledge seemed oblivious that many of King's theological roots lay within the numerous liberal philosophical and theological movements that many evangelicals scorn.[19] Yet this article does point to the fact that Martin Luther King Jr. is a liberal thinker who appeals strongly to evangelical sentiment. This popularity is evident not only in the way that evangelicals have embraced King's nonviolent ethics in the anti-abortion movement, but recently in how a growing number of evangelicals are identifying themselves with traditionally "liberal" causes like environmental activism.[20] As the previous chapter pointed out, dispensationalism might very well be the popular "folk" theology of America, and one factor that has never been carefully studied is the extent to which dispensationalist ideas have penetrated beyond the "sub-cultures" of American evangelicalism to impact mainline denominations. Yet just as liberal Christianity cannot be defined through a "one-size-fits-all" characterization, contemporary evangelicalism reveals an emerging diversity of opinion that moves beyond a fidelity to dispensationalism.

Liberals (or progressives) need to understand the depth of the evangelical heritage, not to mimic it, but to appreciate how the best of that tradition—stressing the centrality of Scripture, personal piety, and engagement with the world—should be central toward understanding the place of contemporary liberalism. Yet liberals need to challenge the historical pessimism and the *negation* of the natural order with theologies that remind evangelical Christianity that a central theme of Christianity is the sanctity of creation. A critical component of liberalism's mission will be to dialogue with those evangelicals that see the ends of faith moving beyond an obsession with the end times, challenging evangelical theology with a hope that the church's mission should be centered on the preservation of creation, not counting down to its destruction. I doubt that liberalism will bring about a wholesale "conversion" of evangelicals (as people like Rauschenbusch hoped). Yet emerging places of dialogue could open up important conversations that might very well lead to important ways on how many mainline churches rethink their mission, as chapter 7 discusses.

Liberalism and Christian Tradition

The late Jaroslav Pelikan made the well-known assertion that "tradition is the living faith of the dead; traditionalism is the dead faith of the living."[21] I open many of my classes with this quote to remind my students that the importance of their work as pastors, ministers, and teachers is dependent on a willingness to understand history not just as a collection of dates, but as something that is living and breathing and continually speaks to circumstances in the present.

And yet, there is no doubt that aspects of liberal theology, both past and present, carry a level of ambivalence toward earlier Christian traditions, seeing the relevance of theology only in terms of what is happening in the here and now. Peter Hodgson stated the argument for Christians to embrace what he referred to as "radical liberalism" as a clear alternative to the orthodoxies and heterodoxies of our time.

> I believe that what needs radicalization is not orthodoxy in the form of patristic creeds and medieval practices but the liberality at the heart of the gospel— a liberality that demands openness to mediation with the modern/postmodern world of which we are critical, and that blocks imperialistic theological claims. Liberal theology is driven to its roots by the crises and traumas of our time. . . . A bland, accommodating, or methodologically preoccupied theology is inadequate in the face of these threats; and the term revisionary . . . seems too weak a description for the kind of liberal theology that is needed today. A radical vision, not merely a revisioning: let that be our goal.[22]

While I find aspects of Hodgson's argument appealing, he epitomizes a tendency of many liberals (both past and present) to dismiss the importance of earlier historical currents in Christian theology.

Liberalism has been at its best when it has not backed away from being religiously and culturally relevant to its context, especially when it has actively raised questions in dialogue with various dominant and oppressed cultures. But Hodgson makes a common error, characteristic of several representatives of liberalism's past, that centers on "modern" secular intellectual sources at the expense of dialoguing with more traditional sources of theology. Historically, proponents of liberal theology often saw themselves as moving beyond the importance of creeds and ancient doctrines, and yet part of the self-correcting impulse within liberal theology is that it stayed in dialogue with these sources. Just as it is impossible to read Walter Rauschenbusch without appreciating his view of the Old Testament prophets and the Synoptic Gospels, Vida Scudder without the ecumenical creeds of the early church, or Reinhold Niebuhr without Augustine, liberal theology in the twenty-first century needs to open itself up to a range of historical sources in church history—and relate these sources to the unique questions of our time. If liberalism is to have any future beyond its academic base, it not only needs to engage the totality of church tradition, but to reflect carefully on the unique challenges and opportunities facing Christian faith communities in the twenty-first century.

One of the core strengths of early theological liberalism was that its chief representatives understood the power of Christian conversion. Unlike many liberals today, they did not shy away from describing themselves as evangelicals, understanding the way that term reflected a sense of continuity with a tradition that could appeal to the life of the mind as well as the heart. In making the case for liberal theologies in the twenty-first century, I am not arguing that we should abandon critical inquiry or seek to mimic the theological rhetoric that emanates from segments of the evangelical church. Rather, liberals need to understand the importance of their historical and theological legacy, not for the purpose of enshrining it as some sort of infallible tradition, but as a basis for the ongoing renewal of liberal theology. For example, it is easy to read documents like the Apostles' and Nicene creeds and dismiss them for their patriarchy and what may seem like antiquated theological assumptions. By the same token, thousands of mainline churches each week recite these creeds in worship without giving a thought to their contemporary meaning (and for that manner, how many people think critically about the theology they sing in their hymns?). And yet, from the lens of liberalism, how might these historical sources be viewed not as putting "God in a box," but as an invitation for all of us who take Christianity seriously to engage in critical reflection on a range of theological questions?

Too often, it is easy for us to castigate what is wrong with tradition, and no one exceeds liberal theology in the task of deconstructing and reconstructing tradition. Yet liberal theology needs to speak with conviction about what it believes in terms of Scripture, tradition, and how the movement can speak to the anxieties of our world. My hope is that liberal theology in upcoming years will not only stress the importance of contextual relevancy, but also not be afraid to use the language of Christian tradition, taking seriously Pelikan's assertion about the important role that tradition can play in the shaping of liberal theologies.

Historically, groups associated with both evangelical and liberal forms of Christianity have suffered from a common problem: religious illiteracy. In particular, many American evangelicals and liberals may differ widely on their views of biblical revelation and scriptural interpretation, yet both remain oblivious of a shared history that tends to see America as the center of God's plan for global salvation. While many liberal Christians looked with disdain to the religious language used by George W. Bush in his war on terrorism, few have picked up on the fact that Bush's unflinching support of spreading American democracy bears uncanny similarities to the missional objectives of an earlier generation of liberal Christianity, especially the close interconnection between the institutions of American democracy with the church's goal of "Christianizing" the world.

Stephen Prothero has recently added his voice to the list of many prominent academics and public figures to call for Americans to address questions of the nation's religious illiteracy. Ironically, many of his arguments sound similar to those made by figures of the Christian Right, like Ralph Reed in the early 1990s, who wrote of America's loss of religious knowledge, "We have lost this common language, and with it our sense of common values. As religion has been pushed to the uttermost edges of intellectual life, the media's explanation for the continued vitality of religion assumes an apocalyptic flavor."[23] Adds Prothero in 2007, "From this nation's beginnings it has been widely understood that the success of the American experiment rested on an educated citizenry. In today's world it is irresponsible to use the word *educated* to describe high school or college graduates who are ignorant of the ancient stories that continue to motivate the beliefs and behaviors of the overwhelming majority of the world's population. In a world as robustly religious as ours it is foolish to imagine that such graduates are equipped to participate fully in the politics of the nation or affairs of the world."[24]

Part of the opportunity that liberal Christianity may have in the twenty-first century is to participate in this conversation, in ways that not only can promote dialogue with evangelicals, but provide forums for disparate Christian and non-Christian faith communities to engage one another about the role of faith in American public life. While Prothero sees this dialogue largely through the ministrations of university religious studies departments, it is evident that the questions of religious literacy that he discusses directly impact the vast number of American congregations. If recent studies on American religion are correct by suggesting that our era is a time when many young people in their twenties and thirties are looking for religious authenticity and meaning, as opposed to virtual stimulation, then liberal congregations, through the valuing of traditions, may have an opportunity to be places that offer meaningful opportunities for persons not only to learn about these traditions, but to find faith communities that can change their lives.

Perhaps the one area that liberals can take from their evangelical brothers and sisters is to take seriously the hunger of Americans to study the Bible. Part of the appeal of the Emergent Church model is not only the ways that the movement seeks to recapture early church traditions (which is an ongoing theme in American religious history), but how these movements show the relationship between the Bible and how one lives out one's faith in the world. The best of Christian tradition, regardless of whether it wears the label "evangelical" or "liberal," occurs when Scripture becomes more than understanding a secret code to salvation or a collection of wise teachings. Rather, Scripture becomes a means for faith communities to understand their place as God's people, striving to grow in their understanding of what it means to be a Christian. In the past, the best aspects of Christian liberalism were able to engage in critical study of the Scriptures and integrate that inquiry with a passion to relate the Bible to the personal and collective faith journeys of men and women. As the twenty-first century progresses, liberalism will have to hold onto that creative tension.

Liberalism and Theological Ambiguity

Liberal theology was born amidst an era of cultural and scientific optimism, a time period when historical forces believed in varying degrees that human social behavior could be "perfected." Yet the best of the liberal heritage challenged an uncritical optimism about the future of humanity.[25] In recent years, however, the self-critical dimension of liberalism has been called into question. As liberalism's establishment base has eroded, mainline denominations often are perceived to speak in a range of voices that affirm everything except the core beliefs of Christianity. In particular, liberalism is often depicted as a movement more interested in cultural, as opposed to theological, power and consequently speaks an empty message in the face of the modern/postmodern world.

Yet the larger problem of liberalism, I believe, goes back to the concern raised by Donald Miller: what makes the liberal heritage an alternative to strict orthodoxy on one hand, and a purely secular worldview on the other? One of liberalism's greatest strength is also its greatest weakness: its ability to question its inherited traditions. Historically, it has allowed room for a diverse range of voices to engage significant questions related to doctrine and mission, but it has also left it vulnerable to the accusation that liberal theology has no real theological backbone. Part of the portrait one has of contemporary liberalism can easily resemble the image of the Tower of Babel from the book of Genesis. While liberalism represents a plurality of theological voices in the early twenty-first century, they are largely alienated and separated from the church and culture that they are, in theory, supposed to serve. As Dorrien notes about our recent context, "While liberal theology became more liberationist, feminist, environmentalist, multi-culturalist, and postmodernist, the mainline Protestant churches . . . often swung toward greater homogeneity and confessional identity."[26] The questions facing liberalism in the future will not be whether the tradition will continue to evolve academically. The major question is whether or not liberalism can still speak with any measure of authority to churches and the larger society.

Yet one of liberalism's greatest strengths (and in my opinion what makes the movement truly radical) is that the movement at its best has not been afraid of theological ambiguity. Many traditions of liberal theology were rooted in a belief that the pursuit of a just world was the ultimate mission of Christianity. Yet liberal theology, contrary to what its critics have said, did not necessarily see history leading to an inevitable "happy ending." History stood in the balance between good and evil, and part of the hope of Christian liberalism was that good people would have the strength to stand up against societal evils (whether generated by individuals or systems). Indeed, I would argue that liberal theology has far outstripped evangelical theology over the last one hundred years in developing comprehensive theologies pertaining to human sin. Whether one is talking about Rauschenbusch's or Niebuhr's understanding of social sin, or how theologians like Paul Tillich engaged in cultural analysis as a means to understand problems of theodicy, or Howard Thurman's appropriation of Christian mysticism, the best of the liberal heritage has not been afraid to engage the ambiguities surrounding human moral behavior, challenging an uncritical optimism in human goodness on one hand, and a predetermined eschatology of the "end times" on the other. Yet in a time of mainline decline, many spokespersons see any theological language that speaks of faith in terms of questioning and doubt—which asserts that at a given time it is impossible to understand the will of God—as a sign of weakness.

Part of the contemporary dilemma facing mainline churches is that in response to membership decline, some church leaders are turning to a rarified language of evangelical virility that denies ambiguity in belief and resorts to a language of theological certainty. "We are sickened unto death," United Methodist Bishop Richard Wilke observed in 1986. Faced with a denomination losing membership (and, while not stated by Wilke, public influence), Wilke chastised the United Methodist Church for not preaching the clear-cut theology that had been Methodism's core during its period of greatest growth in the early nineteenth century. "The churches that are drawing people to them believe in sin, hell, and death. . . . If there is no sin, we do not need a Savior. If we do not need a Savior, we do not need preachers."[27]

Wilke's assertions, manifested by numerous leaders within the citadels of mainline Christianity, represent what I believe is a dangerous temptation for mainline churches. Through the rhetoric of popular evangelicalism (with a tone that at times borders on the apocalyptic), Wilke embodies a faith that a return to an early nineteenth-century popular theology will create a turnaround in mainline church membership decline. Yet he embodies characteristics that counter what I think are essential for the future of liberal Christianity.

Wilke depicts a common ahistorical view within American popular theology, epitomized by what J. Philip Wogaman calls a "nostalgic vision."[28] The ideal of a clear-cut historical past is seen through the myopic lens of a "white-hot" church that scorns theological uncertainty, relying on a straightforward understanding of conversion, and sees missional success solely in terms of size. The problem is that the type of church sought by the likes of Richard Wilke probably *never existed*, and even churches that succeeded in promoting the type of evangelicalism he champions often paid a heavy price. While the early nineteenth-century Methodism that Wilke exalted grew exponentially, like other evangelical traditions of the time, it was also raked by schisms, most notably an inability of that tradition to deal with the most pressing moral dilemma of the nineteenth century: slavery. The best of that earlier evangelical heritage occurred when it was able to reflect critically on moral questions that still plague questions of mission today; mainly, to what point does religious fervor get in the way of the moral imperatives that undergird Christian faith?

Many recent sociologists note that the future of American religion will not fall under a convenient "one-size-fits all" label, and that missional challenges to future vitality will be confronted by all American congregations, regardless of the theological labels they wear. Yet, as the final chapter points out, despite the continued push within mainline churches to embrace neo-conservative theology and the rhetoric of popular evangelicalism, evidence abounds that America is filled with growing congregations who take Christian tradition seriously and are unequivocally liberal.[29] These congregations are not only creating innovative and visionary models of worship, but they are enabling people to ask tough questions, seeing the questions as a means to grow in all dimensions of one's faith.

Liberalism and Public Theology

Cornel West points to Walter Rauschenbusch as "the most influential and important religious public intellectual in early twentieth-century America."[30] West's observation shows the affinity between the rise of liberalism and later twentieth-century incarnations of public theology. Yet Rauschenbusch, and many religious liberals who followed him, represented figures from a historical era in which they took for granted the public status of being a (Protestant) Christian. Today one searches in vain for liberal Christians on the public horizon to replace those of an earlier era. The tendency of many contemporary theologians to equate a figure like Rauschenbusch to later developments in liberation theology is understandable, given Rauschenbusch's focus on economic justice and a belief that theology needed to stand in solidarity with the poor. Yet, many who are quick to identify Rauschenbusch with the tradition of liberation theology gloss over the fact that he was largely tied to and benefited from a Constantinian paradigm of the church—a church that leaders of Rauschenbusch's generation assumed would forever stand at the cultural center of the country. One way to look at the collapse of public church giants is to explain it as a consequence of the loss of mainline Protestant prestige. As one scholar noted, mainline liberals "have remained culturally engaged but not fully aware of their cultural powerlessness."[31] Representatives of the liberal church are still visible on a public level (figures like Cornel West quickly come to mind), and the Internet lacks no shortage of blog sites where the voices of liberal Christianity are in abundance.[32] Yet these voices no longer speak on behalf of the institutional prerogatives of mainline churches.

One of many paradoxes about the history of American liberal theology is that, while many liberal traditions frequently castigated the "secular" culture, they also sought legitimacy from that culture. Today, many liberal mainliners, while bemoaning the influences of the secular world, nevertheless lament the fact that their churches no longer seem to be gaining the attention of that world. For a good part of the twentieth century, it was possible for liberals to take Charles Sheldon's question, "What would Jesus do?" and believe that Christians could wipe out social vice in America and the world (as the Prohibition amendment to the U.S. Constitution attempted to do). By the late twentieth century, however, liberal ministers are apt to find sermon illustrations not from the inspired writings of theologians or Christian "public intellectuals," but through the examples of media celebrities like Oprah Winfrey and Bono.

Many Christians (including some in the liberal-progressive camp) bemoan the role of popular celebrities like Winfrey as a sign that Christianity has surrendered its authority to popular culture. Yet in some ways these public figures embody the tenets of an earlier liberal Christian heritage that hoped that its moral influence would carry beyond the churches. In effect, the way secular figures, be they politicians or entertainers, espouse religious and moral values in their public lives represents a manifestation of what liberals of a previous generation (and evangelicals today) hoped would happen through the process of "Christianization." The difference today is that it is no longer apparent that churches (at least the liberal ones) are driving the engine of theological and social change. Consequently, the question arises, what should be the role of theological liberalism in terms of crafting a public dialogue within the larger society?

For a time in the 1960s and 1970s, it appeared that a secularized vision of liberalism would win the day. In an era when theologians were talking about "the death of God" and "the secular city," many in the liberal church not only found themselves struggling over their political commitments, but also found that they no longer carried a public voice that characterized earlier incarnations of twentieth-century liberalism. Conservative evangelicalism was ready and able to fill the void by offering a clearly defined theological worldview that lay claim to Scripture and the historical witness of the church. Today many "liberal" organizations seek to reclaim a public voice reflective of an earlier Protestant era, but in my judgment it remains doubtful that liberal Christianity will be able to speak in one public voice reflective of an earlier time in American religious history.

Part of the difficulty facing liberal/progressive Christian movements in the years ahead is that they must wrestle with the tension between their affirmation of theological pluralism on one hand and their support of specific social-political pronouncements on the other. Figures such as John Cobb and Delwin Brown stress the need for Christians to engage in spiritual discernment, stressing the importance of scriptural study and theological reflection in their vision of progressive Christianity. Yet how does this important goal relate to organizations such as the Network of Spiritual Progressives, who make the case for religious progressives to support specific political movements? As the next chapter discusses, there is little evidence to support the idea that mainline churches will ever come to a clear consensus about how personal religious commitments relate to specific social-political postures. The ongoing challenge of Christian liberalism will be how it provides a means by which persons of faith can address tough social questions in ways that can lead to personal and social transformation.

In this regard, liberals who strive for a "public theology" can learn much from contemporary evangelicalism. Much of liberalism's response to the so-called evangelical reawakening of the 1980s was to characterize various groups like the Moral Majority and, later, in the 1990s, the Christian Coalition, as theocratic despots out to usurp American liberal democratic institutions. There is no doubt that there are dimensions of these movements that have their darker sides, represented by the tactics of some extremists to bomb abortion clinics and engage in other associated acts of violence against individuals who they perceive are doing Satan's work on earth. Yet surveys on American evangelicalism not only reflect a condemnation of these violent tactics, but a clear sense that for all the passion of their theological beliefs (especially wide-ranging beliefs in premillennialism), evangelicals see their faith as a means of galvanizing them to civic duty and responsibility to serve the world (exactly what social gospelers like Rauschenbusch hoped that Christianity would do in the early twentieth century).[33]

What emerges from the majority of figures associated with the "religious right," by and large, is not theological fanaticism, but a sense that faith should play a role in the public square of America. While liberalism in the twentieth century sought acceptance from secular elites for its justification, popular evangelicalism took to the streets and on a grassroots level was able to connect with a message of faith that extended beyond the subculture of American evangelicalism. If one looks at the public agenda of many conservative evangelicals today, one sees a familiar range of issues: the security of American families (reflected by an opposition to same-sex marriages and a decidedly pro-life posture), the need for educational alternatives to public schools, and, a belief that religious faith (i.e., evangelical Christianity) needs to play a central role in American public discourse.

In my judgment, and in the judgment of many secular and religious liberals, the conservative political agenda is fraught with problems. Part of what characterizes the conservative religious worldview is that it relies on its own incarnation of a "nostalgic vision" in terms of understanding American history and, in particular, the role of Christianity in shaping that history. Within this evangelical worldview is the ubiquitous argument that American greatness was predicated on its unique Christian heritage. Liberal movements have long believed that these simplistic views of American history only recycle earlier arguments of an American manifest destiny that never existed in the first place.

And yet, what many religious liberals don't want to acknowledge is that, for all of their problems, evangelical churches have put forth a compelling vision that addresses the larger concerns that many evangelicals (and Americans) have about the future. Liberals are not only prone to castigate this vision (and the people who promote it), but offer no compelling alternatives to it. As noted by countless commentators, what has characterized many persons associated with the liberal label has been a persistent inability to talk about the importance of faith in contemporary public life.[34]

If liberal theology wants to find ways to challenge the assertions coming from segments of the evangelical community, then it needs to wrestle with how liberalism can address the political and cultural insecurities of our time. Not surprisingly, I believe there is a great deal that we can learn from the example of Walter Rauschenbusch. There is no doubt that many discussions of theological liberalism in American Christianity center upon Rauschenbusch. In part, his appeal did come from his distinctive vision of social justice. Yet to simply study Rauschenbusch's politics outside of his theology is to lose focus on what made his ideas unique and enduring. We study Rauschenbusch not just because he had "radical" political ideas. Rather, his politics were radical because they emanated from a deeply felt commitment to the Christian faith. If the history of the American social gospel was only about its institutional "triumph" within mainline denominations, then one could easily focus on Harry Ward (considering Ward's role in crafting the social creed of the churches). Yet it was Rauschenbusch's piety, his devotion to ancient and modern Christianity, even amidst his questioning of these beliefs, that makes him stand out—and why many today, both liberal and evangelical, desire to study his life.

Ethicists and theologians like Stanley Hauerwas have pointed out liberalism's dependency upon the privileged culture of establishment Protestantism for its existence. Yet I am not as convinced as he is that liberalism becomes irrelevant if it is separated from its Constantinian moorings.[35] I believe liberalism has been strongest historically when it has been able to relate its theologies in ways that seek to dissent from the opinions of the predominant culture while staying in dialogue with that culture. As Mark Toulouse notes, such a public posture for Christianity has not historically been done without making compromises, yet it offers twenty-first-century liberalism the opportunity to keep raising larger public questions about faith and justice that have always been a critical component of American Christianity. "Public 'God-talk' does not have to be used as a bludgeon over peoples' heads. . . . It can, however, raise important questions and contribute to discussions about both the 'plurality' and 'ambiguity' of our common life together. . . ."[36] As the next chapter points out, Christian liberalism will have opportunities in the next century to carry its voice into the public square. However, the question that Christian liberals must confront is not only what their message will say, but what do they hope to accomplish by being heard?

A New Liberal Paradigm?

For all the ways many scholars have called for a renewal of the liberal theological heritage, few have actually sought to directly connect it to specific models of twenty-first-century Christianity. Much discussion about the changing shape of American religion has emphasized a variety of themes, ranging from the theme of seeker religion to the phenomena of megachurches and the Emergent Church movement. As the next chapter discusses, the question of how liberalism participates in these conversations will be critical to the larger question of Christianity's shape in the future. The issue that needs to be addressed head-on, however, is not whether or not liberalism can recapture its spirit of the past. The question is whether or not liberal theology can still accomplish what it has done best historically: engage the present while still acknowledging the importance of the past. The way liberal Christianity confronts the future will begin by formulating and answering the right questions emerging from an anxious culture, including from many within mainline churches who seek easy answers and quick-fix solutions at the expense of critical thinking and discernment. Perhaps the central question liberal theology needs to answer is this: *what makes liberalism relevant to discussions pertaining to the future of American Christianity?*

Seven

Liberalism without Illusions

One day in my office, I was contacted by a local newspaper reporter who was doing a story on the religious history of our region. He inquired about an Episcopal priest named Algernon Crapsey, who in the early twentieth century was tried for doctrinal heresy by the Episcopal Church.[1] The interview was going fine until the reporter asked me whether Crapsey would be considered controversial if he were alive today. I could tell that my response was not what the reporter expected, nor wanted to hear. I noted that if you looked at Crapsey's views on scriptural interpretation, on the nature of Christian doctrines such as the virgin birth, and on the meaning of salvation, you would find that he echoed themes that one hears today from prominent liberals such as Marcus Borg and John Shelby Spong. I noted the ongoing controversy surrounding the views of Borg and Spong, as well as data citing the continued fidelity of many contemporary Americans around literal interpretations of Scripture and beliefs in doctrines such as the virgin birth. After a few more polite questions, the interview ended, and I could tell by the reporter's tone that I had destroyed his storyline.

What I've described, I believe, is typical of how some liberals, both secular and religious, tend to view the twenty-first-century American social, political, and religious context. The reporter's supposition was that I would say that Crapsey's ideas would *not* be controversial today, and would fall into the mainstream of contemporary American religious thought. Yet a cursory Internet search on figures like Borg and Spong would reveal that, despite their strong appeal, many view their theology as way outside the mainstream of contemporary Christianity. For all of the ways in which liberal theology has gone through continuous cycles of adaptation and change, the movement has been very reluctant to concede that a large cross section of Americans still holds vehemently to long-standing notions of theological orthodoxy that show no signs of breaking down in the face of liberal logic or theological acumen. What is clear is that, if an individual's faith in liberalism is tied to the inevitable triumph of human rationality, or that God's kingdom will occur if only we elect more individuals from a particular political party, or that the basis of Christian virility is contingent upon embracing particular positions on political issues, then there would be little basis for carrying on as a liberal Christian in the early twenty-first century.

In exploring the contemporary landscape of American Christianity, there is no such thing as a unified liberal movement. Places where liberal theology resides academically, primarily represented by a small number of elite voices within theological seminaries, as well as some colleges and universities, now represent the heirs to an earlier heritage of American liberal theology. The many labels that theologians wear today, whether it be process, feminist, liberationist, womanist, post-liberal, neo-conservative, neo-evangelical, or postmodern, only scratch the surface of theological movements that in one form or another grew out of some sort of dialogue with the classic heritage of liberal Christianity that was spawned in the nineteenth century and came to maturity in the early twentieth century. As we have seen, few contemporary theologians, Christian ethicists, and church leaders today choose to label themselves primarily as liberals, and even fewer persons use the label to describe themselves on a popular level.

And yet, the broad heritage of liberalism represents a continuing force in American theology, even as it faces significant challenges in the future. As noted in the introduction, Gary Dorrien reflected that liberal theology has moved beyond its academic base only when it has balanced what is "modern" with the imperative to stay grounded in historical themes of Christianity. Dorrien goes on to identify this "transformative" tradition with many names familiar to most students of American religious history: Horace Bushnell, Henry Ward Beecher, Walter Rauschenbusch, Harry Emerson Fosdick, Reinhold Niebuhr, Howard Thurman, and Martin Luther King Jr. I concur with Dorrien's assessment, but given the fact that recent developments in liberal theology have been largely confined to academic circles, what are the prospects of liberalism becoming any sort of transformative movement within twenty-first-century American Christianity?

I certainly understand that theological creativity needs to come through the work of scholars who devote their efforts to critical thinking and reflection that lead to creative theological synthesis. Yet for all the importance of various academic schools of liberalism, if the tradition is going to have any sort of defining role in twenty-first-century American Christianity, it must do what it has shown itself capable of doing in the past. Mainly, liberal theology must be contextually formulated around the needs of specific faith communities, where questions of faith are debated and lived out on a daily basis, while also maintaining a critical engagement with earlier forms of Christian tradition. What has given liberalism its staying power is when it has moved beyond philosophical abstraction and found a way to dialogue with the deep-seated religious and cultural issues of a given historical era. As a historian, my interest lies not only in the study of ideas, but in assessing how particular theological ideas "played out" in terms of their wider impact upon actual faith communities, *and* how successive generations sought to live in tension with the ideas of the past. The future of the liberal tradition in the twenty-first century might very well depend on how church leaders today seek to do what components of liberal theology did well in the past: update the tradition, in light of contextual realities.

Stating the Case for Christian Liberalism in the Twenty-first Century

If I were to suggest one goal that contemporary liberalism needs to abandon, it would be seeking to "take back" or "save" Christianity from the alleged sins of conservative evangelicalism. Over the past several years, there have been efforts to form coalitions of liberal Christians in order to stave off the perceived influence of "right-wing" Christian movements. While I think many of these organizations can serve an important role for disseminating information and networking, I'm not convinced that groups like the Network of Spiritual Progressives stand on the vanguard of a popular liberal (or progressive) movement in America. First, as history shows, the great failing of liberal movements is that they never materialized into sustained grassroots movements in the same manner as conservative evangelicalism. While it is true that a large portion of Americans statistically identify themselves with liberal Christianity (even if they reject the label of being "liberal"), there is no common social, political, or theological thread that ties these liberal Christians together. In fact, as Diana Butler Bass points out, neat correlations between liberal theology and politics seldom emerge within congregations. "In the pews, people do not typically identify with camps or parties, but tend to hold blended views on a variety of issues."[2] Coalitions of "national" liberal groups may succeed in garnering the support of seminary professors,

assorted academics, and well-known church leaders, but I remain unconvinced that such an approach is a viable strategy for liberals who are
concerned with both spiritual renewal and social justice, as well as stok-
ing the fires of faith on a grassroots level. In the heyday of mainline
Protestant influence, liberals craved the idea of cultural respectability and
influence, a goal that, as I highlighted in previous chapters, is no longer
possible for liberalism. Yet the tenor of many liberal church leaders today
still seems to yearn for this vision. Even though the earlier language of
"Christianization" has been dropped by liberal theology, there is still that
residue of an earlier establishment mentality that sees its ultimate goal as
getting the culture to embrace its point of view.

One of the great contributions of liberal theology in the twentieth
century was its influence upon ecumenical and interfaith dialogue. Yet
historically, these emphases have been rooted within the institutional
contours of mainline denominations, as opposed to grassroots faith
communities. For many years, denominational and ecumenical agencies
could live believing in an illusion of institutional permanence, due to
the fact that they had the financial resources to support expansion. But
at a time when denominational resources are declining across the spectrum of North American mainline churches, this earlier vision of faith is
becoming more untenable.[3] One of the reasons evangelical Christianity
has been so effective in mobilizing political support around conservative
candidates is that the movement understood the importance of mobili-
zation on a grassroots level. Loren Mead's often-cited assertion from his
influential 1991 book *The Once and Future Church*, that "ministry begins
at the church's front door," is critical for liberal churches to remember to
reclaim their voices.[4] The danger of Mead's quote is that it can lead to a
parochialism that sees ministry only in terms of what is local. Yet, as many
liberation theologians point out, there can be a false dichotomy between
what is considered "local" and "global." As many American congregations are discovering, the vision of the timeless and idyllic "little church
on the vale" is giving way to the realities in which faith communities
must regularly confront issues of mission in a world facing a global AIDS
pandemic, global economic instability, racism, and, of course, a fear of
terrorism. These issues have and will affect faith communities throughout
the world, and increasingly, American congregations that once viewed
mission primarily through writing a weekly check to address social crises
thousands of miles away are discovering how to interact with these issues
on a daily level within their own communities.

The question of liberalism's future vitality, as well as Christianity's,
will not come about when churches embrace another denominational

program, or when a denominational or ecumenical agency passes another resolution against war, or racism, or some other ism; it will come when these larger global issues meet up with the needs of persons living in specific communities. As Mead suggests, authentic missional change in the future will occur when congregations can impact the direction for the people of God, as opposed to receiving their marching orders from their denominations.[5] At the same time, however, authentic transformation will come when liberals do what liberals are capable of doing best—raising penetrating and relevant questions that not only address the contemporary context, but also, in the tradition of Walter Rauschenbusch, Vida Scudder, Reinhold Niebuhr, Howard Thurman, and Martin Luther King Jr., delve deeply into the traditions of the Christian faith, which can awaken contemporary faith communities to experiences that can increase the life of the mind and of Christian witness.

Many religious and political progressives in America still point to the civil rights movement as the classic example of a national movement that included a diverse cross section of Americans (including many within Catholic and mainline Protestant churches). What is often forgotten, however, is that the civil rights movement was born out of the sweat and blood of grassroots organizations that took place at the Highlander Folk School (where individuals like Rosa Parks received their training in nonviolence), the black churches in cities throughout the American South, as well as countless direct-action groups that emerged in response to the sins of racism and Jim Crow.[6] Historically, social movements seldom begin from a "national platform." Rather, they gravitate around grassroots movements that over time are connected to a larger vision, and can point to concrete successes that galvanize growing waves of support.[7] It is true that the end result of the civil rights movement was the scene of thousands of people on the Washington Mall in August 1963 to hear Martin Luther King Jr.'s "I Have a Dream" speech, as well as the passing of federal civil rights legislation in 1964 and 1965. Yet these events would not have occurred without the efforts of scores of organizations throughout the country, as well as the sacrifices of thousands of persons who labored in places such as Montgomery, Birmingham, and Selma.

Liberalism can't simply "will" Americans to embrace their measures of theological and social reform; they have to live in hope that a time will come when the convictions for change will impact people in a new way. Showing his indebtedness to liberal theology (in particular, the influence of Hegel), Martin Luther King Jr. frequently noted that his larger public success was part of "the Zeitgeist," the spirit of the times, in which the movement he helped galvanize reflected both the imperative for change and the possibilities of the historical moment to realize that vision for change. While many contemporary liberals might feel that their causes have been vanquished, they need to have faith that a time will come when their tradition will speak again with power and clarity—as there are signs in our time that it already has.

Questions for Liberals

For Christian liberalism to grow into the twenty-first century, indeed for it to approximate anything that could be characterized as a religious movement, it needs to counter the often-made accusation that the movement is theologically inaccessible, yet also be unapologetic in expressing itself in ways that are a reflection of deeply rooted theological beliefs. The only way this can happen is for those tied to theological liberalism to ask tough questions related to their tradition. I've included what I consider to be four essential questions in this process.

Are liberals truly addressing the deepest needs and anxieties of the culture?

Segments of religious progressivism embody many of the sins of the past by assuming that there is a broad public consensus around their theological, cultural, and political agendas. When I listen to some of the rhetoric coming from segments of the liberal church (even though I often agree with their particular stands), not only do I ask myself, "who is listening?" but also, "are these organizations asking and answering the right questions?" The identification of many strands of liberal Christianity around the imperative to work for justice, focused on specific political issues, embodies part of contemporary liberalism's dilemma. As Mark Chaves notes, when compared to other activities (such as worship and Christian education), the pursuit of social justice ministries has historically represented a low priority for most congregations (including mainline, evangelical, Catholic, and Jewish). "The Social Gospel image of congregations deeply engaged in serving the needy of communities has been for many a compelling normative vision for more than a century, but we should not let notions of what congregations ought to look like influence our assessment of what they *do* look like."[8]

My point is *not* that the pursuit of social justice should be dropped from the agenda of liberalism. The point is that sustained definitions of ministry centered primarily on questions of social justice have historically been difficult for most congregations to maintain. Part of the major difficulty of the liberal church's emphasis on social justice is not just the question of how these themes relate to the missional priorities of many congregations (often defined around worship, education, spiritual growth, and service), but also the even more difficult question of how one measures the success (or failure) of focusing one's ministry on social justice initiatives: Is the goal of the liberal-progressive church primarily one of public advocacy that will lead to passing certain legislative measures? Is it to get congregations in line with certain social-political goals, or is it merely to raise the consciences of individual members? From the standpoint of widely embraced goals of many liberals, such as eliminating racism, sexism, and homophobia in church and society, how are these going to be accomplished? Not only these questions, but others arise. To what extent does liberalism need to take into account the experiences of numerous Americans, many of them representing younger generations, who view their faith not as belonging to an organization or denomination, but nevertheless are passionate about questions of personal spirituality and social transformation?[9] For all the ways that liberalism has inspired the power of preaching and proclamation, to what extent will liberal churches actually carry the ideas espoused on Sunday morning into the wider culture? (And, in particular, to what extent does the message of liberal theology connect to the concerns of young people, regardless of how they define themselves theologically and politically?)

I believe the greatest challenge *and* potential opportunity of liberalism will come through its ability to engage the culture, not only from the perspective of understanding the larger changes that are happening in our era, but also for ways in which local congregations can discern and define mission in the future. One of the fascinating dimensions about the rise of the Christian Right in the 1980s and 1990s was how the movement shifted its strategy and tactics from national to local politics. When the Moral Majority first emerged in 1980, the organization attempted to build a following predicated on creating a national forum for a cross section of evangelical Christians. While the tactic worked in the short run (not least for the ways that it propelled a dispensationalist preacher named Jerry Falwell to national prominence), in the long run the initial enthusiasm sparked by the Moral Majority waned. Yet the rise of the Christian Coalition, emerging from the ashes of Pat Robertson's failed 1988 presidential candidacy, is a different manner. Thanks in large part to the organizational abilities of Ralph Reed, the Christian Coalition pursued a different strategy of engagement. Rather than seeking headlines on a national forum, the Christian Coalition mobilized its resources locally, including school board and town council elections. While liberals tend to view Reed as another example of a conservative Christian who has gone the road of Falwell, few take the time to recognize the contributions of persons like Reed toward enabling conservative Christians to achieve a voice not only in local, but in national politics. Presidential campaigns for much of the twenty-first century will likely be talking about the politics of evangelicalism, and while contemporary liberalism has paid more attention to these dynamics, liberal Christianity needs to engage in this conversation more than once every four years, when a presidential election comes around.

Yet the question of conservative evangelicalism's tactics is only part of the story. I believe that by and large many segments of the evangelical church have asked the right questions, which touch many American congregations, and these questions go beyond the traditional use of categories like "liberal" and "conservative." They understand that Americans are living in a time of great anxiety and fear, a time when often change is seen as a threat to particular values and worldviews. What the conservative church has done is speak effectively to many who worry about the safety of their families, the education of children, and the security of a country that prides itself on its patriotism. Liberalism not only needs clarity of message, but to find ways to make that message come alive in the faith journeys of those within congregations. It will come out of the type of engagement that Walter Rauschenbusch practiced in his congregation in Hell's Kitchen over a hundred years ago. It will come when congregations, pastors, and laity, understand the fears that many persons have of living in an unstable economy, of losing jobs, of violence in their neighborhoods, and how the reality of a globalized world, while a windfall for some, is desolation for others. It will come when congregations not only advocate for social justice, but embody these commitments through the centrality of worship, prayer, education, and spiritual discipline.

Historically, liberal theologies stress the goodness of humanity and the potential of human beings to reshape and change their world. If liberalism were to lose this emphasis, then we will have lost a tremendous chunk of our identity! Yet too often, the stress on human goodness can obscure another part of the Christian message that parts of the liberal heritage have forgotten: that Jesus was betrayed, crucified, and buried— and then he rose. For all the racial, ethnic, theological, and cultural differences that exist today in the church, in some fundamental way, churches gather to relive this reality. I believe the ways that liberalism connects that foundational story of Christianity to the pressing social and cultural issues of our era is the central question that the liberal church needs to engage diligently and faithfully.

*To what extent can and should liberal churches emulate popular
models of "church growth"?*

One of the most contentious topics within mainline churches today is
the question of whether their congregations can, and should, embrace
strategies of many popular church-growth pundits, especially models that
deemphasize more traditional forms of worship and stress more contemporary models. While many see the so-called church-growth movement
as a recent phenomenon, the themes within it are far from monolithic,
nor are they necessarily contemporary. American religious history, especially its Protestant incarnations, is one characterized not only by innovation, but by controversy that emerges as a consequence of innovation.
The so-called great awakening eras in American history were in large
measure struggles between those who saw innovation (such as the camp
meeting revival) as a means to an end (evangelism), and those who were
concerned that popular innovations detracted from the theological/doc-
trinal heritages coming out of specific traditions. While in some way this
division between "new light" innovators and "old light" traditionalists is
as old as Christianity itself, the history of American Christianity accentuates these tensions in ways that still inform debates about religion in
twenty-first-century America.

As indicated in chapter 1, a chief difficulty for mainline congregations
who seek to emulate the style and model of evangelical megachurches is
that their membership is made up mostly of persons who represent the
remnant of earlier establishment Protestant sensibilities (not to mention
the problems of doing contemporary worship in a one-hundred-year-old
gothic sanctuary). By the same token, one of the dangers of the megachurch model is that it risks throwing away church traditions that, for
liberals, have brought out the best aspects of critical thinking and theological reflection.

What characterizes much research about the future of American religion is the lack of consensus about where the future is taking us. One of
the signs of hope identified by sociologist Diana Butler Bass is what she
describes as a phenomenon of "retraditioning" in contemporary American religion. In juxtaposition to a post-1960s disillusionment with mainline Protestantism, in which many churches abandoned the use of various
forms of traditional liturgy and worship (epitomized by the practices of
"seeker-friendly" liturgies), evidence suggests that there is burgeoning
interest among many seekers to embrace practices associated with earlier
Christian practices that could lead to a rebirth of liberal congregations.[10]
I think what Bass is suggesting about the future of American Christianity

is one aspect of a larger transformation taking place. While one current of American Christianity can be seen through the lens of conservative nondenominational movements that stress contemporary worship and an absence of tradition, another lens, the so-called Emergent Church movement, reflects a deep desire of many to not only study the Bible (the ultimate source of truth for good Protestants), but to also delve into the depths of a Christian tradition that takes seriously both evangelical and liberal aspects of that heritage.[11]

Mainline denominations will not die out in the twenty-first century. Yet they are changing, and one reality that liberalism must face is that the movement cannot and should not seek a return to the days when it lifted up leaders who could find their way onto the cover of *Time* magazine. Rather, the future of liberalism will come through the hard work and dedication of clergy and laity who care passionately about people and are able to address the social and moral issues of the day, but also touch the hearts and souls of those in the pews. In chapter 3, we saw that an underappreciated part of twentieth-century liberalism was how many of its major practitioners lived in the creative tension between prophetic action and pastoral concern. In the future, this theme of ministry will not just be the domain of the clergy. Rather, in reflection of a theology that affirms Martin Luther's doctrine of "the priesthood of all believers," congregations will be filled with laity who will not simply sit passively in the pews on Sunday, but will be working with ordained clergy in ministries of nurture, education, and community outreach. I have no doubt that for some "liberal" congregations, these ministries will utilize themes coming out of the megachurch and Emergent Church movements. But for others, these goals will come out of innovations that await future study by sociologists, historians, and future commentators on "church growth."

Liberalism in the future cannot and should not strive to return to the bygone historical model of establishment Protestantism, nor should it simply embrace change because it has been deemed by some as necessary. Robert Wuthnow sends a dire warning: that many younger Americans, while thriving for spiritual authenticity and starving for faith communities, show a declining interest in participating in the structures of liberal denominations *and* nondenominational evangelical megachurches.[12] The challenge for mainline churches might very well be how they can accommodate the voices of young Americans hungry for tradition, yet impatient with current models of "doing" church. Clearly, there are grassroots models of Christianity that create communities of faith and theological discourse that are lively, evangelistic (broadly conceived), transformative for their members and for the larger community they serve, and liberal in that they respect open theological inquiry, questioning, and the ongoing task of discerning theological truth. Butler Bass is accurate when she suggests that the future of liberal Christianity rests not so much on manning the ramparts in defense of liberal theology. Rather, the future is embodied by how congregations give voice to the questions and spiritual yearnings of its adherents, in hope that persons may experience transformation. "Christianity for the rest of us is not about personal salvation, not about getting everybody else saved, or about the politics of exclusion and moral purity. Christianity for the rest of us is the promise of transformation—that, by God's mercy, we can be different, our congregations can be different, and our world can be different."[13]

To what extent should the future of liberalism be predicated primarily upon specific political agendas?

Many aspects of the liberal heritage attempted to resist identifying their theological and ethical pronouncements with specific political parties and platforms; however, that separation has been impossible to maintain. As I noted in question 1, many liberals today come precariously close to identifying certain political positions or political parties with manifestations of the kingdom of God. But at a time period when both the theological and political temperament of Americans is quite conservative (despite Barack Obama's election), what does that say about liberalism's future mission?

The overarching theme connecting most liberal theologies has been their insistence that God's activity cannot be separated from the events of history. However, the way that liberalism has attempted to keep this tension alive has at times gotten the movement in trouble. While some traditions of evangelical theology relegated history to a secondary role to the activities of God (or the Bible), liberalism stressed the necessity of humanity to discern how the teachings of the Bible and various Christian traditions could be brought to bear on historical events.

By the early twentieth century, many in the liberal camp, especially those connected to the social gospel, saw in American democratic institutions visible signs of the kingdom on earth. Yet for some radicals, American democracy didn't go far enough in its eschatological hopes for a new heaven on earth. The problem, as the example of Harry F. Ward suggests, is that representatives of liberalism were not immune from a harsh condemnation of the culture, to the point that they saw all opposition to their theological and political agendas as demonic. The "God of Battles" theology employed by several liberals like Ward, and some later traditions of liberation theology, while claiming a radical vision of Jesus' ethics, ultimately tore Christianity away from its historical moorings in liturgy, worship, and the devotional life. Instead, the kingdom of God became exclusively rooted not in the ability to ask difficult questions, but embracing specific social-political positions.

One of the great contributions of liberalism was how it contributed to the emerging field of Christian social ethics, crafting a variety of movements that were concerned with how Christianity could shape social-political meaning in the contemporary world. However, I believe that part of the negative view against many forms of liberalism today is rooted partly in a tendency to make the same mistake as Ward—believing that the essence of Christianity can be reduced merely to specific ethical applications.

In the early twentieth century, the genius of classical liberalism was that it not only was a mediating tradition, open to a wide range of intellectual sources and influences, but that it grappled with a range of complex political questions facing contemporary society, questions that many liberal Christians recognized had no easy answers. By the early twenty-first century, however, liberal Christianity has overwhelmingly identified itself with specific social-political programs coming from the political left that are not exactly achieving universal acceptance in the American public square. Peter Hodgson warns the liberal church that "The political, cultural, and environmental problems that we face today are deadly serious, life threatening. Under these circumstances the delusional character of the dominant religiosity of our time, and of the politics it supports, is extremely dangerous."[14] While I agree with aspects of Hodgson's assertion, ultimately the goal of liberal Christianity (indeed the chief goal of Christianity) is not simply the pursuit of specific social-political agendas, however valuable those objectives may be. The reality faced by countless ministers and dedicated members of churches throughout the country is that they share the pews with women and men of good faith and divergent convictions on social-political questions.

The question that Christian liberalism must face head-on is not whether to engage persons on pressing social justice questions; the issue is, *how* will that engagement occur? There is no doubt, as Martin Luther King Jr. exposed during the height of the civil rights era, that Christian complacency to evil is its own form of injustice; however, the fact remains, as Reinhold Niebuhr recognized, that as worthy as the pursuit of justice is for the Christian, does getting our way politically constitute the essence of what it means to call ourselves Christian? This was part of Vida Scudder's warning to Walter Rauschenbusch, reflected in the fact that any sort of Christian engagement with culture needed to be clear about its theological and historical foundation. While Scudder and Rauschenbusch understood this point, later liberal traditions have not, and in part contributed to Donald Miller's concern that liberal Christianity was in danger of disappearing, replaced by a secular humanism predicated on social change, without the spirituality or the humility provided by religious belief.[15]

What the best of the liberal tradition has recognized is not so much that Christians are of one mind on the major political issues of a given era, but that any political question at a given moment is at its core a question of faith. If liberal theology starts with the premise that people of faith need to believe in certain political doctrines before they can enter the kingdom of God, then they will not only alienate themselves from the majority of persons living in America today, but lose an opportunity to engage persons and congregations with questions that might lead them to embrace new visions of faith and practice. Part of the liberal creed has always been that persons are capable of change; twenty-first-century liberal theology needs to take this view seriously, if it ever wants to hold out hope of becoming a popular movement.

How do liberals see themselves continuing to shape the larger Christian heritage?

At the height of the fundamentalist-modernist controversy in the 1920s, J. Gresham Machen raised a critical question that liberals in some way have never really answered: What makes liberal Christianity Christian? Is the tradition of theological liberalism akin to classical Christianity, or does it represent, as Machen argued, something else? During the heated exchanges between liberals and conservatives in the 1920s and 1930s, it was difficult for liberals not to respond with obvious distaste toward Machen's question. Yet, in some way, liberal Christianity has to find ways to address Machen's question as a means of keeping the tradition fresh, and in hopes of sharpening how liberalism responds to emerging cultural realities in the years ahead.

Part of what characterized the staying power of many earlier traditions of liberal theology was not only the way they sought to interpret theology in a "modern" context, but the passion in which these heritages cared deeply for various forms of church tradition and a variety of theological heritages. Certain liberal traditions throughout the twentieth century kept that tension alive, but others were more interested in dialoguing with secular philosophical movements, as opposed to the various components of the Christian heritage that emerged from Nicaea, Rome, Wittenberg, and Geneva. Part of calling oneself a liberal is the desire to mediate between the claims of extreme orthodoxy on one hand and modern rationalism on the other. Yet if liberalism is content to surrender any engagement with earlier traditions of Christianity's diverse historical and theological roots, then aren't we guilty of what Machen argued in 1923? Has liberalism in some way evolved into a totally different religion? Should we look for another label to call ourselves, besides *Christian*? Or, as some contemporary theologians have argued, does liberalism by default imply a movement that is more concerned about being culturally relevant, as opposed to being explicitly Christian?

It is this final point that has prompted some post-liberal theologians to castigate liberalism. Part of the appeal of a post-liberal theologian like Stanley Hauerwas is not only his incisive critique of liberalism (especially what he rightly sees as the folly of many liberals to continue propagating paradigms of Constantinian theology), but the way that he states the case for defining Christianity around a clear definition of the church as a community that can transcend the foibles of postmodern culture. As Hauerwas (and his theological ally, William Willimon) noted in their popular book *Resident Aliens*,

> We want to assert, for the church, politics that is both truthful and hopeful. Our politics is hopeful because we really believe that, as Christians, we are given the resources to speak the truth to one another. Fortunately, hope is not limited to the programs of the right or the left. Hope is described as the church—a place, a *polis*, a new people who are given the means to live without fear that inevitably leads us to violence.[16]

However, for all of the ways that Hauerwas defines himself as against liberalism, he is acting out of a decidedly liberal model. Like many classic evangelical-liberals such as Walter Rauschenbusch, he espouses a "social gospel" theology that is passionate about the Christian pursuit of justice, and identifies the aspects of secular culture that work against that worldview. Despite his dismissal of H. Richard Niebuhr's "Christ transforming Culture" paradigm, Hauerwas largely speaks out of an earlier model of public theology that believed Christian theology could make a difference to various questions of social-political import. If one were to follow Hauerwas's and Willimon's metaphor of "resident aliens" to its sectarian limits, one could possibly raise the question of whether the embrace of this metaphor precludes any sort of public theology, because public theology at its core historically operates out of a "Christ transforming culture" model.

My point is not to engage the extent to which Hauerwas' ethics falls into the liberal camp. But I'm not convinced, as he is, that Christians need to choose between a Niebuhrian model of a "liberal" public church and Hauerwas' vision of a Christian colony of resident aliens living apart from liberal-cultural power structures. Rather, I believe the central question that *all* Christians must live with in the twenty-first century is: how can churches reside in the tension between a desire to carry their beliefs into the public square and staying grounded in a vision of Christian faith that can undergird churches, when the dominant culture does not appear to be in support of the church? As Robert Wuthnow notes, liberal churches "cannot retain a distinctive force in public life if they merely follow popular sentiments that happen to be moving in a liberal or progressive direction." Rather, the power of liberalism can only be realized by "tapping into the deeper truths about love, redemption, reconciliation and justice that are recurrent themes in biblical tradition. Understanding these truths and finding ways to put them into practice requires the church above all to function as a church—preaching and teaching, gathering for worship, praying, and serving."[17] Regardless of whether one defines Christianity through the models centered upon the "public church" of classical liberalism or that of "resident aliens," each will have to engage the challenge Wuthnow accentuates. The specific question for Christian liberalism is not predicated, like it was during the time of Reinhold Niebuhr, on gaining public status. It is how churches understand their identity as something more than public prestige (or, as seems to count for much in mainline churches today, numerical size).

Today in America, Christian communities wrestle over a variety of theological issues pertaining to the nature of God, the purpose of the church, and, most importantly, the meaning of Christ and of salvation. I believe that most congregations that reflect the influence of liberalism do not speak with one mind on these issues. However, liberalism needs to find ways to bring these questions front and center in all of our theological discourse. Milton Coalter, John Mulder, and Louis Weeks noted in the mid-1990s that one of the "vital signs" of an awakening within mainline denominations was a willingness to wrestle with the central question of Matthew 16:15, when Jesus says to his disciples "Who do you say that I am?"[18] Part of the opportunity that liberal congregations may have in the future will not come through their ability to provide the "right" answers to this question. Rather, it will come through an ability of churches to take this question seriously: of what it means to follow Christ, and how the response to that question can not only enable congregations to honor traditions, but where age-old questions of faith and meaning can be engaged and revived in innovative ways.

Ambiguity and Grace

In the 1960s, sociologist Peter Berger warned that Christianity was losing its sense of historical and theological purpose, and in its place the
church only represented a "sacred canopy" that presented the exterior
luster of faith devoid of the theological power of an earlier era.[19] Like
many of his contemporaries, Berger did not anticipate the phenomenal
spread of traditional Christian movements that have swept the globe
in a variety of Protestant and Catholic forms over the past quarter century. Yet Berger's analysis in some way is instructive for understanding
the mindset carried by some in the mainline today that our best years
are already behind us. For the past several decades, mainline denominations have chewed themselves up debating issues like gay-lesbian rights,
war-peace, racism, and economic justice, engaging in protracted battles
that often reflect a nasty dualism reminiscent of an earlier social gospel, liberal emphasis on a "God of Battles," whereby it was easier for
some liberals (like their conservative foes) to identify their enemies, as
opposed to finding common ground in mission. And yet, little thought
sometimes goes into one question: how do these denominational wars
address the doubts and anxieties expressed by many persons in our era?
If Diana Bass is right, a central issue for twenty-first-century Christianity is not what the church is saying in its pronouncements; it is how the
church will help persons live authentic and holistic lives, where faith is
not about coming to the "right" theological and political conclusions,
but how faith empowers persons to use their gifts and talents toward the
creation of a better world.

Part of this model of liberalism will disappoint those who envision
liberalism (i.e., progressivism) on the cusp of a national and international
stage of influence. Yet it provides space for people in local churches to
explore the contours of their own faith experiences, and to help these
persons reach out beyond their own walls to connect with others who
are raising similar questions about God, the church, and how Christianity can make a difference in an unjust world. The dominant perspective
for much of American and Western Christendom was that ministerial
authority rested with the ordained clergy who, in effect, gave people in
the pews their marching orders to change the world. As numerous commentators have noted, this is a dying model for the church, and while I
am a strong advocate for the role of ordained clergy, one of the challenges
that clergy are already facing is, what happens when members of their
congregations get an idea for change—and are ready to act on it? Will
that idea be processed through church committees, or be reshaped to fit

the particular theologies of the ordained minister or denomination? Or will congregational leaders have enough faith to trust those in the church to take that idea and run with it?

Too often, church-growth manuals stress that, if congregations follow prescribed programs (often implying acceptance of a certain theological posture), then they will grow. However, I hope that churches who identify themselves as liberal or progressive will be cautious about buying into this model.

Liberalism has always struggled in terms of how to balance faith in God's sovereign power over history with faith in humanity's ability to change history. Congregations that embrace aspects of liberalism need to wrestle with this tension and struggle intentionally with how to be missionally innovative while also staying grounded in distinctive theological and historical resources. If American religious history teaches us anything, it is that faith traditions, like jazz, often thrive when they are allowed the freedom to improvise. By the same token, while religious innovation has often challenged, stretched, and at times broken the parameters of religious tradition, these traditions have found ways to live on and, on occasion, thrive. I have no doubt that this pattern will continue into the new century, and it is one of which liberal churches need to be mindful whenever conversations turn to the "death" of mainline churches.

Like all forms of Christian theology, liberalism needs to accept a degree of ambiguity in terms of its mission. Like their evangelical counterparts, parts of the liberal tradition have been guilty of embracing a dogmatic certitude surrounding the truth of their theological perspectives (including seeing certain political representatives of the secular world as somehow anointed by God). Such dogmatism may carry the day for a while, but it will likely not lead to the goals that many liberals profess to believe: the transformation of individuals and the larger society.

In the mid 1980s, J. Philip Wogaman warned liberal Christianity that in the quest for theological certitude, it was always possible to seize upon a fragment of the truth, and mistake that fragment for the whole of the Christian gospel. Whether it is worship and liturgy, fidelity to Scripture, or a passion for social justice, if these components become separated from other components of the Christian message, they become isolated fragments, as opposed to means of grace that can change lives and communities.[20]

The liberal church of the twenty-first century will be very different from the liberal church envisioned over a hundred years ago by Walter Rauschenbusch. Instead of a movement that would Christianize America and, by extension, the world, the future of American liberal Christianity is one characterized by a posture of exile, where we no longer can expect that the larger culture cares what we are saying or doing. Part of our tradition will lament the loss of prestige and power that we once appeared to have (and some may die still clinging to the hope that a former glory will be restored), but we need to remember that being in exile is part of the biblical narrative, and that even amidst what might appear to some as defeat, new life and vitality can be and is upon us.

The ultimate illusion that Christian liberalism must abandon is one predicated on winning the church (and the world) back to its point of view, especially the yearning to recapture the perceived glory of a Christendom world. As Loren Mead noted, "faithfulness in the church has always been about following the call. It has rarely meant winning."[21] The future of liberalism will not be about winning and losing, but, in the spirit of the book of Hebrews, about keeping the faith. And yet, in reference to a quote that I used in the beginning of the book, liberal Christianity would do well to remember Reinhold Niebuhr's words: that the pursuit of traditional liberal theological objectives—personal transformation, justice, and the kingdom of God—may not be obtainable in what we do, and yet we must, by faith, pursue these goals, not because we seek to live in a Christian nation or a Christian colony of "resident aliens," but because we are called to live out our faith in a world that not only manifests sin and evil, but also the possibility and the hope of transformation.

A Hopeful Future

Today, in the context of early twenty-first-century American Christianity, signs of hope manifest themselves through individuals, churches, and organizations that in one form or another carry on the legacy of theological liberalism. We see hope in the fact that numerous academicians and popular church leaders are drawn to liberal theology, not just for the purpose of intellectual inquiry, but to raise tough and difficult questions pertaining to faith in twenty-first-century society.[22] We see hope in the fact that many segments of contemporary Christianity are drawn to figures such as Walter Rauschenbusch, Howard Thurman, and Martin Luther King Jr. as exemplars of liberal theology who still speak with power and conviction to the issues of our time.[23] We see hope through the renewing ministries of several mainline churches that strive to connect their local communities to the perplexing social problems of our era, seeing Christian discipleship not only through the utterance of words, but through the doing of deeds.[24] Finally, and most significantly, we see hope in the ministries of countless congregations throughout the nation who articulate in their mission statements key historical tenets of liberal theology, including open theological inquiry, a belief that Christian discipleship can make a lasting difference in the world, and a passion for social justice. An era in which liberal mainline churches could speak in one voice to the nation is long past (if it ever existed in the first place). In its place, however, is a time in the early twenty-first century when congregations live in expectation that God brings change into our lives and our world, even when we don't see or recognize those signs of change. Above all else, liberalism gives to contemporary communities the assurance that the labors of our hearts and minds will bear witness to God's grace in the world, even when we don't see the results of our works. These words from Ernest Fremont Tittle remain as valid today as when he first affirmed them in 1944: "It is not required of us to save the world. It is required of us to say what the world must do to be saved. The event is in the hands of God."[25]

In the tradition of Walter Rauschenbusch, Reinhold Niebuhr, and Martin Luther King Jr., we live in the present moment, knowing that we will not achieve everything that we hope for, yet we stay expectant about the possibilities of how our faith can equip us for the challenges of the future. One of my favorite hymns is Harry Emerson Fosdick's "God of Grace and God of Glory." This hymn captures, in a timeless fashion, the enduring vitality of the liberal heritage reflected in the following verse:

God of grace and God of glory,
On thy people pour thy power;
Crown thine ancient church's story;
Bring her bud to glorious flower.
Grant us wisdom, grant us courage,
For the facing of this hour,
For the facing of this hour.[26]

In microcosm, this verse accentuates the enduring legacy of liberalism and what constitutes its core. It is a heritage that sees itself in continuity with earlier Christian traditions, one that believes in the reality of sin, but also sees a future beyond sin. It is a heritage that sees our ministries as part of an ongoing dialogue with God and with each other, staying hopeful that we can become "means of grace" that contribute to a just world. And it is ultimately a recognition that amidst our own work in the present, what we do today is only a minute manifestation of God's wider vision, which enables us, by faith, to cast a hopeful eye toward the future.

Epilogue

Past Imperfect

Among many of the things we learn from the study of Christian history is that Christians have never been especially prescient at predicting the future. From Paul's belief that Christ would return in his lifetime, to 2,000 years' worth of prophecies about the end of the world, to various projections throughout American history about which churches would grow and which would decline, forecasting the future has always been elusive for scholars, church leaders, and public intellectuals at any given historical moment.[1] In the relatively short history of American Christianity, no prediction has proved more off-base than the reaction of many clergymen in the late eighteenth and early nineteenth centuries to the realities of religious disestablishment brought about by the First Amendment to the U.S. Constitution. For centuries, Christianity largely existed under a rubric that churches could only thrive if supported officially by governments (and for all the "radical" nature of the sixteenth-century reformations, the majority of Protestants never questioned the idea that reformers needed the active support of secular rulers). When Connecticut finally ratified the First Amendment clause in 1818, abolishing the centuries-old Congregational religious establishment, Lyman Beecher, patriarch of one of the great American families of the nineteenth century, was despondent almost to the point of tears, because he felt that the move represented a mortal blow to the future of American Christianity. "It was as dark a day as I ever saw," Beecher recounted. "The injury done to the cause of Christ, as we supposed, was irreparable. For several days I suffered what no tongue can tell."[2] Not only was Beecher proved wrong by subsequent historical events, but he soon became an enthusiastic supporter for many of the measures associated with popular revivalism that in one form or another has been an ongoing characteristic of American Christianity. Yet even Beecher, like most of the central "players" in the story of American religious history, still found lots to complain about in his subsequent career, as he witnessed the proliferation of sects, churches, and religious movements that did not necessarily fit his idea of "respectable" Christianity.[3]

Yet Beecher shares a quality with most figures and movements in the study of religious history, in that he was unable to completely grasp, or control, the historical forces at work during his lifetime. While he fantasized about a nation that would be dominated by an evangelical Protestant worldview, he could not foresee, nor halt, the growth of non-Protestant forms of Christianity, such as those embodied by the Catholic Church, nor the spread of sectarian movements, epitomized by the Church of Jesus Christ of Latter-day Saints, nor comprehend the fact that some of the most dynamic and critical churches to the future of American Christianity would emerge from the antebellum crucible of African American slavery.[4] Most ironic, Beecher had no ability to control the future theological direction of his own son, Henry Ward Beecher, who served as one of the chief pioneers in the spread of liberal theology in the late nineteenth century.

Beecher's life not only reminds us that no matter how influential a person is to a particular historical narrative (and it is very difficult to discuss the history of nineteenth-century Protestantism without some inclusion of Lyman Beecher's story), history often moves in ways that defy human efforts to regulate or control. Part of the great gift of liberal theology was that it challenged earlier models of theological orthodoxy to break away from a deterministic worldview surrounding individuals and the ultimate destiny of our world. The manner in which liberals rethought concepts of God, Christ, the nature of sin, the kingdom of God, and the mission of the church changed the ways that Christianity would be seen as a movement of theological and social change in America. The most notable champions of early twentieth-century liberalism, such as Gladden and Rauschenbusch, largely saw the movement as an engine driving the nation's churches to transform American culture. However, the most significant representative of the liberal theological heritage later on in the century didn't come through the "mainline" churches, represented by persons such as Gladden and Rauschenbusch. It came through an individual whose own faith was rooted in the African American Christianity of the American South: Martin Luther King Jr.

Regardless of whether one identifies oneself as a friend or foe of liberalism, one should take pause before consigning the tradition to America's past. Foes of liberalism will continue to castigate the movement for its inability to handle the demands of postmodernity, its positive orientation to culture, and its stress on theological pluralism rather than fidelity to specific doctrines. Liberals might counter that no other theological heritage allows one to strike a balance between having a "modern" view of the world and raising critical questions that extend beyond our world. Yet friends and foes of liberalism need to be cautious about how they look to the future. The only certainty is that none of us will be one hundred percent accurate about what awaits us in the future, and the chances are high that there are things happening in our religious landscape right now—regardless of the theological labels we wear—that we don't as yet recognize.

When asked to discuss the future of liberal theology in the mid-1980s, the late William Hutchison made this whimsical point. "A famous and often-married actress was asked, during one of her seasons of respite between husbands, whether she would do it all again. She replied that she would—but with different people. Liberalism, like evangelicalism or most other important isms, will perdure, but there's no reason to suppose that it must express itself always and forever through the institutional forms within which it flourished in the past."[5] Hutchison's point affirms the age-old truth from the Apostle Paul that no matter our wisdom, and the depth of our own beliefs, we still see "through a glass darkly." The institutions and beliefs that from the perspective of one generation seemed permanent, from the perspective of a later generation always turn out to be flimsier than first thought. Yet if the study of religious history teaches us anything it is that theological ideas rarely die, but await a day when they will burst forth in what H. Richard Niebuhr called "a pregnant source of a new aggression."[6] My biased hope is that historians and theologians writing at the close of the twenty-first century will be able to apply Niebuhr's assertion toward theological liberalism.

For the historian, hindsight is always easier than foresight, and those who study American religion in the future will surely see something in our era that, at present, eludes our field of vision. And, by grace, providence, or simply the throw of the dice of history, these persons will have a better interpretive lens on what is happening in our current historical era, including a fuller understanding of how liberal theology responded creatively to the religious, theological, social, political and cultural challenges of the twenty-first century.

Notes

Introduction

1   Walter Rauschenbusch, *Christianity and the Social Crisis in the 21st Century*, ed. Paul Raushenbush (New York: HarperOne, 2007), 338–39.

2   Rauschenbusch, *Christianity and the Social Crisis*, 337–38.

3   Reinhold Niebuhr, *Moral Man and Immoral Society: A Study in Ethics and Politics* (New York: Charles Scribner's Sons, 1932), 277.

4   James M. Washington, ed., *A Testament of Hope: The Essential Writings of Martin Luther King, Jr.* (San Francisco: Harper & Row, 1986), 274.

5   As will be developed in subsequent chapters, I concur with the assessment of Gary Dorrien that figures like Reinhold Niebuhr, while frequently seen as liberal critics, represented "a chastened species of liberal theology"; see Dorrien, *The Making of American Liberal Theology: Imagining Progressive Religion, 1805–1900* (Louisville, Ky.: Westminster John Knox, 2001), xxiv.

6   Dorrien, *Imagining Progressive Religion*, xv. The other volumes in Dorrien's three-part series are *The Making of American Liberal Theology: Idealism, Realism, and Modernity, 1900–1950* (Louisville, Ky.: Westminster John Knox, 2003), and *The Making of American Liberal Theology: Crisis, Irony, and Postmodernity, 1950–2005* (Louisville, Ky.: Westminster John Knox, 2006).

7   H. Richard Niebuhr, *The Kingdom of God in America* (New York: Harper & Row, 1937), 193.

8   The range of scholarship on the decline of twentieth-century American Protestant influence includes Robert T. Handy, *A Christian America: Protestant Hopes and Historical Realities* (New York: Oxford University Press, 1971); Robert Wuthnow, *The Restructuring of American Religion: Society and Faith since World War II* (Princeton, N.J.: Princeton University Press, 1988); and William R. Hutchison, ed., *Between the Times: The Travail of the Protestant Establishment in America, 1900–1960* (Cambridge: Cambridge University Press, 1989).

9   Two notable surveys include *"American Piety in the 21st Century,"* conducted by the Baylor University Institute for the Studies of Religion (http://www.isreligion.org/) in 2006, and the *"Pew Religious Landscape"* survey, conducted by the Pew Forum on Religion and Public Life (http://religions.pewforum.org/) in 2007. The Baylor survey noted that 33.6 percent of Americans defined themselves as "evangelical," conforming to an understanding of "Protestant groups that emphasize the authority of the Bible, salvation through a personal relationship with Jesus Christ, personal piety, and the need to share the 'Good News' of Jesus Christ with others." Mainline Protestants, defined by Baylor as "historic Protestant denominations that are more accommodating of mainstream culture," were third in the survey (behind Roman Catholic and National Catholic churches) at 22.1 percent. While the Pew survey placed the percentage of evangelical churches at 26.3 percent, its percentage for mainline Protestantism was also lower, at 18.1 percent (once again in third place behind Catholic churches). The ramifications of these results will be discussed in chapter 1.

10   Barack Obama, *The Audacity of Hope: Thoughts on Reclaiming the American Dream* (New York: Crown, 2006), 356–57.

11   Obama, 208.

12   While Gary Dorrien's three-volume study *The Making of American Liberal Theology* is the definitive work on the intellectual development of liberalism in the United States, he builds upon a solid foundation of earlier scholarship on liberal theology. Kenneth Cauthen's *The Impact of American Religious Liberalism* (New York: Harper & Row, 1962) remains a significant study into the origins and maturing of liberal theology through the early twentieth century. Like Dorrien, I favor a broader view of liberal theology that sees this tradition manifesting itself in a variety of historical and contemporary incarnations, as opposed to petering out in influence between the world wars.

13   For many years, the so-called neo-orthodox theologians of the 1930s were dubbed as "post-liberal" for the ways they challenged the assumptions of earlier liberalism. However, I agree with Gary Dorrien, who views American neo-orthodoxy as a movement more concerned with correcting the excesses of liberalism than overthrowing it. As I will point out in later chapters, the term "post-liberal" more appropriately defines a recent tradition of American theology that takes aim at the theological and cultural suppositions of liberal theology; see, e.g., George Lindbeck, *The Nature of Doctrine* (Philadelphia: Westminster, 1984), and Stanley Hauerwas and William H. Willimon, *Resident Aliens: Life in the Christian Colony* (Nashville: Abingdon, 1990).

14   Dorrien, *Imagining Progressive Religion*, xxiii. Liberalism's role as a mediating heritage reconciling faith and reason represents a consistent theme in most studies of liberal theology. For a helpful nuance to this view, see Peter C. Hodgson, *Liberal Theology: A Radical Vision* (Minneapolis: Fortress, 2007).

15   As will be discussed later in the book, this theme is especially evident within the work of another theologian not frequently associated with liberal theology: Paul Tillich. An excellent historical and theological overview of Tillich's life and thought can be found in volume 2 of Dorrien's *The Making of American Liberal Theology: Idealism, Realism, and Modernity*.

16   The historical connection between liberalism and earlier movements of Reformed Calvinist theology has largely been ignored by recent historians. Yet this linkage was critical to earlier traditions of American religious history writing; see, e.g., Winthrop Hudson, *The Great Tradition of the American Churches* (New York: Harper & Row, 1953), and Sidney E. Mead, *The Lively Experiment: The Shaping of Christianity in America* (New York: Harper & Row, 1963). An important, but largely forgotten, study that highlights liberalism's challenge to this earlier New England heritage is Daniel Day Williams' *The Andover Liberals: A Study in American Theology* (New York: King's Crown Press, 1941).

17   Recent studies of American religious demographics tend to divide American Christianity along four primary groups: mainline Protestant, evangelical (or conservative) Protestant, Catholic, and African American Protestant; see, e.g., Nancy Tatom Ammerman, *Pillars of Faith: American Congregations and Their Partners* (Berkeley: University of California Press, 2005), and Robert Wuthnow, *After the Baby Boomers: How Twenty- and Thirty-Somethings Are Shaping the Future of American Religion* (Princeton, N.J.: Princeton University Press, 2007). While the categories of liberal theology discussed in this book tend to fall under the rubric of mainline Protestant, liberalism's influence extends in some fashion to all of these groups.

18   Ammerman, *Pillars of Faith*, 4.

19   As Glenn T. Miller makes evident, the rise of liberalism was inseparable from the emergence of the modern theological seminary; see Miller, *Piety and Profession: American Protestant Theological Education, 1870–1970* (Grand Rapids: Eerdmans, 2007).

20   Although both Rauschenbusch and Fosdick had academic connections, they reflected a concern, like many of their liberal predecessors, for relating theology to a lay audience. Even though Rauschenbusch wrote most of his major works while on the faculty at Rochester Theological Seminary, his writings clearly showed the influence of his years as a pastor in New York City. One also needs to be reminded that before Reinhold Niebuhr joined the faculty at Union Seminary in 1928, he spent thirteen years as pastor of a local church in Detroit.

21   Liberation theologians such as Cone and Ruether are clear that they represent theological viewpoints that have moved beyond liberalism. By the same token, they derive inspiration from aspects of the liberal theological heritage. Ruether notes that contemporary Christian feminism needs to embrace components of classical liberal theology, while also moving beyond it; see Rosemary Radford Ruether, *Sexism and God-Talk* (Boston:

Beacon Press, 1983). James Cone's work reflects upon many aspects of the legacy of the civil rights movement, especially the impact of Martin Luther King Jr. and Malcolm X; see especially Cone, *Martin and Malcolm and America: A Dream or a Nightmare* (Maryknoll, N.Y.: Orbis, 1991). The relationship between these traditions of liberation theology and the classic liberal heritage will be discussed in chapter 4.

22   Various movements associated with late twentieth-century liberation theology have frequently been critical, if not hostile, toward earlier forms of liberal theology. As chapter 4 points out, however, there are clear affinities between various schools of liberation theology to earlier forms of liberalism, especially pertaining to theological views of social justice. For details on this connection see Dorrien, *Soul in Society: The Making and Renewal of Social Christianity* (Minneapolis: Fortress, 1995).

23   William Newton Clarke, *An Outline of Christian Theology*, 4th ed. (New York: Charles Scribner's Sons, 1899), 123.

24   The connection between liberal theology and earlier incarnations of evangelical theology emerging out of the nineteenth century remains a critical theme toward understanding the development of American Protestant thought; see Timothy Smith, *Revivalism and Social Reform* (Nashville: Abingdon, 1957); Donald Dayton, *Discovering an Evangelical Heritage* (New York: Harper & Row, 1976); and Ralph E. Luker, *The Social Gospel in Black and White* (Chapel Hill: University of North Carolina Press, 1991).

25   See Ernst Troeltsch, *The Social Teachings of the Christian Church* (1931; repr., Louisville, Ky.: Westminster John Knox, 1992); Jaroslav Pelikan, *Reformation of Church and Dogma, 1300–1700* (Chicago: University of Chicago Press, 1984).

26   Perhaps the two classic works dealing with the aspect of Protestant social teaching are H. Richard Niebuhr's books *The Social Sources of Denominationalism* (New York: Henry Holt, 1929) and *The Kingdom of God in America.*

27   Edwin H. Friedman, *From Generation to Generation: Family Process in Church and Synagogue* (New York: Guilford Press, 1985).

28   This positive embrace of history has not been universal among all liberals. Many neo-orthodox theologians (as well as later movements in liberal theology) were galvanized by a tendency to downplay any sort of progressive orientation of history. Nevertheless, part of what I believe united many disparate traditions of liberal theology in the nineteenth and twentieth centuries revolved around a critical engagement with the discipline of church history, especially exploring how the study of history pointed to the ways theological concepts took on new interpretations over different historical eras.

29   Daniel Day Williams, *God's Grace and Man's Hope* (New York: Harper & Brothers, 1949), 22.

30   Martin Luther King Jr., *Stride Toward Freedom: The Montgomery Story* (New York: Harper & Row, 1958), 91.

31   Dorrien, *Crisis, Irony, and Postmodernity*, 538.

32   The idea of liberalism's "decline" after World War I has been a common theme in the writing of American religious history, even though most historians concede that liberalism's influence never fully disappeared from American Christianity; see, e.g., Sydney Ahlstrom, *A Religious History of the American People* (New Haven: Yale University Press, 1972). I concur with the perspective offered by scholars like Dorrien who view later movements of twentieth-century theology (such as neo-orthodoxy/Christian realism) as self-critical movements within American liberalism, as opposed to separately defined theological entities.

33   The numerous dimensions of what has been called the "Protestant establishment" are taken up in the essays in Hutchison, ed., *Between the Times*.

34   See Philip Jenkins, *The Next Christendom: The Coming of Global Christianity* (New York: Oxford University Press, 2002).

35   Glenn T. Miller, *Piety and Profession*, 224–26.

36   Reinhold Niebuhr, *The Irony of American History* (New York: Charles Scribner's Sons, 1952), 63.

CHAPTER ONE

1   Garry Wills, *Under God: Religion and American Politics* (New York: Simon & Schuster, 1990), 51–61.

2   Thomas Frank, *What's the Matter with Kansas? How Conservatives Won the Heart of America* (New York: Henry Holt, 2004).

3   Numerous examples of anti-Wright material saturate the Internet, including blogs and articles from numerous conservative organizations and commentators; see, e.g., Stanley Kurtz, "Wright 101," at http://www.nationalreview .com (accessed October 15, 2008).

4   As Frank's analysis makes clear, the theme that liberals are out of touch with Middle America is a persistent chord struck by many conservative media pundits such as Rush Limbaugh and Ann Coulter.

5   What has frequently been called the "church-growth" movement has been represented by numerous theological perspectives and emphases. At the center of this movement a generation ago was Lyle Schaller, a United Methodist pastor whose work has been followed by a spate of works by popular authors including William Easum, George Hunter III, and Leonard Sweet. What tends to unite the disparate perspectives of these authors is their belief that the ecclesiastical tenets of contemporary denominationalism fail to address many of the theological *and* cultural issues confronted by declining mainline churches (and, as discussed later in the chapter, how congregations should do ministry in a postmodern era for the church). For examples of these authors' perspectives, see Schaller, *21 Bridges to the 21st Century* (Nashville: Abingdon, 1992); Easum, *Dancing with Dinosaurs:*

Ministry in a Hostile and Hurting World (Nashville: Abingdon, 1993); Hunter, *How to Reach Secular People* (Nashville: Abingdon, 1992); and Sweet, *Faithquakes* (Nashville: Abingdon, 1995).

6   The theme that mainline denominations are out of touch with the values and lifestyles of contemporary Americans is a persistent mantra of many church-growth leaders. Most cite the disconnection between an earlier time of cultural Christianity and the recent emergence of a "post-Christian" worldview; see, e.g., Leonard Sweet, *Faithquakes*.

7   This progression toward academia is evident in Dorrien's three-volume study, *The Making of Liberal Theology*. The majority of figures he emphasizes in volume 1 (*Imagining Progressive Religion, 1805–1900* [2001])—William Ellery Channing, Horace Bushnell, Henry Ward Beecher, Theodore Munger, Washington Gladden, and Newman Smyth—spent the bulk of their careers as pastors of churches. The shifting of liberalism toward academia is evident in volume 2 (*Idealism, Realism, and Modernity, 1900–1950* [2003]) and even more so in volume 3 (*Crisis, Irony, and Postmodernity* [2006]), where the majority of Dorrien's subjects are professors of seminaries or university divinity schools (with many closely identified with two institutions central to the history of liberal theology: the University of Chicago and Union Theological Seminary in New York).

8   The top four labels that participants used to describe their beliefs in the Baylor survey "*American Piety in the 21st Century*" were as follows: Bible-Believing, 47.2%; Born Again, 28.5%; Mainline Christian, 26.1%; and Theologically Conservative, 17.6%. Among those who identified themselves as theologically liberal, only 9.1% saw that label as their primary identity.

9   Delwin Brown, *What Does a Progressive Christian Believe? A Guide for the Searching, the Open, and the Curious* (New York: Seabury Press, 2008), 3–4.

10 And as Brown's otherwise insightful book points out, continue to perpetuate common stereotypes of liberalism.

11 R. Laurence Moore, *Religious Outsiders and the Making of Americans* (New York: Oxford University Press, 1986).

12 See Sydney Ahlstrom, *A Religious History of the American People* (New Haven: Yale University Press, 1972); Thomas Tweed, ed., *Retelling American Religious History* (Berkeley: University of California Press, 1997); and Diana Eck, *A New Religious America: How a "Christian Country" Has Become the World's Most Religiously Diverse Nation* (San Francisco: HarperOne, 2001).

13 Winthrop Hudson, *The Great Tradition of the American Churches* (New York: Harper & Row, 1953).

14 While conceding the reality of religious pluralism, William R. Hutchison argues that historically pluralism has always been a contentious ideal that in more recent history has become a means to gloss over deep-seated religious differences; see Hutchison, *Religious Pluralism in America: The*

Contentious History of a Founding Ideal (New Haven: Yale University Press, 2003).

15 William R. Hutchison, ed., *Between the Times: The Travail of the Protestant Establishment in America, 1900–1960* (Cambridge: Cambridge University Press, 1989).

16 The theme of ecumenical unity was also evident in many late nineteenth-century studies of American Christianity; see, e.g., Leonard W. Bacon, *A History of American Christianity* (New York: Charles Scribner's Sons, 1897). Bacon's work served as one of the standard scholarly works on American religion for the first third of the twentieth century.

17 See the Baylor survey *"American Piety in the 21st Century."*

18 Nathan O. Hatch, *The Democratization of American Christianity* (New Haven: Yale University Press, 1989).

19 Roger Finke and Rodney Stark, *The Churching of America, 1776–1990: Winners and Losers in Our Religious Economy* (New Brunswick, N.J.: Rutgers University Press), 3.

20 See Harvey Cox, *Fire from Heaven: The Rise of Pentecostal Spirituality and the Reshaping of Religion in the 21st Century* (Cambridge, Mass.: Da Capo, 1995), and Grant Wacker, *Heaven Below: Pentecostals and American Culture* (Cambridge, Mass.: Harvard University Press, 2001).

21 For an overview of the theological orientation of postmodernity, see J. Richard Middleton and Brian J. Walsh, *Truth Is Stranger than It Used to Be: Biblical Faith in a Postmodern Age* (Downers Grove, Ill.: InterVarsity, 1995), and Paul Lakeland, *Postmodernity: Christian Identity in a Fragmented Age* (Minneapolis: Fortress, 1997).

22 Stanley Hauerwas and William H. Willimon, *Resident Aliens: Life in the Christian Colony* (Nashville: Abingdon, 1990), 38–39.

23 The irony is that, while some Christian postmodern commentators embrace the idea of seeker religion within institutional Christianity, others see it as just another example of the church's desire to make the culture "relevant," as opposed to affirming, without apology, the truths of historical Christianity. (Note the differing perspectives of Leonard Sweet in *Faithquakes* and Hauerwas and Willimon in *Resident Aliens*.)

24 In fairness, this perspective is not just a part of postmodern thought, but reflects how many evangelicals and liberals view the early church.

25 See Stephen Prothero, *Religious Literacy: What Every American Needs to Know—And Doesn't* (New York: HarperCollins, 2007).

26 E. Brooks Holifield, *God's Ambassadors: A History of the Christian Church in America* (Grand Rapids: Eerdmans, 2007).

27 Richard Rorty, "Buds That Never Opened," in Walter Rauschenbusch, *Christianity and the Social Crisis in the 21st Century*, ed. Paul Raushenbush (New York: HarperOne, 2007), 349.

28 Christopher Hitchens, *God Is Not Great: How Religion Poisons Everything* (New York: Twelve Books, 2007).

29   Frank, *Polity and Practice in the United Methodist Church* (Nashville: Abingdon, 1997).

30   For a discussion on the role of American megachurches, see Stephen Ellingson, *The Megachurch and the Mainline: Remaking Religious Tradition in the Twenty-First Century* (Chicago: University of Chicago Press, 2007). Although the so-called Emergent Church phenomenon defies easy classification, it seeks to reclaim numerous patterns of historical Christianity, while moving outside the structures of mainline Christianity. Perhaps the classic text toward understanding this growing phenomenon is Brian D. McLaren, *A Generous Orthodoxy* (Grand Rapids: Zondervan, 2004).

31   Nancy Tatom Ammerman, *Pillars of Faith: American Congregations and Their Partners* (Berkeley: University of California Press, 2005); Diana Butler Bass, *Christianity for the Rest of Us: How The Neighborhood Church Is Transforming the Faith* (New York: HarperCollins, 2006).

32   Willowcreek Community Church in suburban Chicago is the prototypical example of a church built around this concept of niche marketing; see the church's Web site at http://www.willowcreek.org.

Chapter Two

1   See, e.g., H. Richard Niebuhr, *The Kingdom of God in America* (New York: Harper & Row, 1937); Hauerwas and Willimon, *Resident Aliens*.

2   The role of John Locke's philosophy on emerging patterns of eighteenth-century revivalism is highlighted in George Marsden's study of Jonathan Edwards; see Marsden, *Jonathan Edwards: A Life* (New Haven: Yale University Press, 2003).

3   This is not to say that Kant believed reason was somehow a substitute for God; it did mean, however, that reason provided humans with an intellectual foundation in the certainty of a creation where God existed; see, e.g., Immanuel Kant, *Critique of Practical Reason* (1788; repr., Indianapolis: Bobbs-Merrill Educational Publishing, 1956).

4   John Macquarrie, *Twentieth-Century Religious Thought* (Harrisburg, Penn.: Trinity Press International, 2002), 23.

5   Peter C. Hodgson, *Liberal Theology: A Radical Vision* (Minneapolis: Fortress, 2007), 36.

6   Schleiermacher's views on ministerial training also had an impact on the later developments in American theological education by the end of the nineteenth century; see Glenn T. Miller, *Piety and Profession: American Protestant Theological Education, 1870–1970* (Grand Rapids: Eerdmans, 2007), 47–49.

7   Jon Butler, *Awash in a Sea of Faith: Christianizing the American People* (Cambridge, Mass.: Harvard University Press, 1990), 225–26.

8   On the rise of popular revivalism in the early nineteenth century, see Nathan O. Hatch, *The Democratization of American Christianity* (New Haven: Yale University Press, 1989). On the rise of Methodism, see John Wigger, *Taking Heaven by Storm* (New York: Oxford University Press, 1998).

9   Two important studies that explore the growth of American theology prior
      to the Civil War are Mark Noll, *America's God: From Jonathan Edwards
      to Abraham Lincoln* (New York: Oxford University Press, 2002), and E.
      Brooks Holifield, *Theology in America: Christian Thought from the Age of the
      Puritans to the Civil War* (New Haven: Yale University Press, 2003).

10   Charles M. Sheldon, *In His Steps* (1897; repr., New York: Barnes & Noble,
      2004), 8–9; this edition of Sheldon's novel is the latest in numerous edi-
      tions that have been published since the 1890s.

11   Ironically, the late 1990s' explosion of "WWJD" bracelets, popular among
      evangelical youth, made no connection to this expression's popular origins
      in America, reflected in the culture of late nineteenth-century theological
      liberalism.

12   Excellent primary sources on the rise of American Unitarianism are offered
      in Sydney Ahlstrom and Jonathan Carey's edited compilation, *An Ameri-
      can Reformation: A Documentary History of Unitarian Christianity* (Middle-
      town, Conn.: Wesleyan University Press, 1985).

13   As Gary Dorrien points out, much of early Unitarian theology tended
      toward Arianism, that is, a belief that while Christ was divine, he was sub-
      servient to God as creator; see Dorrien, *Imagining Progressive Religion*, 24.

14   Dorrien, *Imagining Progressive Religion*, 33.

15   Theodore Parker's impact upon the post-Christian turn in Unitarianism is
      analyzed in Dean Grodzins, *American Heretic: Theodore Parker and Tran-
      scendentalism* (Chapel Hill: University of North Carolina Press, 2003).

16   Robert Bruce Mullin, *The Puritan as Yankee: A Life of Horace Bushnell*
      (Grand Rapids: Eerdmans, 2002).

17   Major works by Horace Bushnell include *Nature and the Supernatural*
      (New York: Charles Scribner's Sons, 1858), and *Christian Nurture* (New
      York: Charles Scribner's Sons, 1860).

18   Mullin, *The Puritan as Yankee*, chap. 6; Dorrien, *Imagining Progressive Reli-
      gion,* chap. 3.

19   Dorrien, *Imagining Progressive Religion*, 137.

20   In the decades following Bushnell's death, a variety of forum movements
      flourished in the U.S. that provided popular venues for many of the coun-
      try's prominent political and religious leaders. The most well-known of
      these was the Chautauqua movement, initially founded in the 1870s by
      Methodist leaders as an institute in western New York for promoting
      Christian education. Today, the Chautauqua Institute still carries on much
      of its original mission: to be a center promoting a progressive ethos; see the
      Chautauqua Web site, http://www.ciweb.org.

21   Mullin, *The Puritan as Yankee,* 230.

22   See Ernest Lee Tuveson, *Redeemer Nation: The Idea of America's Millennial
      Role* (Chicago: University of Chicago Press, 1968). Recent studies on the
      American Civil War note how Bushnell contributed to a larger tradition
      of American civil religion, associating the sacrifices of the North with the

"atonement" of the nation; see Harry S. Stout, *Upon the Altar of the Nation: A Moral History of the American Civil War* (New York: Viking, 2006), and Drew Gilpin Faust, *This Republic of Suffering: Death and the American Civil War* (New York: Alfred A. Knopf, 2008).

23   See Robert T. Handy, *A Christian America: Protestant Hopes and Historical Realities* (New York: Oxford University Press, 1971); Robert Jewett, *Mission and Menace: Four Centuries of American Religious Zeal* (Minneapolis: Fortress, 2008).

24   William Newton Clarke, *Outline of Christian Theology*, 4th ed. (New York: Charles Scribner's Sons, 1899), 359.

25   See Mark Noll, A *History of Christianity in the United States and Canada* (Grand Rapids: Eerdmans, 1992).

26   On the role of Beecher, see Debbie Applegate, *The Most Famous Man in America: The Biography of Henry Ward Beecher* (New York: Doubleday, 2006). The circumstances behind Beecher's libel trial are marvelously reconstructed in Richard W. Fox, *Trials of Intimacy: Love and Loss in the Beecher-Tilton Scandal* (Chicago: University of Chicago Press, 1999).

27   Washington Gladden, *Recollections* (Boston: Houghton Mifflin, 1909), 231.

28   William R. Hutchison, *The Modernist Impulse in American Protestantism* (Cambridge, Mass.: Harvard University Press, 1976), 49.

29   Kenneth Cauthen, *The Impact of American Religious Liberalism* (New York: Harper & Row, 1962), 29.

30   See Glenn T. Miller, *Piety and Profession: American Protestant Theological Education, 1870–1970* (Grand Rapids: Eerdmans, 2007), 88–112.

31   Hutchison, *The Modernist Impulse*, 52.

32   The case of Newman Smyth is especially illuminating related to liberalism's emergence within churches *and* historically orthodox Protestant seminaries like Andover; see Glenn T. Miller, *Piety and Profession*, 134–53, and Daniel Day Williams, *The Andover Liberals: A Study in American Theology* (New York: King's Crown Press, 1941).

33   For excellent summaries of Mathews' thought, see Dorrien, *Soul in Society: The Making and Renewal of Social Christianity* (Minneapolis: Fortress, 1995), 30–38; Dorrien, *Idealism, Realism, and Modernity*, 181–99; and William D. Lindsey, *Shailer Mathews' Lives of Jesus: The Search for a Theological Foundation for the Social Gospel* (Albany: State University of New York Press, 1997).

34   On the Jesus Seminar, see http://www.westarinstitute.org.

35   As will be discussed in chapter 5, these apocalyptic themes represent a dominant theme in American religious history.

36   For a discussion on the relationship between liberalism and the study of church history, see Henry Bowden's *Church History in the Age of Science* (Chapel Hill: University of North Carolina Press, 1971). Bowden's work also discusses the significance of Philip Schaff, longtime professor at the

German Reformed Seminary in Mercersburg, Pennsylvania (and later in his career at Union Seminary in New York), whose work was essential in the development of church history as a critical academic discipline in America.

37   Albert Schweitzer, *The Quest of the Historical Jesus*, 3rd ed. (London: SCM Press, 1981).

38   Lindsey, *Shailer Mathews' Lives of Jesus*, 87.

39   Lindsey, *Shailer Mathews' Lives of Jesus*, 102.

40   For a discussion of Foster's thought, see Hutchison, *The Modernist Impulse*, 215–20.

41   See William McGuire King, "The Biblical Basis for the Social Gospel," in *The Bible and Social Reform*, ed. Ernst Sandeen (Philadelphia: Fortress, 1982), 59–79.

CHAPTER THREE

1   While the term "social gospel" is mostly associated with a particular historical movement in American Christianity, it is often used in a contemporary context to refer to a heritage of liberal Christianity that sees the pursuit of social justice as central to its mission; see Christopher H. Evans, ed., *The Social Gospel Today* (Louisville, Ky.: Westminster John Knox, 2001).

2   For a summary of scholarship on the social gospel, see Ralph E. Luker, "Interpreting the Social Gospel: Reflections on Two Generations of Historiography," in *Perspectives on the Social Gospel*, ed. Christopher H. Evans (Lewiston, N.Y.: Edwin Mellen Press, 1999), 1–13.

3   Charles Howard Hopkins, *The Rise of the Social Gospel in American Protestantism* (New Haven: Yale University Press, 1940).

4   Susan Hill Lindley, "Deciding Who Counts: Toward a Revised Definition of the Social Gospel," in *The Social Gospel Today*, 17–26.

5   Paul T. Phillips, *A Kingdom on Earth: Anglo-American Social Christianity* (University Park: Pennsylvania State University Press, 1996).

6   Ronald White and C. Howard Hopkins, eds., *The Social Gospel: Religion and Reform in Changing America* (Philadelphia: Temple University Press, 1976), 30.

7   White and Hopkins, *The Social Gospel*, 71.

8   Perhaps no work of the social gospel era reflects this wedding of evangelical themes toward an imperative to address the era's social problems more than Josiah Strong's 1885 book, *Our Country: Its Possible Future and Its Present Crisis* (New York: Baker & Taylor, 1885). While later commentators would dismiss the book for its ethnocentrism (that at times borders on racism), the book was seen by many later leaders of the liberal social gospel as their introduction to the world of Christian social reform on a systemic level; see Wendy J. Deichmann Edwards, "Manifest Destiny, the Social Gospel and the Coming Kingdom: Josiah Strong's Program of Global Reform, 1885–1916," in *Perspectives on the Social Gospel*, 81–116.

9   Timothy Smith, *Revivalism and Social Reform* (Nashville: Abingdon, 1957);
       Donald Dayton, *Discovering an Evangelical Heritage* (New York: Harper &
       Row, 1976).

10   See Ralph E. Luker, *The Social Gospel in Black and White* (Chapel Hill:
       University of North Carolina Press, 1991).

11   Nathan O. Hatch, *The Democratization of American Christianity* (New
       Haven: Yale University Press, 1989).

12   Gary Dorrien, "Social Salvation: The Social Gospel as Theology and Eco-
       nomics," in *The Social Gospel Today*, 101.

13   Quoted in Dorrien, "Social Salvation," 107.

14   See Hopkins, *The Rise of the Social Gospel in American Protestantism*; Henry
       F. May, *Protestant Churches and Industrial America* (New York: Harper &
       Row, 1949).

15   William T. Stead, *If Christ Came to Chicago!* (Chicago: Laird & Lee, 1894),
       444.

16   For examples of how late nineteenth- and early twentieth-century women
       embodied the ethos of the social gospel, see Eleanor J. Stebner, *The Women
       of Hull House* (Albany: SUNY, 1997); Rosemary Skinner Keller, "Women
       Creating Communities—and Community—in the Name of the Social
       Gospel," in *The Social Gospel Today*, 67–85; and Wendy Deichmann
       Edwards and Carolyn DeSwarte Gifford, eds., *Gender and the Social Gospel*
       (Urbana: University of Illinois Press, 2003).

17   Peter J. Frederick, *Knights of the Golden Rule: The Intellectual as Christian
       Social Reformer in the 1890s* (Lexington: University of Kentucky Press,
       1976), 10.

18   Henry May defines the social gospel as the middle ground between conser-
       vative and radical social Christianity that emerged by the end of the nine-
       teenth century (see May, *Protestant Churches and Industrial America* [New
       York: Harper & Row, 1949]). Although his analysis helps one understand
       the range of different political responses taken by these church leaders, it
       doesn't fully analyze the differences in theological orientation that sepa-
       rated earlier and later representatives of social Christianity.

19   On Gladden, see Jacob H. Dorn, *Washington Gladden: Prophet of the Social
       Gospel* (Columbus: Ohio State University Press, 1967).

20   Dorn, "The Social Gospel and Socialism: a Comparison of the Thought of
       Francis Greenwood Peabody, Washington Gladden, and Walter Rauschen-
       busch," *Church History* 62 (1993): 82–100.

21   On the significance of Gladden's theology to questions of economic jus-
       tice, see Dorrien, "Social Salvation," in *The Social Gospel Today*, 101–13.

22   George Fry, "The Social Gospel at the Crossroads of Middle America: Wash-
       ington Solomon Gladden and the First Congregational Church, Colum-
       bus, Ohio, 1882–1918," in *Perspectives on the Social Gospel*, 61–62.

23   Washington Gladden, "O Master Let Me Walk with Thee" (originally pub-
       lished, 1879).

24 Evans, *The Kingdom Is Always but Coming: A Life of Walter Rauschenbusch* (Grand Rapids: Eerdmans, 2004), xxvii.

25 Casey Nelson Blake, "New Century, Same Crisis: Walter Rauschenbusch and the Social Gospel," in *Commonweal: A Review of Religion and Culture* (October 26, 2007).

26 Daniel Day Williams, *God's Grace and Man's Hope* (New York: Harper & Brothers, 1949), 22; Dorrien, *Imagining Progressive Religion*, xix.

27 See Luker, "Interpreting the Social Gospel"; William McGuire King, "'History as Revelation' in the Theology of the Social Gospel," *Harvard Theological Review* 76:1 (1983): 109–29.

28 Walter Rauschenbusch, *A Theology for the Social Gospel* (New York: Macmillan, 1917), 1.

29 H. Richard Niebuhr, *The Kingdom of God in America* (New York: Harper & Row, 1937), 194.

30 See Rauschenbusch, *Christianizing the Social Order* (New York: Macmillan, 1912), 142–47.

31 Quoted in Evans, *The Kingdom Is Always but Coming*, xxvii.

32 Rauschenbusch, *Christianizing the Social Order*, 464.

33 Walter Rauschenbusch, *Prayers of the Social Awakening* (Boston: Pilgrim, 1910), 12–13. Rauschenbusch's emphasis on the connection between prayer and social action in the context of twenty-first-century American Christianity is explored in Christian Iosso and Elizabeth Hinson-Hasty, eds., *Prayers for the New Social Awakening* (Louisville, Ky.: Westminster John Knox, 2008).

34 Walter Rauschenbusch, *Dare We Be Christians?* (Boston: Pilgrim Press, 1914), 50–51.

35 Winthrop S. Hudson, ed., *Walter Rauschenbusch: Selected Writings* (New York: Paulist Press, 1984), 46–48.

36 Martin Luther King Jr., *Stride Toward Freedom: The Montgomery Story* (New York: Harper & Row, 1958), 91.

37 Stanley Hauerwas, "Repent. The Kingdom Is Here," in Rauschenbusch, *Christianity and the Social Crisis in the 21st Century*, 176.

38 William McGuire King, "'History as Revelation,'" 129.

39 Evans, *The Kingdom Is Always but Coming*, 301.

40 William McGuire King, "Enthusiasm for Humanity: The Social Emphasis in Religion and Its Accommodation in Protestant Theology," in *Religion and 20th-Century American Intellectual Life,* ed. Michael J. Lacey (Cambridge: Cambridge University Press, 1989), 68.

41 The argument that later movements of "neo-orthodoxy" shared an organic relationship to the earlier social gospel is taken up in the next chapter; see also William McGuire King, "The Emergence of Social Gospel Radicalism: The Methodist Case," *Church History* 50:4 (1981): 436–49.

42 For a discussion of personalism as a theological heritage, see Paul Deats and Carol Robb, eds., *The Boston Personalist Tradition in Philosophy, Social*

Ethics, and Theology (Macon, Ga.: Mercer University Press, 1986), and Rufus Burrows Jr., *Personalism: A Critical Introduction* (St. Louis: Chalice Press, 1999).

43   Evans, *The Kingdom Is Always but Coming*, 280.

44   Elizabeth Hinson-Hasty, *Beyond the Social Maze: Exploring Vida Dutton Scudder's Theologcal Ethics* (New York: T&T Clark, 2006), 127.

45   Hinson-Hasty, *Beyond the Social Maze*, 32.

46   Hinson-Hasty, *Beyond the Social Maze*, 33.

47   See, e.g., Kenneth Leech, *Subversive Orthodoxy: Traditional Faith and Radical Commitment* (Toronto: Anglican Book Centre, 1992).

48   On Howard Thurman, see his *Jesus and the Disinherited* (New York: Abingdon-Cokesbury Press, 1949) and *With Head and Heart: An Autobiography* (San Diego: Harcourt Brace Jovanovich, 1979); Alton B. Pollard III, *Mysticism and Social Change: The Social Witness of Howard Thurman* (New York: Peter Lang, 1992); and Walter Earl Fluker and Catherine Tumber, eds., *A Strange Freedom: The Best of Howard Thurman on Religious Experience and Public Life* (Boston: Beacon Press, 1998).

49   Although Rauschenbusch was dead by the time Thurman attended Rochester Theological Seminary, he was heavily influenced by other theological liberals on the faculty who were contemporaries of Rauschenbusch, in particular, George Cross; see Thurman, *With Head and Heart*.

50   Thurman, *The Great Incarnate Words* (San Francisco: Howard Thurman Educational Trust, 1972).

51   Thurman, *With Head and Heart*, 269.

52   On Peale's role in American religious history, see Carol George, *God's Salesman: Norman Vincent Peale and the Power of Positive Thinking* (New York: Oxford University Press, 1994).

53   See, e.g., Rauschenbusch, *A Theology for the Social Gospel.*

54   First Church, Evanston, Illinois, was also a congregation with an extensive history in late nineteenth-century social reform movements, including the settlement house movement. One of its most prominent parishioners was Frances Willard, president of the Woman's Christian Temperance Union and leading advocate for women's rights; see Christopher H. Evans, *Social Gospel Liberalism and the Ministry of Ernest Fremont Tittle: A Theology for the Middle Class* (Lewiston, N.Y.: Edwin Mellen Press, 1996).

55   See Robert Moats Miller, *How Shall They Hear Without a Preacher?* (Chapel Hill: University of North Carolina Press, 1971), and Evans, *Social Gospel Liberalism.*

56   See Joseph C. Hough Jr. and John B. Cobb Jr., *Christian Identity and Theological Education* (Chico, Calif.: Scholars Press, 1985); E. Brooks Holifield, *God's Ambassadors: A History of the Christian Church in America* (Grand Rapids: Eerdmans, 2007).

57   Evans, *Social Gospel Liberalism*, 212.

58   James K. Wellman Jr.'s account of Fourth Presbyterian, Chicago (a church

with a very similar status in American Protestantism as First Methodist, Evanston), shows how one liberal Protestant pulpit adapted to changing twentieth-century contexts within American Protestantism; see Wellman, *The Gold Coast Church and the Ghetto: Christ and Culture in Mainline Protestantism* (Urbana: University of Illinois Press, 1999).

59   See, e.g., "Alex's Death," William Sloane Coffin's sermon on the death of his son, in *The Courage to Love* (San Francisco: Harper & Row, 1984), 93–98.

60   Donald Gorrell, *The Age of Responsibility: The Social Gospel in the Progressive Era* (Macon, Ga.: Mercer University Press, 1988).

61   Sidney E. Mead, *The Lively Experiment: The Shaping of Christianity in America* (New York: Harper & Row, 1963), 177–78.

62   See Gladden, *Recollections* (Boston: Houghton Mifflin, 1909).

63   On Reverdy Ransom, see Luker, *The Social Gospel in Black and White*.

64   This fascinating chapter of American religious history is reconstructed in Evelyn Brooks Higginbotham, *Righteous Discontent: The Women's Movement in the Black Baptist Church, 1880–1920* (Cambridge, Mass.: Harvard University Press, 1993).

65   Janet Fishburn, *The Fatherhood of God and the Victorian Family: The Social Gospel in America* (Philadelphia: Fortress, 1981).

66   By the same token, the "recovery" of Rauschenbusch's legacy owes a great deal not only to Martin Luther King Jr., but to another prominent African American religious leader, Benjamin Mays, who published one of the first anthologies of Rauschenbusch's work in 1950; see Benjamin Mays, ed., *A Gospel for the Social Awakening* (New York: Association Press).

Chapter Four

1   The question of how American Protestantism wrestled with the shifting historical and theological terrain of the mid-twentieth century is taken up by numerous scholars; see, e.g., William R. Hutchison, ed., *Between the Times: The Travail of the Protestant Establishment in America, 1900–1960* (Cambridge: Cambridge University Press, 1989), and David W. Lotz, Donald W. Shriver Jr., and John F. Wilson, eds., *Altered Landscapes: Christianity in America, 1935–1985* (Grand Rapids: Eerdmans, 1989).

2   Many recent theologians and ethicists have argued against the use of the term "neo-orthodoxy" as a descriptive term to describe the emerging theological currents of the 1930s, preferring the term "Christian realism"; see Stanley Hauerwas, *A Better Hope: Resources for a Church Confronting Capitalism, Democracy, and Postmodernity* (Grand Rapids: Brazos Press, 2000).

3   Dorrien, *Idealism, Realism, and Modernity*, 436. Niebuhr himself was quick to distance himself from European neo-orthodox leaders like Karl Barth. As Niebuhr confided to a colleague, "I have never thought of myself in their category. I think when it comes to the crux I belong to the liberal tradition more than to theirs"; see Richard Fox, *Reinhold Niebuhr: A Biography* (San Francisco: Harper & Row, 1985), 214.

4   In the revised preface to the 1956 edition of *An Interpretation of Chris-
     tian Ethics*, Reinhold Niebuhr noted that the original work, published in
     the mid-1930s, "was meant to express both the author's general adhesion
     to the purposes of the 'Social Gospel' of which Rauschenbusch was the
     most celebrated exponent, and to spell out some of the growing differences
     between the original social gospel and the newer form of social Christian-
     ity"; see Niebuhr, *An Interpretation of Christian Ethics* (New York: Merid-
     ian Books, 1956), 9.

5   In a study on the theology of Karl Barth, Dorrien makes the point that
     neo-orthodoxy, associated with the heritage of Barth, was devoted to restat-
     ing "the principles of Reformation teaching in modern forms." Noting the
     relationship of Barth to traditions of nineteenth-century German theology
     (especially the legacy of Hegel), Dorrien argues that Barth signaled a dis-
     tinctive approach that was both indebted to, and a protest of, earlier liberal
     theologies; see Dorrien, *Theology without Weapons: The Barthian Revolt in
     Modern Theology* (Louisville, Ky.: Westminster John Knox, 2000), 7.

6   Dorrien, *Theology without Weapons*. In another work, Dorrien examines the
     idea that many strands of evangelical theology that broke with liberalism
     during the course of the twentieth century had no love for Barth, with many
     evangelicals seeing Barth's theology as a compromise on several tenets of
     evangelical theology, such as biblical inerrancy; see Dorrien, *The Remaking
     of Evangelical Theology* (Louisville, Ky.: Westminster John Knox, 1998).

7   See Richard Fox, *Reinhold Niebuhr: A Biography*. A definitive biography on
     H. Richard Niebuhr remains to be written.

8   Ronald White and Charles Howard Hopkins, eds., *The Social Gospel: Reli-
     gion and Reform in Changing America* (Philadelphia: Temple University
     Press, 1976), 267–68.

9   The continued vitality of liberal idealism in the 1920s and 1930s is dis-
     cussed in Paul Carter, *The Decline and Revival of the Social Gospel: Social
     and Political Liberalism in American Protestant Churches, 1920–1940*
     (Ithaca, N.Y.: Cornell University Press, 1954), and Robert Moats Miller,
     American Protestantism and Social Issues: 1919–1939 (Chapel Hill: Uni-
     versity of North Carolina Press, 1958). The liberal idealism of the social
     gospel was also evident in the international ecumenical movement, as illus-
     trated by the 1925 Life and Work Conference in Stockholm, Sweden; see
     Paul Bock, *In Search of a Responsible World Society: The Social Teachings of
     the World Council of Churches* (Philadelphia: Westminster, 1974).

10   Reinhold Niebuhr, *Moral Man and Immoral Society: A Study in Ethics and
     Politics* (New York: Charles Scribner's Sons, 1932), 3.

11   Robert Jewett, *Mission and Menace: Four Centuries of American Religious
     Zeal* (Minneapolis: Fortress, 2008), 229–30.

12   In his final years, Niebuhr himself became disillusioned with American
     aims and objective in Vietnam; see Fox, *Reinhold Niebuhr: A Biography*,
     283–84.

13 Reinhold Niebuhr, *The Irony of American History* (New York: Charles Scribner's Sons, 1952), 143.

14 See Rosemary Skinner Keller, *For Such a Time as This: The Life of Georgia Harkness* (Nashville: Abingdon, 1992).

15 Georgia Harkness, *Understanding the Christian Faith* (Nashville: Abingdon, 1947), 48.

16 While Harkness lived in Evanston, she became a close friend and parishioner of Ernest Fremont Tittle; see Keller, *For Such a Time as This*.

17 Harkness, "Hope of the World" (original publication, 1954).

18 Neo-orthodoxy as a tradition is most associated with individuals coming out of the tradition of Reformed theology. These traditions tended to place greater stress on human sinfulness and manifested earlier incarnations of their Calvinist heritages. In juxtaposition, traditions that came more out of movements emphasizing Christian perfection, the idea that individuals could increase in God-like righteousness (such as Methodism), were somewhat reluctant to embrace the teachings of American and continental neo-orthodoxy. A study that reflects on this theological pattern within American Methodism (taking a very critical view toward liberalism) is Robert Chiles, *Theological Transition in American Methodism: 1790–1935* (Nashville: Abingdon, 1965).

19 Daniel Day Williams, *God's Grace and Man's Hope* (New York: Harper & Brothers, 1949), 35.

20 Martin Luther King Jr. was probably typical of many church leaders of his generation when he remarked, "The prophetic and realistic elements in Niebuhr's passionate style and profound thought were appealing to me, and I became so enamored of his social ethics that I almost fell into the trap of accepting uncritically everything he wrote"; see King, *Stride Toward Freedom* (New York: Harper & Row, 1958), 97–98.

21 Williams, *God's Grace and Man's Hope*, 134.

22 John B. Cobb Jr., *Liberal Christianity at the Crossroads* (Philadelphia: Westminster, 1973).

23 John B. Cobb Jr., "Process Theology," in *The Encyclopedia of Protestantism*, vol. 3, ed. Hans J. Hillerbrand (New York: Routledge, 2004), 1567. Cobb's later work has shown a deep interest in discussing the affinity between process thought and earlier movements of Christian theology, in particular, John Wesley's doctrine of sanctification (i.e., Wesley's view of perfection that the Christian, through the interplay of faith and works, could grow toward the perfect knowledge and love of God); see Cobb, *Grace and Responsibility: A Wesleyan Theology for Today* (Nashville: Abingdon, 1995).

24 Douglas John Hall, *The Steward: A Biblical Symbol Come of Age* (Grand Rapids: Eerdmans, 1990), 113; while Hall is not usually identified with process thought, his analysis here shows an affinity with that tradition, as well as the extent to which themes in process thought have become a feature of many late twentieth-century traditions of liberalism.

25 See Dorrien, *Crisis, Irony, and Postmodernity*.

26 H. Richard Niebuhr, *Christ and Culture* (Harper & Brothers, 1951). The five historical paradigms noted by Niebuhr were "Christ against Culture," associated with radical sectarian Protestantism, "Christ of Culture," associated with predominant strands of theological liberalism, "Christ above Culture," associated with medieval Catholicism, "Christ and Culture in Paradox," associated with Luther, and "Christ the Transformer of Culture," with a tradition that he associated with Augustine.

27 H. Richard Niebuhr, *Christ and Culture*, 191.

28 The term "magisterial" refers to ecclesiastical movements of the sixteenth century that represented churches that relied on direct state support in order to propagate their mission.

29 See Joseph C. Hough Jr. and John B. Cobb, *Christian Identity and Theological Education* (Chico, Calif.: Scholars Press, 1985).

30 Quoted in Kelton Cobb, *The Blackwell Guide to Theology and Popular Culture* (Malden, Mass.: Blackwell Publishing, 2005), 105.

31 Paul Tillich, *Dynamics of Faith* (New York: Harper & Row, 1957), 48.

32 See Donald E. Miller, *Reinventing American Protestantism: Christianity in the New Millennium* (Berkeley: University of California Press, 1997); Stephen Ellingson, *The Megachurch and the Mainline: Remaking Religious Tradition in the Twenty-First Century* (Chicago: University of Chicago Press, 2007).

33 The two most prominent radicals to emerge after World War I were Norman Thomas and A. J. Muste. Thomas, a former Presbyterian minister, became a leader in the Socialist Party for several decades. Muste, an individual who drew heavily on various traditions of social gospel liberalism, was instrumental in the establishment of several political leftist movements from the 1920s through the 1960s; see James Tracy, *Direct Action: Radical Pacifism from the Union Eight to the Chicago Seven* (Chicago: University of Chicago Press, 1996).

34 See Tracy, *Direct Action*.

35 See Taylor Branch, *Parting the Waters: America in the King Years, 1954–63* (New York: Simon & Schuster, 1988).

36 William McGuire King, "The Emergence of Social Gospel Radicalism: The Methodist Case," *Church History* 50 (1981): 436–49.

37 For an overview of Harry F. Ward's "mature" radicalism, see Ward, *In Place of Profit: Social Incentives in the Soviet Union* (New York: Charles Scribner's Sons, 1933).

38 While lacking objective criticism, Eugene P. Link's biography, *Labor-Religion Prophet: The Times and Life of Harry F. Ward* (Boulder, Colo.: Westview Press, 1984), represents a detailed account of Ward's life, written by one of his former students. The definitive biography of Ward is David Nelson Duke's *In the Trenches with Jesus and Marx: Harry F. Ward and the Struggle for Social Justice* (Tuscaloosa: University of Alabama Press, 2003).

39 Duke, *In the Trenches*, 144.

40 Duke, *In the Trenches,* 233–34.

41 Erik Gritsch, *Reformer without a Church: The Life and Thought of Thomas Muentzer* (Philadelphia: Fortress, 1967).

42 Duke, *In the Trenches,* 237.

43 William McGuire King, "Enthusiasm for Humanity: The Social Emphasis in Religion and Its Accommodation in Protestant Theology," in *Religion and 20th-Century American Intellectual Life,* ed. Michael J. Lacey (Cambridge: Cambridge University Press, 1989), 70.

44 William McGuire King, "Enthusiasm for Humanity," 70.

45 The classic statement of this theme within liberation theology comes from the Latin American theologian Gustavo Gutierrez; see, e.g., Gutierrez, *A Theology of Liberation: History, Politics, and Salvation* (rev. ed., Maryknoll, N.Y.: Orbis, 1988); Gutierrez and other Latin American liberation theologians stress the concept of base communities, indigenous faith communities that affirm that God stands with those who struggle for social-political power. As I argue, I believe that American liberation theologies have *not* been successful in connecting with grassroots communities in ways comparable to Latin American liberationist theologies.

46 The two classic branches of American liberation theology that emerged in the 1970s were African American and feminist theologies. Among the theologians who have been especially skillful in defining these specific traditions of Christian liberation theology are James Cone and Rosemary Radford Ruether; see Cone, *God of the Oppressed* (Minneapolis: Fortress, 1975), and Ruether, *Sexism and God-Talk: Toward a Feminist Theology* (Boston: Beacon Press, 1983). An excellent summary of numerous traditions of feminist and African American liberation theology can be found in Susan Brooks Thistlethwaite, *Sex, Race, and God: Christian Feminism in Black and White* (New York: Crossroad, 1989). Queer theology is represented by an emerging range of theological perspectives. Marcella Althaus-Reid's work is notable for her engagement with postmodern theory and many insights from Latin American liberation theology; see, e.g., Althaus-Reid, *The Queer God* (New York: Routledge, 2003). Interestingly, the Metropolitan Community Church, a denomination founded on the premise of openness to gays and lesbians, has a very traditional mission statement, predicated on fidelity to historical statements coming from the Apostles' and Nicene creeds; see http://www.mccchurch.org (accessed January 26, 2009).

47 As Duke points out in his biography, aspects of Harry F. Ward's political radicalism were not matched by a cultural radicalism, especially in his Victorian views toward women.

48 Mark Chaves, *Congregations in America* (Cambridge, Mass.: Harvard University Press, 2004).

49 Paul Ramsey, *Who Speaks for the Churches?* (Nashville: Abingdon, 1967).

50 See Jose Miguez Bonino, "Reflections on the Church's Authoritative Teaching on Social Questions," in *What Should Methodists Teach?* ed. M. Douglas Meeks (Nashville: Kingswood Press, 1990), 67.

51   Ironically, H. Richard Niebuhr developed a far more optimistic view regarding the role of institutional Christianity later in his career. In the late 1920s, Niebuhr had largely seen institutional churches in the form of denominations as structures more intent on preserving institutional order, as opposed to carrying the radical passion that he associated with more sectarian forms of Christianity; see Niebuhr, *The Social Sources of Denominationalism* (New York: Henry Holt, 1929).

CHAPTER FIVE

1   It is interesting that Sydney Ahlstrom, in his two-volume *A Religious History of the American People* (New Haven: Yale University Press, 1972), which still stands out as one of the best comprehensive treatments of American religion, recognized the impact of the 1960s upon the American religious terrain, especially its impact on what he called a "post-Puritan" America. Yet even as his conclusion lamented the eclipse of a tradition of American theology associated with the heritage of the Protestant mainline, he largely ignored the upsurge in popular evangelicalism that characterized the broader history of twentieth-century American Christianity.

2   See Harry Emerson Fosdick, *The Living of These Days: An Autobiography* (New York: Harper & Brothers, 1956); Robert Moats Miller, *Harry Emerson Fosdick: Preacher, Pastor, Prophet* (New York: Oxford University Press, 1985).

3   Fosdick, *The Living of These Days.*

4   Fosdick, "Shall the Fundamentalists Win?" http://historymatters.gmu .edu/d/5070/ (accessed March 4, 2008).

5   The one figure who epitomized this earlier theological unity was Dwight Moody. While considered to be the architect for many movements of popular evangelicalism that arose in the twentieth century, Moody maintained close relationships with many liberal leaders, and also was the mover behind numerous missional organizations, such as the Student Volunteer Movement, which young Christians out of numerous theological backgrounds enthusiastically embraced. A fascinating first-person account of the theological changes taking place in America during the late nineteenth and early twentieth centuries is offered by Gaius Glenn Atkins, *Religion in Our Times* (New York: Round Table Press, 1932).

6   See Joel A. Carpenter, *Revive Us Again: The Reawakening of American Fundamentalism* (New York: Oxford University Press, 1997). Robert Wuthnow points out that the so-called evangelical resurgence, often associated with a reaction against the cultural dislocation of the 1960s, needs to be viewed with caution. Evangelicals were not only growing in number before the 1960s, but their growth rate had already surpassed the liberal mainline; see Wuthnow, *After the Baby Boomers: How Twenty- And Thirty-Somethings Are Shaping the Future of American Religion* (Princeton, N.J.: Princeton University Press, 2007).

7   Martin E. Marty, *Righteous Empire: The Protestant Experience in America* (New York: Dial, 1970); Jean Miller Schmidt, *Souls of the Social Order: The Two-Party System in American Protestantism* (Brooklyn, N.Y.: Carlson, 1991).

8   See Robert T. Handy, *A Christian America: Protestant Hopes and Historical Realities* (New York: Oxford University Press, 1971).

9   On the early history of American pentecostalism, see Harvey Cox, *Fire From Heaven: The Rise of Pentecostal Spirituality and the Reshaping of Religion in the 21st Century* (Cambridge, Mass.: Da Capo, 1995), and Grant Wacker, *Heaven Below: Pentecostals and American Culture* (Cambridge, Mass.: Harvard University Press, 2001).

10   The development of this genre of Protestant orthodoxy in American history is traced in Mark Noll, *America's God: From Jonathan Edwards to Abraham Lincoln* (New York: Oxford University Press, 2002), and E. Brooks Holifield, *Theology in America: Christian Thought from the Age of the Puritans to the Civil War* (New Haven: Yale University Press, 2003).

11   In a historical sense, the term "evangelical" could encompass two very different historical movements that emerged in the early twentieth century, the "liberal" social gospel and "conservative" pentecostalism; see Martin E. Marty, *Modern American Religion: The Irony of It All* (Chicago: University of Chicago Press, 1986).

12   See Robert Jewett, *Mission and Menace: Four Centuries of American Religious Zeal* (Minneapolis: Fortress, 2008); note esp. chap. 8.

13   Garry Wills, *Under God: Religion and Politics in America* (New York: Simon & Schuster, 1990), 144–45.

14   These verses read, "For the Lord himself shall descend from heaven with a shout, with the voice of the archangel, and the trump of God; and the dead in Christ shall rise first: then we which are alive and remain shall be caught up together with them in the clouds, to meet the Lord in the air; and so shall we ever be with the Lord" (KJV).

15   Paul Boyer, *When Time Shall Be No More: Prophecy Belief in Modern American Culture* (Cambridge, Mass.: Belknap Press, 1992).

16   Glenn T. Miller provides a useful overview to the intellectual progression of dispensationalist thought, noting that even before the so-called fundamentalist-modernist split of the 1920s, the movement had strong institutional bases in Bible colleges, biblical institutes, and parachurch structures; see Miller, *Piety and Profession: American Protestant Theological Education, 1870–1970* (Grand Rapids: Eerdmans, 2007), 179–200.

17   Boyer, *When Time Shall Be No More*, 97–98.

18   I. M. Haldeman, *The Coming of Christ: Both Pre-Millennial and Imminent* (New York: Charles C. Cook, 1906), 114.

19   Randall Balmer, *Mine Eyes Have Seen the Glory: A Journey into the Evangelical Subculture in America* (New York: Oxford University Press, 1989); see also the PBS documentary *Mine Eyes Have Seen the Glory* (1992), based upon Balmer's book.

20   *A Thief in the Night* (Mark IV Films, 1972).

21   Balmer, *Mine Eyes Have Seen the Glory*, 57–68.

22   Arthur T. Pierson, "The Testimony of the Organic Unity of the Bible to its Inspiration," in *The Fundamentals: A Testimony to the Truth* (Chicago: Testimony Publishers, 1910).

23   Noll, *The Scandal of the Evangelical Mind* (Grand Rapids: Eerdmans, 1994), 132.

24   This is not to say that dispensationalism does not have its academic centers. Numerous Christian colleges and theological seminaries stress the centrality of dispensationalism in their theology and mission statements; see, as an example, Randall Balmer's discussion of Dallas Theological Seminary in *Mine Eyes Have Seen the Glory*, 31–49.

25   See the Baylor survey *"American Piety in the 21st Century"* and the Pew Study, *"Pew Religious Landscape."*

26   See, e.g., Michael Barkun, *Culture of Conspiracy: Apocalyptic Visions in Contemporary America* (Berkeley: University of California Press, 2003).

27   See George Marsden, *Understanding Fundamentalism and Evangelicalism* (Grand Rapids: Eerdmans, 1991); Marty and R. Scott Appleby, *The Glory and the Power: The Fundamentalist Challenge to the Modern World* (Boston: Beacon Press, 1992).

28   From his research on Protestant churches in the Pacific Northwest, James K. Wellman Jr. notes how many evangelicals hold in tension their apocalyptic beliefs with their desire to live in the culture; see Wellman, *Evangelical vs. Liberal: The Clash of Christian Cultures in the Pacific Northwest* (New York: Oxford University Press, 2008).

29   Quoted in William R. Hutchison, *The Modernist Impulse in American Protestantism* (Cambridge, Mass.: Harvard University Press, 1976), 262.

30   J. Gresham Machen, *Christianity and Liberalism* (New York: Macmillan, 1923), 172–73.

CHAPTER SIX

1   See Gibson Winter, *The Suburban Captivity of the Churches: An Analysis of Protestant Responsibility in the Expanding Metropolis* (Garden City, N.Y.: Doubleday, 1961); Pierre Berton, *The Comfortable Pew: A Critical Look at the Church in the New Age* (Philadelphia: Lippincott, 1965).

2   Harvey Cox, *The Secular City* (New York: Macmillan, 1965); Peter Berger, *The Sacred Canopy* (New York: Doubleday, 1967).

3   Dean Kelley, *Why Conservative Churches Are Growing* (New York: Harper & Row, 1972); Dean Hoge and David A. Roozen, eds., *Understanding Church Growth and Decline, 1950–1978* (New York: Pilgrim Press, 1979).

4   For examples of theological assessments of liberalism that appeared from the 1960s through the 1980s, see Lloyd J. Averill, *American Theology in the Liberal Tradition* (Philadelphia: Westminster,1967); John B. Cobb Jr., *Liberal Christianity at the Crossroads* (Philadelphia: Westminster, 1973); and

Donald E. Miller, *The Case for Liberal Christianity* (San Francisco: Harper & Row, 1981).

5   See Amanda Porterfield, *The Transformation of American Religion: The Story of a Late-Twentieth-Century Awakening* (New York: Oxford University Press, 2001).

6   Two differing interpretations of so-called "seeker" culture are offered by Robert Bellah, *Habits of the Heart: Individualism and Commitment in American Life* (Berkeley: University of California Press, 1985), and Wade Clark Roof, *Spiritual Marketplace: Baby Boomers and the Remaking of American Religion* (Princeton, N.J.: Princeton University Press, 1999).

7   Donald E. Miller, *The Case for Liberal Christianity*, 152.

8   See, e.g., Marcus Borg, *Meeting Jesus Again for the First Time* (San Francisco: Harper, 1994); John Spong, *Here I Stand: My Struggle for a Christianity of Integrity, Love, and Equality* (San Francisco: HarperSanFrancisco: 2000).

9   See, e.g., Donald E. Miller, *Reinventing American Protestantism: Christianity in the New Millennium* (Berkeley: University of California Press, 1997); Stephen Ellingson, *The Megachurch and the Mainline: Rethinking Religious Tradition in the Twenty-First Century* (Chicago: University of Chicago Press, 2007).

10   Dorrien, *Crisis, Irony, and Postmodernity*, 190.

11   No figure of contemporary liberalism has been more vocal in asserting the need for liberal theology to interface with faith communities than John Cobb; see, e.g., Cobb's book *Reclaiming the Church: Where the Mainline Church Went Wrong and What to Do About It* (Louisville, Ky.: Westminster John Knox, 1997).

12   Glenn T. Miller, *Piety and Profession: American Protestant Theological Education, 1870–1970* (Grand Rapids: Eerdmans, 2007), 226.

13   Cobb, *Reclaiming the Church*, 31.

14   Peter Hodgson, *Liberal Theology: A Radical Vision* (Minneapolis: Fortress, 2007), 9–10.

15   Mark Silk, "The Rise of the 'New Evangelicalism,'" in *Between the Times: The Travail of the Protestant Establishment in America, 1900–1960*, ed. William R. Hutchison (Cambridge: Cambridge University Press, 1989), 297.

16   Winthrop Hudson, ed., *Walter Rauschenbusch: Selected Writings* (New York: Paulist Press, 1984), 85. Reinhold Niebuhr made similar points in his critique of dispensationalism; see Paul Boyer, *When Time Shall Be No More: Prophecy Belief in Modern American Culture* (Cambridge, Mass.: Belknap Press, 1992).

17   Dorrien, *The Remaking of Evangelical Theology* (Louisville, Ky.: Westminster John Knox, 1998).

18   Fleming Rutledge, "When God Disturbs the Peace," *Christianity Today* 52 (2008): 32.

19   Additionally, many evangelicals overlook much of the political radicalism of Martin Luther King Jr., especially his growing disillusionment with

political gradualism in his final years; see James Cone, *Malcolm and Martin and America: A Dream or a Nightmare?* (Maryknoll, N.Y.: Orbis, 1990).

20   A highly publicized blog dialogue between Paul Raushenbush and Bill Hybels on beliefnet.com (www.beliefnet.com/Search/Blogs) reflects aspects of this emerging dialogue.

21   Jaroslav Pelikan, *The Vindication of Tradition* (New Haven: Yale University Press, 1984).

22   Hodgson, *Liberal Theology: A Radical Vision*, 9–10.

23   Ralph Reed, *Politically Incorrect: The Emerging Faith Factor in American Politics* (Dallas: Word Publishing, 1994), 64.

24   Stephen Prothero, *Religious Literacy: What Every American Needs to Know—and Doesn't* (New York: HarperCollins, 2007), 146.

25   Note the most recent edition of Walter Rauschenbusch, *Christianizing the Social Order* (Waco, Tex.: Baylor University Press, 2010).

26   Dorrien, *Crisis, Irony, and Postmodernity*, 529.

27   Richard Wilke, *And Are We Yet Alive? The Future of the United Methodist Church* (Nashville: Abingdon, 1986), 98.

28   J. Philip Wogaman, *Faith and Fragmentation: Christianity for a New Age* (Philadelphia: Fortress, 1985), 12–14.

29   See Robert Wuthnow and John H. Evans, eds., *The Quiet Hand of God: Faith-Based Activism and the Public Role of Mainline Protestantism* (Berkeley: University of California Press, 2002).

30   Cornel West, "Can These Dry Bones Live?" in Rauschenbusch, *Christianity and the Social Crisis in the 21st Century*, 231.

31   Phillip E. Hammond, *The Protestant Presence in Twentieth-Century America: Religion and Political Culture* (Albany: State University of New York Press, 1992), 167.

32   See, e.g., the "Progressive Revival" blog site hosted by Paul Raushenbush on beliefnet.com.

33   In a recent analysis of evangelical and liberal congregations in the Pacific Northwest, James K. Wellman Jr. notes the relationship between the evangelical's beliefs in premillennialism and the liberal's desire to "save" the world through active civic engagement; see his *Evangelical vs. Liberal: The Clash of Christian Cultures in the Pacific Northwest* (Oxford: Oxford University Press, 2008).

34   See Jim Wallis, *God's Politics: Why the Right Gets It Wrong and the Left Doesn't Get It* (San Francisco: HarperOne, 2005).

35   Stanley Hauerwas, *After Christendom? How the Church Is to Behave if Freedom, Justice, and a Christian Nation are Bad Ideas* (Nashville: Abingdon, 1991).

36   Mark G. Toulouse, *God in Public: Four Ways American Christianity and Public Life Relate* (Louisville, Ky.: Westminster John Knox, 2006).

Chapter Seven

1   For an interesting depiction of the events surrounding the Crapsey trial, see Gaius Glenn Atkins, *Religion in Our Times* (New York: Round Table Press, 1932), 101–5.

2   Diana Butler Bass, *The Practicing Congregation: Imagining a New Old Church* (Herndon, Va.: Alban Institute, 2004), 75.

3   See Robert Wuthnow, *The Restructuring of American Religion: Society and Faith since World War II* (Princeton, N.J.: Princeton University Press, 1988); Donald E. Miller, *Reinventing American Protestantism: Christianity in the New Millennium* (Berkeley: University of California Press, 1997); and Wuthnow and John H. Evans, eds., *The Quiet Hand of God: Faith-Based Activism and the Public Role of Mainline Protestantism* (Berkeley: University of California Press, 2002).

4   Loren Mead, *The Once and Future Church: Reinventing the Congregation for a New Mission Frontier* (Herndon, Va.: Alban Institute, 1991).

5   Loren Mead, *The Once and Future Church*, 82.

6   What many studies on the civil rights era make clear is that a large measure of Martin Luther King Jr.'s success came as a consequence of a diverse range of leadership networks that emerged prior to the Montgomery Bus Boycott; see Taylor Branch, *Parting the Waters: America in the King Years, 1954–63* (New York: Simon & Schuster, 1988); Tracy, *Direct Action*; and Charles Marsh, *God's Long Hot Summer: Stories of Faith and the Civil Rights Movement* (Princeton, N.J.: Princeton University Press, 1997).

7   Luther Gerlach and Virginia Hine, *People, Power, Change: Movements of Social Transformation* (Indianapolis: Bobbs-Merrill, 1970).

8   Mark Chaves, *Congregations in America* (Cambridge, Mass.: Harvard University Press, 2004), 93. Chaves points out that congregations who engage in social justice ministry are frequently in partnership with secular agencies.

9   See Wuthnow, *After the Baby Boomers*.

10 Bass, *The Practicing Congregation* and *Christianity for the Rest of Us: How The Neighborhood Church Is Transforming the Faith* (New York: HarperCollins, 2006).

11 See Brian McLaren, *A Generous Orthodoxy* (Grand Rapids: Zondervan, 2004).

12 Wuthnow, *After the Baby Boomers*, 214–15.

13 Bass, *Christianity for the Rest of Us*, 281.

14 Peter C. Hodgson, *Liberal Theology: A Radical Vision* (Minneapolis: Fortress, 2007), 97–98.

15 Ironically, the rhetoric of religious liberals like Harry F. Ward sounds a great deal like that of secular liberals like Christopher Hitchens.

16 Hauerwas and Willimon, *Resident Aliens*, 156.

17   Wuthnow and Evans, eds., *The Quiet Hand of God*, 21–22.

18   Milton J. Coalter, John M. Mulder, and Louis B. Weeks, *Vital Signs: The Promise of Mainline Protestantism* (Grand Rapids: Eerdmans, 1996), 130.

19   Peter Berger, *The Sacred Canopy* (New York: Doubleday, 1967).

20   J. Philip Wogaman, *Faith and Fragmentation: Christianity for a New Age* (Philadelphia: Fortress, 1985).

21   Mead, *The Once and Future Church*, 80.

22   For some of the most significant contemporary liberal voices to demonstrate that the Christian life can be lived not only by asking tough questions, but by understanding the importance of humor, see Anne Lamott, *Traveling Mercies: Some Thoughts on Faith* (New York: Pantheon, 1999), and Becky Garrison, *Red and Blue God, and Black and Blue Church: Eyewitness Accounts of How American Churches are Hijacking Jesus, Bagging the Beatitudes, and Worshipping the Almighty Dollar* (San Francisco: Jossey-Bass, 2006).

23   The interest in these figures historically associated with liberalism can be seen in the ministries of several prominent evangelicals, in particular Tony Campolo and Jim Wallis.

24   The Church of the Resurrection, a United Methodist congregation located in Leawood, Kansas, and one of the largest mainline congregations in America, reflects a mission that seeks to connect its 15,000-member community to larger social gospel themes of personal and social transformation. Although the church's website avoids identifying its mission through the labels of "progressive" or "liberal," the church is unapologetic in its embrace of its denominational identity, and defining its mission, in terms of "renewing the mainline church"; see the church's Web site, http://www.cor.org.

25   Christopher H. Evans, *Social Gospel Liberalism and the Ministry of Ernest Fremont Tittle: A Theology for the Middle Class* (Lewiston, N.Y.: Edwin Mellen Press, 1996), 293.

26   Harry Emerson Fosdick, "God of Grace and God of Glory" (originally published, 1930).

Epilogue

1   Note, as one example, Thomas Jefferson's confident prediction that churches aligned with Unitarianism would become the dominant religious groups in America.

2   Winthrop Hudson, *The Great Tradition of the American Churches* (New York: Harper & Row, 1953), 63.

3   Nathan O. Hatch, *Democratization of American Christianity* (New Haven: Yale University Press, 1989).

4   Albert Raboteau, *Slave Religion: The "Invisible Institution" in the Antebellum South* (New York: Oxford University Press, 1978).

5   William R. Hutchison, "Past Imperfect: History and the Prospect for Liberalism," in *Liberal Protestantism: Realities and Possibilities*, ed. Robert S. Michaelsen and Wade Clark Roof (New York: Pilgrim Press, 1986), 66.

6   H. Richard Niebuhr, *The Kingdom of God in America* (New York: Harper & Row, 1937), 198.

Selected Bibliography

PRIMARY SOURCES

Choosing a list of primary sources for American Christian liberalism depends, in large measure, upon one's interests. What I have presented here is a cross section of significant primary (and in some cases secondary) works on Christian liberalism, especially corresponding to the historical and theological themes discussed in chapters 2 through 5 in this volume. While not an exhaustive bibliography, it can serve as a good overview of liberalism's role in the history of American Christianity, as well as a useful guide for further study by students, scholars, and church leaders.

Early to Middle Nineteenth Century (American Foundations)

One of the best starting points for understanding the rise of American theological liberalism is Sydney Ahlstrom and Jonathan Carey's anthology, *An American Reformation: A Documentary History of Unitarian Christianity* (Middletown, Conn.: Wesleyan University Press, 1985). The book contains primary sources from the major figures associated with early New England Unitarianism, including William Ellery Channing and Henry Ware (whose appointment to the faculty of Harvard Divinity School in 1805 was a catalyst to the founding of Andover Seminary).

If any theologian deserves the label of being the father of American liberalism, it is Horace Bushnell. Yet as one scholar noted, Bushnell tends to be a figure that more people have read about than to have actually read. Before reading Bushnell, a reader might first want to consult Robert Bruce Mullin's biography, *The Puritan as Yankee: A Life of Horace Bushnell* (Grand

Rapids: Eerdmans, 2002), to appreciate Bushnell's historical context and the nuances of his thought. Two of Bushnell's most important books are *Nature and the Supernatural* (New York: Charles Scribner's Sons,1858), and *Christian Nurture* (New York: Charles Scribner's Sons,1860). These works reflect upon key concepts critical to the later rise of American liberalism, specifically, the metaphorical nature of theological language and a mediating view of Christianity.

Mid- to Late Nineteenth Century (Theological Transitions, "New Theology" Liberalism)

After Bushnell, Theodore Munger represents perhaps the most well-known representative of what was called "the New Theology." A good overview of his thought can be found in his book, *The Freedom of Faith* (Boston: Houghton Mifflin, 1883). Munger's work paralleled many other prominent ministers of that era who were widely published in their lifetimes, including George Gordon and Newman Smyth. William R. Hutchison's work *The Modernist Impulse in American Protestantism* (Cambridge, Mass.: Harvard University Press, 1976) remains a superlative treatment of liberalism's late nineteenth-century rise, especially its shift from churches to the academy. An anthology that shows useful connections between various strands of nineteenth-century liberalism and the legacies of the social gospel is Ronald White and Charles Howard Hopkins, eds., *The Social Gospel: Religion and Reform in Changing America* (Philadelphia: Temple University Press, 1976). Daniel Day Williams' account of liberalism's ascendancy at Andover Seminary in the 1880s, *The Andover Liberals: A Study in American Theology* (New York: King's Crown Press, 1941), provides readers a view, in microcosm, of liberalism's ascendancy within a seminary that prided itself as caretaker of an earlier New England Calvinist heritage.

Late Nineteenth and Early Twentieth Century (Evangelical and Modernist Liberalism)

Although scholars frequently differentiate between evangelical and modernist schools of liberalism, many figures within these traditions often shared strong affinities with one another. Of all the church leaders associated with the rise of Christian liberalism at the end of the nineteenth century, few could match the impact of William Newton Clarke. His major work, *An Outline of Christian Theology* (New York: Charles Scribner's Sons, 1898), represents a summation of key tenets of evangelical liberalism's beliefs in God, Christ, the atonement, and the nature of Christian mission that guided many liberal movements well into the twentieth century.

The period around the late nineteenth and early twentieth centuries is frequently seen as a time of theological schism between Christian conservatives and liberals. Two works written by liberals that give the reader a unique glimpse into this historical period are Washington Gladden, *Recollections* (Boston: Houghton Mifflin, 1909), and Gaius Glenn Atkins, *Religion in Our Times* (New York: Round Table Press, 1932). These books recount some of the major heresy incidents of the late nineteenth century, as well as how liberalism developed on both an institutional and, to a degree, a popular level in American Protestantism.

Although Shailer Mathews would be seen by many later theologians as embodying the worst aspects of religious modernism, he introduced many themes of German liberalism to an American audience—especially in terms of New Testament studies. The most well known of Mathews' works is *The Social Teaching of Jesus* (New York: Macmillan, 1897; revised as *Jesus on Social Institutions* [New York: Macmillan, 1928]). Mathews' autobiography, *New Faith for Old* (New York: Macmillan, 1936), like earlier such works by Gladden and Atkins, provides a unique window toward understanding a tumultuous period in American religion. (This book also shows how Mathews, frequently dismissed as a "modernist liberal," displayed an affinity with other currents of evangelical liberalism of the late nineteenth and early twentieth centuries.)

Early Twentieth Century (Social Gospel)

For many years, historians focused on the social gospel as a historical response to the conditions of modern American industrialization. However, more recent scholarship has come to appreciate the social gospel as a distinctive genre of liberalism in its own right. Although Gladden was probably the most prolific of the social gospelers, the majority of his books came from his sermons. Gladden's splendid autobiography, *Recollections* (referenced above), is not only an excellent guide to the major theological battles of the late nineteenth century, but also accentuates how a key component of the social gospel emerged out of a parish setting. While Walter Rauschenbusch is perhaps best known today for his 1907 book, *Christianity and the Social Crisis* (most recently republished as *Christianity and the Social Crisis in the 21st Century*, ed. Paul Raushenbush [New York: HarperOne, 2007]), a more detailed overview of Rauschenbusch's theology is found in his last major work, *A Theology for the Social Gospel*

(New York: Macmillan, 1917). The full scope of Rauschenbusch's theological and social agenda was fleshed out in his 1912 work, *Christianizing the Social Order* (New York: Macmillan, 1912; to be reissued by Baylor University Press in 2010). Finally, the scope of Rauschenbusch's theological interests, including his deep-seated piety, can be found in Winthrop S. Hudson's edited volume, *Walter Rauschenbusch: Selected Writings* (New York: Paulist Press, 1984).

Compared to Rauschenbusch, Vida Scudder's life and thought is mostly relegated to a select number of dissertations and monographs. For an excellent introduction to her thought, including a comprehensive bibliography of Scudder's work, see Elizabeth Hinson-Hasty, *Beyond the Social Maze: Exploring Vida Dutton Scudder's Theological Ethics* (New York: T&T Clark, 2006).

Mid-Twentieth Century (Crisis Theology and Response)

I share with other scholars a belief that what is commonly referred to as neo-orthodoxy was more of a corrective to earlier liberal theologies, as opposed to a conscious effort to overthrow the movement. Any discussion of American neo-orthodoxy must begin and end with Reinhold Niebuhr, and a Niebuhr novice would do well to read Richard Fox's excellent work, *Reinhold Niebuhr: A Biography* (San Francisco: Harper & Row, 1985). Although Fox does not pay as close attention to some of the theological sources that shaped Niebuhr's thought, the book connects Niebuhr's rise to the liberal model of the "public church intellectual" that Niebuhr, more than any other figure in American history, epitomized. Another excellent primer on Niebuhr's thought is Harlan Beckley's *Passion for Justice: Retrieving the Legacies of Walter Rauschenbusch, John A. Ryan, and Reinhold Niebuhr* (Louisville, Ky.: Westminster John Knox, 1992).

For all the ways that Reinhold Niebuhr shifted his focus in many of his writings (particularly between theology-ethics and politics), the one book that still serves as the best introduction to him is his *Moral Man and Immoral Society: A Study in Ethics and Politics* (New York: Charles Scribner's Sons, 1932). This book underscores the classic themes that underscored Niebuhr's later work, including the themes of human sin, historical irony, and theological paradox. Other Reinhold Niebuhr works that display the development of these themes include *An Interpretation of Christian Ethics* (New York: Harper & Brothers, 1935), a work that shows much affinity with earlier traditions of the social gospel; *The Children of Light and the Children of Darkness* (New York: Charles Scribner's Sons,

1944); and *The Irony of American History* (New York: Charles Scribner's Sons, 1952).

In the opinion of this author, H. Richard Niebuhr's writings contain a less polemical treatment of liberalism compared to his brother's, and a more nuanced assessment of liberalism. His 1937 work, *The Kingdom of God in America* (New York: Harper & Brothers, 1937), provides a classic assessment of liberalism that too often has been viewed as a blanket condemnation of the tradition. Additionally, Niebuhr's much discussed work *Christ and Culture* (Harper & Brothers 1951) still provides useful insights on the historical and theological relationship between Christianity and dominant social, political, and cultural processes. Along with H. Richard Niebuhr, Paul Tillich helped shape much of American Christianity's dialogue with secular culture in the mid-twentieth century, and his work remains frequently cited by contemporary scholars of religion and culture. For an excellent study showing the interface between Tillich's theology and the study of popular culture, see Kelton Cobb, *The Blackwell Guide to Theology and Popular Culture* (Malden, Mass.: Blackwell, 2005).

Despite the polemical nature of his attacks against liberalism, Reinhold Niebuhr's work had a profound impact on movements of liberalism to emerge in the mid-twentieth century. The ways in which Niebuhr's worldview was embraced *and* challenged can be seen in works such as Georgia Harkness, *Understanding the Christian Faith* (Nashville: Abingdon, 1947), and Daniel Day Williams, *God's Grace and Man's Hope* (New York: Harper & Brothers, 1949). Both of these works provide appreciative and substantive critiques of the Niebuhrian tradition that are still germane today.

More than any other work in this bibliography, the one work that perhaps best embodies the broader public influence of Christian liberalism during the first half of the twentieth century is Harry Emerson Fosdick's *The Living of These Days: An Autobiography* (New York: Harper & Brothers, 1956). In a similar vein to the autobiographical work of Gladden and Atkins, Fosdick takes the reader on a journey through many of the major theological controversies of his lifetime, including his account of the fundamentalist-modernist battles of the 1920s.

At the same time that Christian liberals like Fosdick propagated a vision of liberalism for a large following within mainline Protestantism, dissenting traditions of liberal theology attempted to build movements of political radicalism that found themselves at odds with liberals within the churches. No better example of this tension can be found than that of Harry F. Ward. David Nelson Duke's biography, *In the Trenches with Jesus and Marx: Harry F. Ward and the Struggle for Social Justice* (Tuscaloosa: University of Alabama Press, 2003), provides a fascinating historical overview of Ward's life, from his early career as a social gospel preacher in the tradition of Walter Rauschenbusch to an individual who ultimately reconciled the ethics of Jesus with those of Marxism. (In addition, Duke provides a fascinating glimpse into the often antagonistic relationship between Ward and Reinhold Niebuhr at Union Seminary.)

Of all the figures to emerge out of twentieth-century Christianity, no one is more worthy of rediscovery than Howard Thurman. Thurman's *With Hand and Heart: An Autobiography* (San Diego: Harcourt Brace Jovanovich, 1979) displays the range of his theological influences, from the black church and the social gospel to religious mysticism. Thurman's work not only provides a window to understanding how a Christian worldview can come into dialogue with world religions in the West, but also offers a compelling argument for what would later become known as liberation theology. Thurman's *Jesus and the Disinherited* (New York: Abingdon-Cokesbury Press, 1949) shows how the integration of an earlier social gospel tradition was applied to address issues of racial justice.

Late Twentieth-Century Liberal Movements and Critics

Martin Luther King Jr. stands out as the most prominent exponent of a prophetic Christian liberal tradition that impacted the world. However, his relationship to classical traditions of Christian liberalism has become obscured with the passing of time. King's first major work, *Stride Toward Freedom* (New York: Harper & Row, 1958), allowed King, in his own words, to explain his philosophy of nonviolence and highlight his indebtedness to liberal theological sources, including Rauschenbusch, Niebuhr, and personalism. An excellent one-volume anthology to King's works remains James Washington, ed., *A Testament of Hope: The Essential Writings of Martin Luther King, Jr.* (San Francisco: Harper, 1985).

Perhaps no other individual did more to show the ongoing resiliency of an earlier tradition of the liberal social gospel than William Sloane Coffin. A good example for understanding his thought is his *The Courage to Love* (San Francisco: Harper & Row, 1984), a collection of his sermons from Riverside Church. Although the relationship between liberalism and liberation theology has been somewhat contentious, many liberation theologians have conceded the importance and vitality of earlier liberal efforts to their own work. See, for example, Rosemary Radford Ruether, *Sexism and God-Talk* (Boston: Beacon, 1983). Although Ruether is clear about the limitations of liberalism, she also provides an example of a liberationist perspective that is in dialogue with that heritage.

Part of my hope for the recovery of a twenty-first-century Christian liberalism is that it will speak to the cultures of American congregations (and emerge out of them). One individual who represents this integration in his work is J. Philip Wogaman. His *Faith and Fragmentation: Christianity for a New Age* (Philadelphia: Fortress, 1985) outlines many of the theological challenges facing church leaders who seek to navigate competing claims of faith and culture.

SECONDARY SOURCES

Survey Texts (History of American Christian Liberalism)

These works represent comprehensive treatments of American liberalism, with Gary Dorrien's three-volume *The Making of American Liberal Theology* being the most comprehensive and detailed. With the exception of Dorrien's work, the rest of these studies tend to tie liberalism mostly to movements of the late nineteenth and early twentieth centuries.

Averill, Lloyd J. *American Theology in the Liberal Tradition*. Philadelphia: Westminster Press, 1967.

Cauthen, Kenneth. *The Impact of American Religious Liberalism*. New York: Harper & Row, 1962.

Dorrien, Gary. *Soul in Society: The Making and Renewal of Social Christianity*. Minneapolis: Fortress, 1995.

———. *The Making of American Liberal Theology: Imagining Progressive Religion, 1805–1900*. Louisville, Ky.: Westminster John Knox, 2001.

———. *The Making of American Liberal Theology: Idealism, Realism, and Modernity, 1900–1950*. Louisville, Ky.: Westminster John Knox, 2003.

———. *The Making of American Liberal Theology: Crisis, Irony, and Postmodernity, 1950–2005*. Louisville, Ky.: Westminster John Knox, 2006.

Critical Assessments: American Theological Liberalism/Mainline Protestantism

Since the 1960s, there have been periodic studies on the future of liberal theology, especially surrounding the renewal of mainline churches. This list provides some well-known studies in this regard (including some significant contemporary studies). As noted in this book, the term "progressive" has become the accepted designation for "liberal" in recent years.

Bass, Diana Butler. *The Practicing Congregation: Imagining a New Old Church.* Herndon, Va.: Alban Institute, 2004.

———. *Christianity for the Rest of Us: How the Neighborhood Church Is Transforming the Faith.* New York: HarperCollins, 2006.

Brown, Delwin. *What Does a Progressive Christian Believe? A Guide for the Searching, the Open, and the Curious.* New York: Seabury Press, 2008.

Chapman, Mark D., ed. *The Future of Liberal Theology.* Burlington, Vt.: Ashgate, 2002 (a work that includes contributors from the U.S. and Great Britain).

Cobb, John B., Jr. *Liberal Christianity at the Crossroads.* Philadelphia: Westminster Press, 1973.

———. *Reclaiming the Church: Where the Mainline Church Went Wrong and What to Do about It.* Louisville, Ky.: Westminster John Knox, 1997.

Hodgson, Peter C. *Liberal Theology: A Radical Vision.* Minneapolis: Fortress, 2007.

Michaelsen, Robert S., and Wade Clark Roof, eds. *Liberal Protestantism: Realities and Possibilities.* New York: Pilgrim Press, 1986.

Miller, Donald E. *The Case for Liberal Christianity.* San Francisco: Harper & Row, 1981.

Van Dusen, Henry P. *The Vindication of Liberal Theology: A Tract for the Times.* New York: Charles Scribner's Sons, 1963.

Contemporary American Religion (works that include substantive discussions on Christian liberalism)

Finally, as I tried to outline in this study, it is impossible to discuss the role of any theological heritage without taking seriously its larger historical and sociological context. These resources display some significant recent works by sociologists that add an important dimension to the possibilities and pitfalls faced by church leaders who seek to revive Christian liberalism in the years ahead.

Ammerman, Nancy Tatom. *Pillars of Faith: American Congregations and Their Partners.* Berkeley: University of California Press, 2005.

Chaves, Mark. *Congregations in America*. Cambridge, Mass.: Harvard University Press, 2004.

Wellman, James K., Jr. *Evangelical vs. Liberal: The Clash of Christian Cultures in the Pacific Northwest*. New York: Oxford University Press, 2008.

Wuthnow, Robert. *After the Baby Boomers: How Twenty- and Thirty-Somethings Are Shaping the Future of American Religion*. Princeton, N.J.: Princeton University Press, 2007.

Wuthnow, Robert, and John H. Evans, eds. *The Quiet Hand of God: Faith-based Activism and the Public Role of Mainline Protestantism*. Berkeley: University of California Press, 2002.

Index

Abbot, Lyman, 60
abortion, 28, 110, 112, 127, 136–37
academia, 5, 8, 12–13, 15, 33, 50, 54, 56, 85, 87, 103–4, 111, 121–25, 129–32, 142–44, 158, 167n20, 170n7, 186n24
Addams, Jane, 61
African Americans, 58, 71–72, 75, 77, 95, 102, 162, 167n17, 179n66, 183n46
Ahlstrom, Sydney, 22, 184n1, 193
Ammerman, Nancy Tatom, 30
Atkins, Gaius Glenn, 195, 197
Augustine, 70, 81, 82, 87–88, 123, 129, 182n26

Balmer, Randall, 109
Baptists, 38, 43, 56, 63, 77, 100–101, 103, 105–7
Barth, Karl, 80–81, 83, 88, 179n3, 180nn5–6
Bass, Diana Butler, 30, 143, 149, 151, 156
Beecher, Henry Ward, 8, 47, 60, 73, 119, 142, 162, 174n26
Beecher, Lyman, 47, 161–62
Berger, Peter, 156

biblical literalism, 8, 41, 104, 106
"big steeple" churches, 75–76, 88
Blake, Casey Nelson, 64
Bonino, Jose, 96
Bono, 92, 135
Borg, Marcus, 50, 119, 141
Bowne, Borden Parker, 69, 121
Brooks, Phillips, 8, 47, 62
Brown, Delwin, 21, 136, 170n10
Bush, George Herbert Walker, 19, 28
Bush, George W., 130
Bushnell, Horace, 8, 42–46, 48, 142, 170n7, 173n20, 174–75n22, 193–94
Buttrick, George, 74

Calvin, John, 33, 38, 80, 87–88, 110–11, 123
Calvinism, 6–7, 10, 22, 34, 38, 40–42, 47, 87, 167n16, 181n18, 194; see also Reformed theology
Carter, Jimmy, 112, 125
Case, Shirley Jackson, 70
Catholicism, 6, 10, 12, 22, 23–24, 25, 37, 46, 51, 71, 79, 117, 123, 145, 146, 156, 162, 166n9, 167n17, 182n26; anti-Catholicism, 52, 71
Cauthen, Kenneth, 48

Channing, William Ellery, 8, 41–42, 57, 170n7, 193
Chaves, Mark, 146, 189n8
Christian Coalition, 136, 147
Christian realism, 3, 9, 69, 169n32, 179n2; *see also* neo-orthodoxy
Church of England 34, 56
civil rights movement, 79, 91, 95, 122, 145, 152, 167–68n21, 189n6
Civil War, 38, 45–47, 58–59, 102, 105, 173–74n22
Clarke, William Newton, 9, 45, 100, 194–95
Clinton, Hillary, 28
Coalter, Milton, 155
Cobb, John B., Jr., 85–86, 88, 122, 123, 136, 181n23, 187n11
Coe, George Albert, 91
Coffin, William Sloane, 76, 94, 179n59, 198
Cone, James, 9, 122, 167–68n21, 183n46
congregational ministry, 21, 157
Congregationalism, 38–40, 42, 47, 56, 60–61, 161
Crane, Henry Hitt, 74
Crapsey, Algernon, 141

Darby, John Nelson, 105–6
Darwin, Charles, 7, 47, 49, 50
dispensationalism, 104–13, 115, 125–26, 128, 147, 185n16, 186n24, 187n16
Dorrien, Gary, 2, 6, 13–14, 21, 59, 80–81, 121–22, 132, 142, 165n5, 166nn12–13, 169n32, 170n7, 173n13, 180nn5–6, 199
Dukakis, Michael, 19, 28
Duke, David Nelson, 93

Ely, Richard, 61, 64
Emergent Church, 30, 56, 120, 131, 139, 150, 172n30
Emerson, Ralph Waldo, 41, 43

environmentalism, 86, 111, 128, 132, 152
Episcopalians, 47, 57, 61, 141
evangelicalism, 3, 8, 10, 15, 21–27, 29, 31, 33–34, 38, 40–42, 46–47, 54, 55–56, 58, 60, 63, 65–66, 73, 80, 89, 99–113, 115, 117–20, 123–24, 125–28, 130–31, 133–38, 142, 143–44, 146, 147–48, 149–51, 157, 162, 163, 166n9, 167n17, 168n24, 171n24, 173n11, 180n6, 184nn1, 5, 6, 185n11, 186n28, 188n19, 188n33; evangelical liberalism, 9, 14, 41, 67, 84, 129, 154, 175n8, 190n23, 194–95

Falwell, Jerry, 147–48
feminism, 28, 95, 122, 132, 142, 167–68n21, 183n46; anti-feminism, 77, 184n47; women's rights, 58, 83, 178n54
Fosdick, Harry Emerson, 8, 62, 74–75, 94, 100–101, 111, 113, 119, 124, 142, 159, 167n20, 197
fundamentalism, 8, 10, 15, 100–104, 112–13, 153, 185n16, 197

gay-lesbian rights, 28, 95, 112, 127, 147, 156, 183n46; same-sex marriage, 110, 137
gender, 11, 40, 77–78, 95; *see also* feminism, womanist theology, women's organizations and activism
Gladden, Washington, 8, 47–48, 56, 59, 62–64, 65, 66, 77, 119, 162, 170n7, 195, 197
Gordon, George, 8, 47, 49, 194
Griffin, David Ray, 122

Haldeman, I. M., 107–8
Hall, Douglas John, 86, 181n24
Harkness, Georgia, 83–85, 119, 181n16, 197

Harnack, Adolf von, 52, 68
Hatch, Nathan, 24
Hauerwas, Stanley, 26, 66, 67, 138,
    154–55, 171n23
Hegel, Georg, 35–36, 85, 121, 145,
    180n5
Hinson-Hasty, Elizabeth, 70
Hitchens, Christopher, 29, 118,
    190n15
Hodgson, Peter C., 35, 124, 128–29,
    152
Hough, Joseph, 88
Hudson, Winthrop, 22
Hull House, 61
Hutchison, William R., 48, 49, 163,
    170–71n14, 194
Hybels, Bill, 188n20

Jenkins, Jerry, 108
just war theory, 82

Kant, Immanuel, 35–36, 121, 172n3
King, Henry Churchill, 69
King, Martin Luther, Jr., 2, 4,
    12–13, 14, 17, 67, 69, 72, 91, 101,
    127, 142, 145, 152, 158, 159, 162,
    167–68n21, 179n66, 181n20,
    187–88n19, 189n6, 198
King, William McGuire, 68, 94
kingdom of God, 1, 3, 11, 50–53, 55,
    59, 64–66, 68–70, 77, 80, 90, 92,
    97, 102, 108, 142, 151–53, 158, 162

LaHaye, Tim, 108
Latitudinarianism, 34
Left Behind (novels), 108
liberation theology, 9, 56, 79, 94–98,
    120, 122–23, 132, 135, 142,
    144, 151, 167–68n21, 168n22,
    183nn45–46, 198–99
Lindbeck, George, 26
Lindsey, Hal, 108
Locke, John, 34, 172n2
Luther, Martin, 52, 80, 182n26

Machen, J. Gresham, 113–15, 120,
    153–54
mainline Protestantism, 3, 8, 13–15,
    20–21, 23, 25–27, 29–31, 37–38,
    75–76, 78, 79–80, 84, 88, 93–96,
    99, 101, 103, 108–9, 117–20, 123–
    25, 128, 130, 132–36, 138–39,
    144–46, 149–50, 155–59, 162,
    166n9, 167n17, 169n33, 169–70n5,
    170nn6, 8, 172n30, 184nn1, 6,
    190n24, 197, 199–200
Marty, Martin, 102, 107
Marx, Karl, 61; Marxism, 35, 92, 198
Mathews, Shailer, 50, 53–54, 55–56,
    64, 195
May, Henry, 176n18
Mays, Benjamin, 179n66
Mead, Loren, 144–45, 158
Mead, Sidney, 22, 76
Methodists, 28, 34, 38, 43, 74, 83,
    91–92, 133–34, 169–70n5, 172n8,
    173n20, 181n18, 190n24
millennialism, 58–59, 104–5, 110,
    126; *see also* premillennialism,
    postmillennialism
Miller, Donald E., 118–19, 132, 153
Miller, Glenn T., 16, 123, 167n19,
    185n16
Miller, William, 105, 107; Millerites,
    105
modernism, 47–48, 54, 100, 153,
    185n16, 194–95, 197
Moody, Dwight L., 46, 63, 103, 106,
    184n5
Moral Majority, 136, 147
Mulder, John, 155
Mullin, Robert Bruce, 42, 193
Munger, Theodore, 8, 49, 170n7, 194
Muste, A. J., 182n33

neo-orthodoxy, 3, 69–70, 79–85,
    97, 120, 166n13, 169n32, 177n41,
    179n2, 180n5, 181n18, 196

Niebuhr, H. Richard, 3, 5, 7, 65, 78, 80–81, 85, 87–89, 98, 124, 154–55, 163, 180n7, 182n26, 184n51, 197

Niebuhr, Reinhold, 1–5, 9, 13, 14, 17, 23, 50, 68, 78, 80–85, 90, 92, 93, 101, 129, 133, 142, 145, 152, 155, 158, 159, 165n5, 167n20, 179n3, 180nn4, 12, 181n20, 188n16, 196–98

Noll, Mark, 110

nonviolence, 91, 127, 145, 198; *see also* pacifism

Obama, Barack, 4, 20, 127, 151

Ogden, Schubert, 122

ordination of women, 61, 83

Oxnam, G. Bromley, 23

pacifism, 74, 82; *see also* nonviolence

Parker, Theodore, 41, 43, 46, 173n15

Parks, Rosa, 91, 145

Peale, Norman Vincent, 73

Pelikan, Jaroslav, 128, 130

pentecostalism, 24–25, 77, 102, 106, 120, 185nn9, 11

perfectibility of humanity and society, 1, 70, 93, 107

Pierson, Arthur T., 106, 109

postmillennialism, 104, 110

postmodernity, 5, 25–27, 30, 129, 132, 142, 154, 162–63, 169–70n5, 171nn23–24, 183n46

premillennialism, 105, 110, 137, 188n33

Presbyterians, 38, 47, 49, 100, 101, 103, 106, 178–79n58, 182n33

process theology, 85–87, 120, 122–23, 142, 181n23, 181–82n24

progressivism, 12, 21, 44, 80, 86, 101, 112, 119–20, 127–28, 135–36, 143–47, 155–57, 168n28, 173n20, 190n24, 200; Network of Spiritual

Progressives, 136, 143; Progressive Era, 1, 65, 83

Prothero, Stephen, 130–31

queer theology, 95, 183n46

Ramsey, Paul, 96–97

Rauschenbusch, Walter, 1–2, 4, 8, 10, 13, 17, 21, 29, 31, 56, 63–74, 76–77, 81, 83, 88, 90–92, 96–98, 101, 104, 119, 126, 128, 129, 133, 134–35, 137, 138, 142, 145, 148, 152–53, 154, 157–58, 159, 162, 167n20, 177n33, 178n49, 179n66, 180n4, 195–96, 198

Raushenbush, Paul, 188nn20, 32

Reagan, Ronald, 112, 125

Reed, Ralph, 131, 147–48

Reformed theology, 6, 38, 87, 89, 167n16, 174–75n36, 181n18

revivalism, 22, 24–25, 34, 38, 42–44, 46–47, 58, 63, 103, 106, 161, 172nn2, 8

Riis, Jacob, 60

Ritschl, Albrecht, 51–53, 68, 87, 121

Rorty, Richard, 29

Ruether, Rosemary Radford, 9, 122, 167–68n21, 183n46, 198–99

Rutledge, Fleming, 127

Ryan, John, 71, 196

Schaller, Lyle, 169–70n5

Schleiermacher, Friedrich, 36–37, 41, 51, 121, 172n6

Schuller, Robert, 73

Scofield, Cyrus, 106–7

Scudder, Vida, 70–71, 91, 92, 129, 145, 152–53, 196

Second Vatican Council (Vatican II), 23–24, 79, 117

Sheldon, Charles, 39–40, 42, 45, 53, 55, 59, 60, 135

Smyth, Newman, 8, 49, 170n7, 174n32, 194

social gospel, 9–11, 14, 21, 29, 40, 52, 54, 55–78, 79, 81, 83–84, 90–93, 102, 104, 107, 111, 126, 137, 138, 146, 151, 154, 156, 175nn1–2, 8, 176nn16, 18, 177n41, 180nn4, 9, 182n33, 185n11, 190n24, 194–96, 198; social salvation, 9, 55, 66, 68
social justice, 4, 10, 72, 76, 93, 95, 111, 123, 138, 144, 146–48, 152, 157, 159, 168n22, 175n1, 189n8
socialism, 40, 57, 61–62, 66, 71, 81, 182n33
Sockman, Ralph, 74
Spong, John Shelby, 50, 119, 141
Stead, William, 60
Strong, Josiah, 175n8
Suchocki, Marjorie, 122
Sunday, Billy, 106
Sweet, Leonard, 169–70n5, 170n6, 171n23
Swing, David, 47–49, 100

therapeutic ministry models, 11, 73, 88
Thief in the Night, A, 108–9, 113
Thomas, Norman, 182n33
Thompson, Donald, 108
Thurman, Howard, 14, 71–73, 133, 142, 145, 158, 178nn48–49, 198
Tillich, Paul, 14, 88–90, 133, 167n15, 197
Tilton, Theodore, 47
Tittle, Ernest Fremont, 74–75, 82, 159, 181n16
Troeltsch, Ernst, 68

Unitarianism, 34, 40–44, 46, 49, 53, 57, 173nn12–13, 15, 190n1, 193

Van Dusen, Henry P., 23, 101

Vietnam War, protests against, 79, 82, 91, 95, 96, 180n12
Voltaire, 35

Ward, Harry F., 91–97, 138, 151–52, 182n38, 183n47, 189n15, 197–98
Warfield, Benjamin, 104, 106
Warren, Rick, 127
Weeks, Louis, 155
Wellhausen, Julius, 48
Wellman, James K., Jr., 178–79n58, 186n28, 188n33
Wesley, John, 16, 33, 34, 109, 181n23
West, Cornel, 134–35
Whitehead, Alfred North, 85, 121, 122
Wilke, Richard, 133–34
Williams, Daniel Day, 12, 64, 84, 85, 194, 197
Willimon, William, 26, 154, 171n23
Wills, Garry, 105
Winfrey, Oprah, 90, 135
Wogaman, J. Philip, 134, 157, 199
womanist theology, 95, 142
women's organizations and activism, 60–61, 176n16, 178n54
World Council of Churches, 74, 84, 96
World War I, consequences of, 3, 14, 55–56, 60, 67, 69, 74, 79, 83, 88, 90–91, 92, 99, 103, 166n12, 169n32
World War II, consequences of, 25, 74–75, 79, 82–83, 86, 88, 91, 92, 118, 125
Wright, Jeremiah, 4, 20, 169n3
Wuthnow, Robert, 150, 155, 184n6